WIN

EVERY

ARGUMENT

WIN

THE ART OF DEBATING,

EVERY

PERSUADING, AND

ARGUMENT

PUBLIC SPEAKING

MEHDI HASAN

HENRY HOLT AND COMPANY
NEW YORK

Henry Holt and Company
Publishers since 1866
120 Broadway
New York, New York 10271
www.henryholt.com

Library of Congress Cataloging-in-Publication Data

Names: Hasan, Mehdi, 1979– author.
Title: Win every argument : the art of debating, persuading, and public
  speaking / Mehdi Hasan.
Description: First edition. | New York : Henry Holt and Company, 2022. |
  Includes bibliographical references and index.
Identifiers: LCCN 2022035989 (print) | LCCN 2022035990 (ebook) |
  ISBN 9781250853479 (hardcover) | ISBN 9781250853486 (ebook)
Subjects: LCSH: Persuasion (Rhetoric) | Reasoning. | Debates and debating. |
  Public speaking.
Classification: LCC P301.5.P47 H378 2022 (print) | LCC P301.5.P47 (ebook) |
  DDC 808.53—dc23/eng/20220831
LC record available at https://lccn.loc.gov/2022035989
LC ebook record available at https://lccn.loc.gov/2022035990

Our books may be purchased in bulk for promotional, educational, or busi-
ness use. Please contact your local bookseller or the Macmillan Corporate and
Premium Sales Department at (800) 221-7945, extension 5442, or by e-mail at
MacmillanSpecialMarkets@macmillan.com.

First Edition 2023

Designed by Gabriel Guma

Printed in the United States of America

3   5   7   9   10   8   6   4

To my wife, the love of my life, and the only person I can never seem to win an argument with.

CONTENTS

Introduction

THE ART OF THE ARGUMENT

> I'm not arguing, I'm just explaining why I'm right.
>
> —Anonymous

What would you do if tens of thousands of lives depended on *you* winning an argument?

In 428 BCE, Ancient Greece was in the midst of the Peloponnesian War. The city-states of Athens and Sparta were locked in all-out conflict, struggling for the upper hand. With the two powerhouses distracted, the tiny city of Mytilene, on the Greek island of Lesbos, saw an opportunity. The oligarchs in charge of the city wanted to throw off Athenian rule and make a push to take full control of the island. "Egged on" by their Spartan allies, the oligarchs launched what became known as the Mytilenean Revolt.

It was a disaster for the Mytileneans. Athens wasn't as distracted as the oligarchs had hoped. The Athenian forces besieged Mytilene from all sides, before the city was even ready for battle. And it crushed Mytilene's nascent insurrection. The Mytilenean leaders were forced to surrender to Athenian general Paches, but the general didn't take it upon himself to decide how to punish the rebels. Athens was still a democracy, after all. He allowed the defeated city to send a delegation of a thousand men to Athens to beg for mercy.

As the ancient Greek historian Thucydides narrates in his *History of the Peloponnesian War*, the Athenian assembly gathered to vote on what action to take against Mytilene. It didn't take long to decide. The Athenians were infuriated by the Mytilenean Revolt— and they were also afraid. What if other cities in their empire followed Mytilene's lead and rebelled against Athens? It would be the end of the Athenian empire.

The members of the assembly voted hurriedly and unanimously for a stark punishment—to execute all the men in Mytilene and to enslave the women and children. Straight after the vote, a trireme— the fastest ship of that era—was dispatched to Lesbos with orders for Paches: wipe out the adult male population of Mytilene.

By the next morning, however, many Athenians were second-guessing the sheer brutality they had voted to inflict on the people of Mytilene. They wanted to consider a softer penalty. Athens being Athens, two orators were picked to debate the issue in front of the assembly.

The first was the general Cleon, described by Thucydides as "the most violent man at Athens," who wanted to stick with the original punishment: killing and enslaving the Mytileneans. He addressed the assembly at length and urged his fellow Athenians to resist the calls for leniency. Cleon raged against Athenian democracy itself if it were to back down from the demands of war: "I have often before now been convinced that a democracy is incapable of empire, and never more so than by your present change of mind in the matter of Mytilene." And he warned his listeners against becoming "very slaves to the pleasure of the ear, and more like the audience of a rhetorician than the council of a city."

"Punish them as they deserve," Cleon argued, "and teach your other allies by a striking example that the penalty of rebellion is death."

Pity poor Diodotus. This leader of a more moderate Athenian political faction was tasked with making the case for clemency, and he had to speak right after Cleon's rant. Thousands of lives hung in the balance—and time was not on his side. The trireme was already on its way to Lesbos. For that matter, Diodotus was now defending the soul of Athenian democracy, in the face of the vengeful anger of his opponents. Can you imagine the pressure he was under?

Despite that pressure, Diodotus began slowly, his calmness a stark contrast to Cleon's rage: "I do not blame the persons who have reopened the case of the Mytileneans," he said, "nor do I approve the protests which we have heard against important questions being frequently debated"—a dig at Cleon's scorched earth tirade. Diodotus instead built his argument around the importance of free and open debate, warning his audience how "haste and passion" were the two biggest obstacles to "good counsel."

For Diodotus, the case against a mass execution didn't rest on the guilt or innocence of the Mytileneans. He conceded that they had indeed revolted against Athens—but he argued only for the oligarchical ringleaders to be punished. His was an argument of expediency, of realpolitik: killing *all* the Mytilenean men would not be in the "interests" of the Athenians. It would be a "blunder," he said, to exclude rebels in other revolting cities "from the hope of repentance and an early atonement of their error." Nor, he added, was there any evidence that a mass execution would act as a deterrent to future insurrections.

The coolheaded Diodotus knew his audience—and what they needed to hear. He also understood the importance of rational argument, and he set the tone for it, eloquently deflecting Cleon's call for vengeance. "The good citizen," argued Diodotus, "ought to triumph not by frightening his opponents but by beating them fairly in argument."

"And beat Cleon he did," notes one writer. The assembly voted again—and, this time, narrowly decided in Diodotus's favor. A second trireme with new orders was then "sent off in haste" to Lesbos, writes Thucydides, with "wine and barley-cakes" provided to the oarsmen and "great promises made if they arrived in time." Thankfully, their trireme pulled into port just as Paches was reading the original decree brought to him by the first ship. The massacre was prevented, with only moments to spare.

Thousands of innocent lives were saved. All thanks to a single argument made back in Athens. An argument that Diodotus was able to win because he excelled at the art of debating, persuading, and public speaking. He knew not just how to craft a reasoned argument but also how to compose himself under pressure. He knew how to reach his audience, in their hearts, their minds, and the very core of their identity. He knew how to roll with his opponent's haymakers and pick the critical opening to strike back. And when he did, Diodotus knew exactly how to use Cleon's weaknesses to his advantage. He knew how to go in the underdog and come out the victor.

The point of this book is to show you all the tools and tactics that Diodotus, and all the world's greatest speakers and debaters, employed. So you, too, can win every argument. Even when thousands of lives *aren't* riding on it.

....

Every single person on the face of the planet—every man, woman, and child—has, at some moment or another, *tried* to win an argument. Whether it is in the comments section on Facebook, or in the marble hallways of Congress, or at the Thanksgiving dinner table. Whether they've trounced their opponent or walked away sullen, everyone might then imagine all the things they could and should have said. We've all been there. We cannot escape the human urge, need, and—yes—desire to argue.

But arguing itself tends to get a bad rap. It's blamed for everything from political polarization to marital breakdown. In his 1936 classic, *How to Win Friends & Influence People*, Dale Carnegie wrote: "I have come to the conclusion that there is only one way under high heaven to get the best of an argument—and that is to avoid it. Avoid it as you would avoid rattlesnakes and earthquakes."

I take issue with Carnegie's conclusion—if he were still alive, maybe we could debate it.

I prefer not to avoid arguments. I seek them out. Rush toward them. Relish and savor them.

I have been arguing my whole life, in fact. I've even made a career of it—first, as an op-ed columnist and TV pundit in the UK; then as a political interviewer for Al Jazeera English; and now as a cable anchor for MSNBC in the United States. I've argued with presidents, prime ministers, and spy chiefs from across the world. I've argued inside the White House; inside Number 10 Downing Street; inside the . . . Saudi embassy!

Philosophically, I consider argument and debate to be the lifeblood of democracy, as well as the only surefire way to establish the truth. Arguments can help us solve problems, uncover ideas we would've never considered, and hurry our disagreements toward (even begrudging) understanding. There are also patent practical benefits to knowing how to argue and speak in public. These are vital soft skills that allow you to advance in your career and improve your lot in life. There are very few things you cannot achieve when you have the skill and ability to change people's minds. Or to quote Winston Churchill, "Of all the talents bestowed upon men, none is so precious as the gift of oratory. He who enjoys it wields a power more durable than that of a great king."

But when it comes down to it, a good argument, made in good faith, can also simply be *fun*. I actually *enjoy* disagreeing with others, poking holes in their claims, exposing flaws in their logic. Maybe it makes me an outlier, but I happen to think there is intrinsic value to disagreement. I'm in the same camp as the nineteenth-century French essayist Joseph Joubert, who is said to have remarked: "It is better to debate a question without settling it than to settle a question without debating it."

I learned this lesson early on. I was raised in, one might say, a disputatious household. To put it plainly: we Hasans love to argue!

My father would challenge and provoke my sister and me at the dinner table, on long car journeys, on foreign holidays. He never shied away from an argument over the merits or demerits of a particular issue. It was he who taught me to question everything, to be both curious and skeptical, to take nothing on blind faith, and to relish every challenge and objection.

In the late 1980s, when British Muslims were denouncing Salman Rushdie's notorious Islamophobic novel *The Satanic Verses*, with some of them even burning copies of it on the streets of northern English cities, my father purchased a copy, read it cover to cover, and kept it in a prominent spot on his bookshelf. His Muslim friends would visit our home, see the book, and their eyes would bulge. "Why . . . why . . . would you buy that book?" they would splutter. "Because you can't dismiss something you haven't read," my father would calmly reply.

You could say my father is a living, breathing embodiment of the dictum outlined by John Stuart Mill in his classic philosophical treatise *On Liberty*:

> He who knows only his own side of the case, knows little of that. His reasons may be good, and no one may have been able to refute them. But if he is equally unable to refute the reasons on the opposite side; if he does not so much as know what they are, he has no ground for preferring either opinion.

I grew up appreciating the value of being able to "refute the reasons on the opposite side" and thereby learned to familiarize myself with both sides of any argument. It's a skill I took with me first to university, where I debated at the Oxford Union alongside the great and the good of the British establishment, and then to a career in the UK and U.S. media where, in recent years, I have earned a reputation as one of the toughest interviewers on television.

. . . .

There are millions of people across America, and the world, who want to learn how to win an argument, who are keen to improve their debating techniques, as well as master the art of public speaking in general—but who need a push.

You may be one of them. But why read this particular book to get that push? I'll admit there are plenty of books already out there on how to argue or debate or give speeches that have been authored by academics and writers and debate coaches. Indeed, you'll see that I cite from many of them in the pages and chapters ahead. But this book builds on my own unique set of experiences: from my student days debating with the likes of future British prime minister Boris Johnson and former Pakistani prime minister Benazir Bhutto, to the highlights from a career spent interviewing some of the biggest names from the worlds of politics, finance, and, yes, Hollywood.

So that's reason number one: I've had to learn every debating technique in this book to be able to step in front of the camera and challenge leaders from around the globe.

But here's an even bigger reason: while there are also, admittedly, plenty of books already out there that focus predominantly on the art of persuasion, or negotiation, or compromise, this book isn't one of them. Simply put, this book is all about teaching you how *to win*.

So this book is intended as a practical guide—for trial lawyers who want to triumph in the courtroom; for corporate executives who want to dominate in the boardroom; for political candidates who want to run for office and win their TV debates; for teachers and lecturers who want to succeed in getting their point across; for students who want to excel in speech and debate tournaments or at Model UN; for spouses who . . . well, you know the rest.

My goal is to turn you, the reader, no matter your background or ability, into a champion of debate, a master of rhetoric, a winner in the art of argument.

In the first section of the book, on the fundamentals, I'll show you how to captivate an audience, distinguish between pathos and logos, and become a better listener as well as a better speaker. I'll explain why humor is often key to winning a debate, and I'll also mount a defense of the much-maligned ad hominem argument.

The second section will introduce you to time-tested tricks and techniques—from the "Rule of Three" to the "Art of the Zinger" to the "Gish Gallop"—and show you how to wield and weaponize them in the real world. You'll come to recognize the value of a triad as well as the power of synchoresis—and also learn what Rambo has to contribute to the world of argument and debate.

The third section focuses on the work you need to conduct behind the scenes to ensure you're ready for prime time. I'll teach you how to build up your confidence, rehearse your delivery, and research your arguments. To me, there is nothing—*nothing!*—more important than practice and preparation.

Finally, there's the conclusion, or the "Grand Finale." How do you bring everything to a close? How do you leave your audience wanting more? I'll lay out the different ways to end a speech on a high—and with listeners on *your* side.

This book is chock-full of behind-the-scenes anecdotes and examples from my own debates—which have ranged from the Oxford Union in England to Kyiv in Ukraine. I'll share secrets from my televised bouts with the likes of Erik Prince, John Bolton, Michael Flynn, Douglas Murray, Slavoj Žižek, Steven Pinker, and Vitali Klitschko, among many others. I'll also unpack lessons on the art of rhetoric from luminaries ranging from the ancient Greek philosopher Aristotle to the British comedian John Cleese to the Barbadian pop star Rihanna.

People often ask me: "Can what you do really be taught?"

The short answer is: yes.

The longer answer is: yes, if you have the right teacher and are willing to listen, learn, and put in the hours.

Anyone can win an argument.

Let me teach you how.

WIN

EVERY

ARGUMENT

Part One

THE FUNDAMENTALS

1

WINNING OVER AN AUDIENCE

Designing a presentation without an audience in mind
is like writing a love letter and addressing it "to whom
it may concern."

—Ken Haemer, design expert

It was a cold, wintry evening in rural southwest England in February 2012. I had been invited to join BBC Radio 4's flagship political panel show, *Any Questions?* The show is broadcast in front of a live audience that is allowed to ask questions of the panelists, who tend to be a mix of politicians and pundits.

That night we were in the small town of Crewkerne—population seven thousand—and, as I walked onstage at the Wadham Community School, I turned to scan the audience in the hall. The house was packed, but it took only three words to describe the whole of the crowd: *elderly, white, conservative.*

I leaned over to fellow panelist David Lammy, a Black Labour member of Parliament, and whispered: "We may be the only people of color, and the only people under the age of forty, in this entire room."

As the show began, so did the contentious political arguments. One of the big stories in the news that week was the fate of extremist preacher Abu Qatada, a Jordanian asylum-seeker who had been dubbed "Osama bin Laden's spiritual ambassador to Europe" and held in the UK without trial for a decade. The Conservative-led coalition government wanted to have Abu Qatada deported to Jordan—despite a credible fear that he might be tortured by the authorities back in Amman. And, on just the second question of the night, a member of the audience rose and asked about the issue directly: "Should the British government ignore the instruction of the European Court of Human Rights and simply deport Abu Qatada to Jordan?"

My mind was racing. I was in the hot seat, center stage. I knew that millions were listening on the radio, many of whom would agree with my own liberal stance: Abu Qatada should be tried in the UK and not tortured in Jordan. But how could I convince the *Daily Mail*–reading, conservative audience facing me down in Crewkerne? How could I get them on board with my argument?

When the questioner had spoken, the audience had clapped rousingly. They seemed to want Abu Qatada gone! I knew that if I simply cited reports from Amnesty International or the articles of the European Convention on Human Rights, I would lose this crowd. Instead, I had to adapt my usual liberal arguments and appeal to what I knew that particular audience would value and cherish—namely, British tradition, British history.

So, when host Jonathan Dimbleby came to me for an answer to that provocative question from the audience, this is how I answered. I said it was "absurd" to claim Abu Qatada could not be prosecuted in a UK court. Why?

The bigger point for me is the principle. When I was in school—we're in a school—I learned about the Magna Carta; I learned about trial by jury; I learned about habeas corpus; I learned about free speech. The "glorious history of liberty" in this country. And I find it amazing that twenty years later, such is the pernicious impact of the "War on Terror" that I have to come back on a program like this, I have to go into TV studios, and debate certain journalists, and say, "Wait a minute, what happened to those liberties? Why have we suddenly abandoned those liberties that made this country great?"

The audience erupted in applause. By bringing it back to the Magna Carta, England's first ever bill of rights, I had connected with them. I now had their full attention and loud support, so I pushed on.

No matter how odious and nasty Abu Qatada may be, the whole point of human rights is that it is the nasty and odious people who need human rights the most, and need the protection of the law the most, because if we don't extend it to them, there's no point [in having them].

This is how you make an argument in front of a skeptical audience. You have to be able to adapt, you have to be agile, and to do that, you have to know your audience and cater to it.

I was able to win over most of that audience in Crewkerne, seemingly against the odds, not because those locals liked me or agreed with my politics but because I understood who they were, where they were coming from, and what they wanted, what they *needed*, to hear in order to be persuaded.

It isn't always easy to do that—but it isn't rocket science either.

....

In this chapter, I am going to outline three main ways in which you can win over a live audience—whether it's your family in your living room, or a crowd of hundreds in a lecture hall, or even millions of people watching you at home on television.

Remember: anytime an audience is present, you cannot, *cannot*, afford to ignore them or take them for granted. The audience is the key. Even if you're in a one-on-one debate, *they* are the people who have been described as "judge and jury." They are who you're trying to convince, persuade, and bring on board with your arguments.

So how do you do all of that? How do you win them over?

KNOW YOUR AUDIENCE

Above all, you have to try to understand where your audience is coming from. If, say, you're in a competitive debate, you'll want to get inside the head of the judge or the audience members whose votes you're seeking. This means that to succeed in "knowing your audience," you'll have to do some legwork before you even enter the room, before you start speaking in front of a crowd.

First, find out who is going to be in the audience. These are the kind of questions I ask the organizers of every event that I'm invited to speak at:

- *How big is the audience?*
- *What kind of people constitute the audience?*
- *What's the rough demographic? Are they young or old? Students or professionals? Political or apolitical? Male or female? White, Black, or Brown?*

It all matters, because once you have a detailed breakdown of the members of your prospective audience, you can focus your language and tailor your arguments toward them.

For example, if I'm speaking to a group of high school or college students, I probably shouldn't make references to events from my childhood, which occurred before most of them were born. And I should definitely avoid patronizing or talking down to them. On the other hand, if I'm speaking to a group of adults, or older people, on a serious matter, I should avoid making references to movies or memes that might go over their heads.

The key benefit of knowing your audience is that it grants you the ability to modify the *language* you use to make your case.

Whether you're trying to sell an argument or, for that matter, sell a product, you should also change *how* you present your speech, depending on who is in front of you. You cannot, writes business speaker Ian Altman, just take a "one-size-fits-all" approach. You have to be agile and be able to target different arguments to different audiences.

Everything from varying tone and volume, to varying content and emphasis, matters. Think about it this way: you wouldn't pitch your ideas to your spouse the same way you would present them to a corporate executive. You would adjust your *tone*—strong or soft, serious or conversational, more passionate or less. Just as important is your *volume*, depending on whether you're addressing five people in a small conference room, five hundred people in a university auditorium, or five million people watching you at home on television.

Making these adjustments is necessary, even when you are trying to make the same argument in front of each of those very different audiences. And these strategies speak to the hardest part of public speaking: adapting. Whenever you take the spotlight—proverbially or literally—you need to be flexible. Be willing to customize your presentation—even the shape of your arguments—to whoever it is you want to win over.

You probably know how to convince your kids or your partner to do something, right? It's because you know those people better than anyone else. If you learn as much as you can about the audience members who you are trying to address, persuade, and convince, you'll find that it's much easier to make headway.

To be clear: I don't want you to *change* your entire argument, or just tell people what they want to hear. What I'm saying is that you should present your argument in such a way that people feel comfortable getting on board with that argument, because you've specifically tailored it to their interests or identities. It would be a huge mistake, as Ian Altman notes, to give the same speech to different types of people in different types of venues.

Take the issue of immigration. I'm not suggesting you should be pro-immigration in front of a liberal crowd and anti-immigration in front of a conservative one. I'm saying that if you're addressing a right-wing or conservative crowd on the merits of immigration, if you're trying to make a pro-immigration case to them, it might not make sense to quote, say, Barack Obama or Alexandria Ocasio-Cortez. Instead, try quoting a prominent conservative, like Ronald Reagan, from his famous pro-immigration speech at Liberty State Park in New Jersey in 1980.

You could say: "Don't take my word for it: Remember how Ronald Reagan in front of the Statue of Liberty praised immigrants for bringing 'with them courage, ambition and the values of family, neighborhood, work, peace and freedom' and helping 'make America great again'?"

By changing your approach, and finding a common language, you immediately make the issue much more palatable.

So remember: cite facts, figures, and quotes that not only bolster your own argument but also appeal to the specific audience in front of you. This works beyond politics, as well—beyond Republican versus Democrat, or Tory versus Labour. If you are debating faith or religion with a Jew, a Christian, or a Muslim, you might want to quote the Bible or the Quran to them. However, if you are debating an atheist, there really is no point quoting a holy book, is there?

In the summer of 2014, I was invited to give a speech to the World Affairs Council of Greater Houston, in Texas, on the topic of Muslim integration in Europe and the United States. I did my homework beforehand and learned that I would be addressing an audience not just of liberals but conservatives, too: people more skeptical of my message. So I made sure I peppered my talk with references to right-wing journalists and news sources—boosting my case for why it was a myth to suggest that Muslims are unable to integrate in the West.

"Don't take my word for it," I said (always a useful phrase in front of a skeptical audience). "Just two weeks ago, in the *Daily Telegraph* newspaper, the leading right-wing, conservative British journalist and columnist, Fraser Nelson, editor of the right-wing *Spectator* magazine, published a piece headlined 'The British Muslim Is Truly One among Us—and Proud to Be So.' Nelson wrote, and I quote: 'The integration of Muslims can now be seen as one of the great success stories of modern Britain.'"

Their ears pricked up when they heard the word *conservative* and the references to publications like the *Telegraph* and the *Spectator*. They didn't expect it, and I had their undivided attention.

I was also told ahead of the event that there would be a fair number of Jewish audience members, too, so I decided to tell this (true) story from the UK.

> Look at what happened last year when the tiny Jewish community in the northern city of Bradford was facing the closure of their historic synagogue, first built in 1880. Its roof was leaking, and the few dozen remaining regulars could not afford the repairs. The chairman of the synagogue, Rudi Leavor, made the decision to sell the building; it was on the verge of being purchased and turned into a block of luxury apartments when, out of nowhere, the synagogue was saved after a fundraising campaign led by a local mosque. Zulfi Karim, the secretary of Bradford's Council of Mosques, who was behind the campaign, now refers to Leavor, who fled to the UK from Nazi-occupied Europe during the Second World War, as his "newfound brother."

From behind my podium, I could see their eyes widen, unexpected smiles appearing on their faces. They were nudging and nodding to each other in approval.

Getting to know your audience is of absolute importance, but it is only the first step. It's what you have to do before you even get up onstage, or on camera, or at the podium. The next step is about what you do once you're up there.

GRAB THEIR ATTENTION

I have some bad news for you. You may have heard that viral stat about how a goldfish only has an attention span of nine seconds. But, according to a study conducted by researchers at Microsoft, the average human loses "concentration after eight seconds." You have very, *very* little time to capture an audience's attention before they tune you out and start thinking about what they're going to have for dinner or, more likely, scrolling through Instagram.

We live in an online era, where everyone, everywhere, is on their smartphone almost all the time. You'll be speaking for twenty, thirty, forty minutes, yes, but if the people you're addressing get distracted or—worse—*bored* at the very start, the rest of your presentation will end up being a huge waste of time. For you, and for them.

Whether giving a presentation in a boardroom or constructing an argument with friends, you want to start in a very clear, direct, and unique manner. As a group of comms experts point out, you want to avoid rote remarks, empty platitudes, and tired clichés.

- "Thank you for inviting me."
- "I'm so glad to be here with you today."
- "How are you all doing?"

No. No. *No.*

You must grab your audience in the very first minute, ideally in the very first ten or twenty seconds.

How?

1.Start with a strong opening line

Something unexpected, provocative, contrary even. To quote the legendary Dale Carnegie, "Begin with something interesting in your first sentence. Not the second. Not the third. The First! F-I-R-S-T! First!"

Here's how British celebrity chef and food campaigner Jamie Oliver kicked off his 2010 TED Talk.

> Sadly, in the next eighteen minutes when I do our chat, four Americans that are alive will be dead from the food that they eat. My name's Jamie Oliver. I'm thirty-four years old. I'm from Essex in England, and for the last seven years I've worked fairly tirelessly to save lives in my own way. I'm not a doctor; I'm a chef, I don't have expensive equipment or medicine. I use information, education.

Wouldn't you want to sit up and listen to more of that?

2. Start with a question

Ideally, a "provocative" question, say those comms experts. "Starting with a question creates a knowledge gap: *a gap between what the listeners know and what they don't know*," adds Akash Karia in his book *How to Deliver a Great TED Talk*. "This gap creates curiosity because people are hardwired with a desire to fill knowledge gaps."

Former NASA scientist James Hansen knows he's not the greatest of orators, but he managed to use that very quality to grab his audience's attention in a 2012 TED Talk on climate change. How? With these opening questions:

> What do I know that would cause me, a reticent midwestern scientist, to get myself arrested in front of the White

House protesting? And what would you do if you knew
what I know?

Wouldn't you want to hear the answers to those stark questions?
Wouldn't you look up from your iPhone for those?

3. Start with a story

Ideally, a personal anecdote. You get bonus points if it's funny, able
to get people laughing and relaxed—and paying attention—from
the get-go. Storytelling helps with instant engagement because everyone loves a great yarn. Plus, our brains are built to fall in love with
a good story—one that taps into imagination and empathy from the
very beginning.

Entrepreneur Ric Elias accomplished this in his 2011 TED Talk
with a very personal recollection of a terrifying flight.

Imagine a big explosion as you climb through three thousand feet. Imagine a plane full of smoke. Imagine an engine
going clack, clack, clack, clack, clack, clack, clack. It sounds
scary. Well, I had a unique seat that day. I was sitting in 1D.

Aren't you instantly transfixed and transported to a plane in
the sky?

Pay close attention to your first sentence if you want anyone else
to pay attention to what you have to say. Surprise your audience with
a striking one-liner, an irresistible question, or a visceral story. You'll
see people's eyes turn to you, instead of to their phones—and then
the room is yours.

But, of course, getting people's attention is one thing. Keeping
people's attention is another. How do we do that?

CONNECT WITH THEM

Remember, the goal is to get your audience on your side, especially in a debate. The point is to change not your opponent's mind but the minds of those watching and listening in the audience. This is especially true if you are participating in a competitive debate in which the audience will decide the outcome—but it applies to any forum, be it a TV talk show or a Thanksgiving dinner table.

To keep an audience's attention and to keep them on your side, the name of the game is to *connect*. You want to appeal to them with arguments that tap into their beliefs, and that, as we've seen, are built upon a clear knowledge of your audience. But even once you've done your homework—perfected your facts, found your sources, prepared your counterarguments—there are important strategies to employ in real time.

1. Make eye contact

You have to try and look people in the eye when you speak to them. And also try and make eye contact with people across the whole room. Don't leave some parts of the audience feeling left out.

As speech coach Fia Fasbinder has pointed out, eye contact "makes the audience feel heard and involves them in your presentation." It is, Fasbinder says, "the nonverbal equivalent of saying somebody's name aloud."

Try your hardest to avoid the "death by presentation" phenomenon. That means: do *not* read from your notes, or from PowerPoint slides. Remember: your audience could read your notes or your slides themselves if they wanted to. You could circulate hard copies of your main points and go home and take a nap! The audience came to see you—and, to quote speech coach Craig Valentine, they want to be "seen by you." So, keep your eyes on them as much as possible.

But—and I must stress this point!—when you are looking at them, please do not imagine them naked. Many people—wrongly citing Winston Churchill—say it's a good way to confidently address a big audience while also dealing with your nerves. They say it's a way of empowering a speaker and tackling a sense of "vulnerability" onstage, writes Fasbinder. They're wrong.

I've never met anyone who says it actually works for them. Also, I tend to have friends and family in the audience—and you probably will, too. My parents have often sat in the front row. Why would I want to picture any of *them* naked? How is that supposed to help me stay focused on delivering my speech?

Instead, you want to make sure you've prepared enough beforehand that you can avoid reading your slides, so you can feel comfortable enough to look out at your audience without going into panic mode. You want to reach the point where you can meet their eyes like you would in any one-on-one conversation. And, as in most conversations, you're headed in the wrong direction if Plan A is to picture them naked.

2. Heap praise

What do you tend to do when you want to charm a person or win them over? You heap praise on them. You're nice toward them. You make them feel special.

The same applies to an audience. Praise can be one of the simplest and most powerful tools to engage an audience—or any group of people!

I cannot tell you the number of U.S. cities where I have been invited to speak or debate, and where I opened my remarks by suggesting that *this* particular city was my favorite city in America.

In Detroit, Michigan, on a visit from the UK almost a decade ago, I told the crowd that everything I knew about the great Motor City came from Detective Axel Foley. They erupted in laughter and cheers. *This British guy with the funny accent knows* Beverly Hills Cop *and also knows the Detroit reference?* they thought to themselves as they settled in to listen to me speak on some obscure political issue.

When I visited Canada in 2017 and 2018, I told the liberal Torontonians who attended my events how lucky they were to live in a country with legalized marijuana, tolerance toward Syrian refugees, and Justin Trudeau—whereas I had just landed from . . . Trump's America. There was an instant connection.

Of course, part of the audience will know what you're doing, but that's more than okay if you do it well. Your point is to tailor your praise so that it reflects actual familiarity with the place or with the audience—and how they see themselves.

3. Get personal

There is simply no better way to influence or stir an audience—instantly, powerfully, authentically—than by opening up to them with a personal story or anecdote.

To be clear: I'm not saying you need to tell them long stories about your family vacations or show them baby pictures from the stage. I'm saying that you can share a key biographical detail, or an emotion that you're feeling in the moment, or a self-deprecating joke. It is a tried-and-tested way of bonding with an audience of strangers—and of laying the groundwork for you to then *persuade* them.

The harsh reality is that people won't bond with your arguments in a vacuum, but they *will*, says speech coach Bas van den Beld, "bond with you"—the person making those arguments. By sharing a revealing story or a personal flaw, you allow audience members a way to identify with you. You show how *you* are no different to *them*.

Here I am speaking at the Oxford Union in 2013, in a debate-winning speech that subsequently went viral and—at the time of writing—is approaching ten million views on YouTube. The motion was "The House believes Islam is a religion of peace," and this is how I chose to make it personal with the audience of students crowded inside a packed chamber. As I approached my concluding remarks, I told them:

> Let me just say this to you: think about what the opposite of this motion is. If you vote "no" tonight, think about what you're saying the opposite of this motion is. That Islam isn't a religion of peace; it is a religion of war, of violence, of terror, of aggression. That the people who follow Islam—me, my wife, my retired parents, my six-year-old child, that 1.8 million of your fellow British residents and citizens, that 1.6 billion people across the world, your fellow human beings—are all followers, promoters, believers in a religion of violence. Do you really think that? Do you really believe that to be the case?

The personal touch is snuck in there—as I discuss myself, my family, my child—but it pulls them into their own personal decision, in real time. At this point, they have already listened to me speak for ten minutes, and (spoiler alert) there was no violence or aggression or terror on that stage. I was making them apply the motion not just to some vague Other but also to *me* and to the millions of other Muslims they shared a country with.

Of course, you can use a personal touch for lighter purposes. When I appeared on NBC's *Late Night with Seth Meyers* comedy show in 2018, I invoked my other daughter to make an important point about the presidency—and to get a laugh while connecting with an audience that did not know me.

> ME: Trump makes George Bush look good. Trump makes everyone look good! I don't think we should lower the bar so much that we say . . . "Oh, Trump went to a funeral and didn't tweet or insult anyone or drool, therefore he's act-

ing presidential." If that's the criteria, I have a six-year-old daughter at home and she's ready for the Oval Office.

SETH MEYERS (laughing): Well, we would love to meet her. She sounds fantastic.

To connect to your audience, you want them to relate to you. *You.* Not just your arguments.

. . . .

So there you have it. Get to know your audience; grab their attention from the outset; and connect with them throughout. These are the three simple steps to winning them over.

For that matter, you really do want to win them over if you want to win your argument. It is difficult to overstate the power and impact of having an audience on your side, knowing they agree with you, seeing them nodding along to your statements. It gives you an edge over your opponent.

In my view, the audience is the equivalent of what military strategists like to call a "force multiplier"—it is an added element that boosts the effect of the power you can deploy, while at the same time also curbing your opponent's.

Too often, we put all our time and energy into defeating our opponent in an argument. But in doing so we ignore the audience—when the members of the audience are the true judge of who has won and who has lost. Just as often, says author Jay Heinrichs, we put all our energy into crafting a speech that sounds appealing to us—rather than one that will sound appealing to a group of strangers.

How important is the audience? Let me conclude with this quote from movie director Billy Wilder. "An audience is never wrong," he remarked. "An individual member of it may be an imbecile, but a thousand imbeciles together in the dark—that is critical genius."

FEELINGS, NOT (JUST) FACTS

> When dealing with people, let us remember we are not
> dealing with creatures of logic. We are dealing with
> creatures of emotion.
>
> —Dale Carnegie, author

T he legendary American political columnist Roger Simon crowned it "the question that ended a presidential campaign." It was "the most controversial ever asked at a presidential debate."

He was referring to a query posed by CNN anchor Bernard Shaw at the second and final presidential debate between Vice President George Bush and Massachusetts governor Michael Dukakis. The candidates were in Los Angeles, in October 1988, and Shaw was well known already as a tough and blunt interviewer. But the question he'd penned the night before, at 2:00 a.m., while sitting in his Holiday Inn hotel room, would ensure him a place in debate history.

Here is how the veteran broadcaster kicked off the debate that night in LA.

SHAW: For the next ninety minutes we will be questioning the candidates following a format designed and agreed to by representatives of the two campaigns. However, there are no restrictions on the questions that my colleagues and I can ask this evening, and the candidates have no prior knowledge of our questions. By agreement between the candidates, the first question goes to Governor Dukakis. You have two minutes to respond. Governor, if Kitty Dukakis were raped and murdered, would you favor an irrevocable death penalty for the killer?

There was an audible shock in the press room. The live audience sat agape. Such a personal and provocative question seemed to cross an invisible line. Shocked viewers watching the debate on television wanted to see the look on Kitty Dukakis's face at that very moment. But, as Simon noted for Politico in 2007, "reaction shots of the candidate's families were expressly forbidden by the debate agreement. So the camera stayed locked on Dukakis."

And the Democratic presidential nominee gathered himself to respond to Shaw's curveball.

DUKAKIS: No, I don't, Bernard. And I think you know that I've opposed the death penalty during all of my life. I don't see any evidence that it's a deterrent, and I think there are better and more effective ways to deal with violent crime. We've done so in my own state. And it's one of the reasons why we have had the biggest drop in crime of any industrial state in America; why we have the lowest murder rate of any industrial state in America. But we have work to do in this nation. We have work to do to fight a real war, not a phony war, against drugs. And that's something I want to lead, something we haven't had over the course of the past many years, even though the vice president has been at least allegedly in charge of that war. We have much to do to step up that war, to double the number of drug enforcement agents, to fight both here and abroad, to work with our neighbors in this hemisphere. And I want to call a hemispheric summit just as soon after the twentieth of January as possible to fight that war. But we also have to deal with drug education prevention here at home. And that's one of the things that I hope I can lead personally as the president of the United States. We've had great success in my own state. And we've reached out to young people and their families and been able to help them by beginning drug education and prevention in the early elementary grades. So we can fight this war, and we can win this war. And we can do so in a way that marshals our forces, that provides real support for state and local law enforcement officers who have not been getting that support, and do it in a way which will bring down violence in this nation, will help our youngsters to stay away from drugs, will stop this avalanche of drugs that's pouring into the country, and will make it possible for our kids and our families to grow up in safe and secure and decent neighborhoods.

It's a long response, two minutes and 360 words. But notice anything missing? Yep. Any kind of emotion whatsoever!

It was a terrible, *terrible* answer. In the first couple of lines, it might have seemed impressive just that Dukakis could keep his poise. But that poise quickly spoiled, turning into something else entirely. None of the voters in that audience needed to hear the governor restate his position on the death penalty for the hundredth time. They certainly didn't need to hear a dry and scripted response about falling crime rates in Massachusetts, or plans for a "hemispheric summit" on drugs.

What they were desperate to see and hear was their future commander-in-chief's reaction! How would *he* "feel" if his own wife were violently raped and killed? And what would he say to Shaw himself, who had come out swinging and made it personal?

Where was the passion or anger? Where was the heart? Where was Dukakis, the person, beneath all his talking points?

During that 1988 campaign, no one was questioning the Democratic candidate's brainpower or his command of policy. But, to quote *Washington Post* columnist Richard Cohen in the days after the debate, the public *was* questioning Dukakis's "warmth, humanity, a willingness to declare who he is as a person." The candidate didn't live in a vacuum. He could have answered by referencing his elderly father, who had been violently mugged; or his brother Stelian, who had been "killed by a hit-and-run-driver." But he didn't.

"I meant the question to Dukakis to be a stethoscope to find out what he was feeling on this issue," Shaw himself later explained in an interview. "Bush had been beating Dukakis severely about the head and shoulders, charging he was soft on crime. Many voters perceive seeing and hearing Dukakis but not feeling him. I asked that question to see if there was feeling."

There wasn't. And it cost him. Dukakis's approval ratings, noted Simon, dropped by 7 percentage points the day after the debate. "It was a question about Dukakis's values and emotions," Susan Estrich, his campaign manager, later conceded. "It was a question that was very much on the table by that point in the campaign. When he answered by talking policy, I knew we had lost the election."

Still, even years later, when Dukakis reflected on his answer, he didn't get it: "I have to tell you, and maybe I'm just still missing it . . . I didn't think it was that bad."

This chapter is all about explaining why it was indeed *that* bad.

． ． ． ． ． ． ． ． ． ． ．

These days you often hear the phrase "facts don't care about your feelings." The point is that the truth is *the truth*, and whether you want to believe it or not, the facts don't lie. But in the realm of debate, it's not so simple. Anyone who's ever tried to change a friend's mind and gotten nowhere has learned this all too well. You might have all your facts in hand, an argument that's unassailable—and make no dent at all. People are stubborn, and wary, and reactive, and bored, and overconfident, and afraid of change—all at once.

Sure, facts might *not* care about any of those feelings, but consider this: our feelings rarely care about the facts.

If you want to win an argument, convince an audience, or give a pitch or presentation that actually persuades anyone . . . facts alone aren't going to be enough. To move people to your side, you need to make them care. You'll need your facts, your figures, your argument to be rock solid. But you'll also need an approach that goes back millennia: you have to appeal to people's hearts, not just their heads.

PATHOS ALL THE WAY

Aristotle was ahead of the curve on much of this. In his landmark treatise *Rhetoric*, published more than two millennia ago, the ancient Greek philosopher developed what he believed were the three main ways that a speaker can engage an audience. He called these his three proofs or "modes" of persuasion: ethos, pathos, and logos.

An appeal to *ethos* relies on the "character" and "credibility" of the speaker. The word *ethics*, as online speech coach Gini Beqiri has noted, is derived from *ethos*. In this realm, Aristotle writes, "persuasion is achieved by the speaker's personal character when the speech is so spoken as to make us think him credible." When a professional such as a physician appeals to her expertise—"You should get vaccinated. I'm a doctor who's been studying this for years, and I know it's safe."—this is an argument centered on ethos.

An appeal to *pathos* relies on our human emotions and feelings: fear, anger, joy, and the rest. The words *empathy* and *sympathy*, notes Beqiri, derive from *pathos*. Aristotle says that in pathos-based arguments, "persuasion may come through the hearers, when the speech stirs their emotions. Our judgements when we are pleased and friendly are not the same as when we are pained and hostile." If that same doctor were to get visceral, moving us through fear or compassion, she'd be making an argument centered on pathos: "You should get vaccinated. Otherwise you may end up like Kevin and Misty Mitchem, an unvaccinated couple from Virginia, who tragically died fifteen days apart and left four children orphaned."

An appeal to *logos* is founded on logic and reason, on facts and figures. In fact, the word *logic* itself comes from *logos*, the Greek word meaning "reason." According to Aristotle, when it comes to logos, "persuasion is effected through the speech itself when we have proved a truth or an apparent truth by means of the persuasive arguments suitable to the case in question." When the doctor speaks of studies and statistics, she is rooting her argument in logos: "You should get vaccinated. Multiple studies show that the COVID vaccines result in a 90 percent decrease in the risk of hospitalization and death."

In our speeches, our presentations, and our debates and arguments, we tend to rely on logos above all else. We extol the use of reason and logic, statistics and data—and for good reason. We want our arguments to be based in bedrock truth. But when we're trying to change people's minds, that's not enough. It's not how our minds work.

In fact, this is where I differ from the great Aristotle. He tended to give equal treatment to all three of his modes of persuasion. But the reality is that pathos beats logos almost every time.

To be clear: I am not suggesting that facts aren't important, or that they're not the foundation of your argument. They are—and should be. And, in the next chapter, I'll discuss how best to deploy your facts to develop killer arguments.

But even when you have your facts locked down, they won't have any impact unless you incorporate feelings as well. Pathos not only beats logos when it comes to influencing your audience, but pathos is also perhaps the best way to *deliver* logos to your audience. It is the perfect vehicle for it. Study after study shows that if you can tap into your audience's emotions, you are more likely to win over their minds.

THE SCIENCE OF PERSUASION

Remember the original *Star Trek* series? Before all the sequels and spin-offs came along? There were two main characters on that show: Commander Spock, the ultralogical, uber-rational Vulcan; and Captain Kirk, the red-blooded, hotheaded human. Many of us, when we prepare a speech or a presentation, end up taking Spock's approach. We focus on facts, stats, and data, when, really, we should be channeling Captain Kirk and making an emotional appeal to our audience.

Why pretend we're Vulcans when we're not? We're humans who rely on our gut reactions; on our emotions, our feelings, our instincts. And that isn't just science fiction either. It's *actual* science.

In recent years, a growing body of evidence from the worlds of neuroscience and cognitive psychology shows that our behavior and our beliefs are governed more by Kirk-like emotions than they are by Vulcan-style rationality. Our feelings affect our decision-making in multiple ways. How fast or slow we make decisions—as well as how able we are to recall facts and figures while doing so. And they do all this by influencing us at a subconscious level. Perhaps without realizing it, argues brand strategist Douglas Van Praet, we often feel, rather than think, our way toward a particular position or viewpoint.

Much of the academic heavy lifting on feelings over facts has been done by the acclaimed Portuguese American neuroscientist Antonio Damasio, who heads the Brain and Creativity Institute at the University of Southern California. "Humans are not either thinking machines or feeling machines," says Damasio, "but rather feeling machines that think."

In his acclaimed book *Descartes' Error: Emotion, Reason, and the Human Brain*, Damasio writes about patients he examined who had suffered damage to the prefrontal cortices of their brains, disrupting their emotional processing. He found that their lack of emotions prevented them from making even simple choices and easy decisions. He tells the story of a patient referred to as "Elliot," a family man with a corporate job, who had surgery to remove a benign tumor from the frontal lobe region of his brain.

The operation was a seeming success and left Elliot with his speech, memory, and arithmetic skills all intact. His IQ score was high. And yet, in the ensuing years, Elliot's life and career had collapsed around him. By the time he began sessions with Damasio, Elliot couldn't hold down a job, his wife had left him, and he was "living in the custody of a sibling." Damasio discovered that Elliot had lost the ability to empathize with the plight of others; he had become a passive, "uninvolved spectator" of his own life. He wasn't able to make *any* decisions—from the mundane to the major.

Elliot had become a "real-life Mr. Spock," says one science writer. And yet, despite having not a "tinge of emotion," to quote Damasio, he wasn't able to make better or more *rational* decisions. Instead, "the cold-bloodedness of Elliot's reasoning prevented him from assigning different values to different options, and made his decision-making landscape hopelessly flat." He wrote: "We might summarize Elliot's predicament as *to know but not to feel*."

Damasio concluded that "reason may not be as pure as most of us think." Our emotions and feelings may not be "intruders in the bastion of reason" but rather "indispensable for rationality." They are critical to guiding and influencing our decisions.

....

None of us rely only on logic and reason to guide our decisions. You can line up as many facts and data points as you'd like. But Damasio and his fellow neuroscientists tell us that we *need* a jolt of emotion to get off the fence and make a decision.

So, what does this mean when it comes to persuasion and debate? When you're looking to win an argument, you're trying to guide your listeners to make a decision. You want them to choose *you* over your opponent. And *that* choice requires an appeal to feelings and emotions. The heart steers the head. And if it's heart *versus* head, I promise you, pure logic is losing nine times out of ten.

The question, then, is: How do you reach the heart? How do you connect with an audience on an emotional level and appeal to their feelings? I've worked for years to find the right balance, and I have three lessons to share on how you can master pathos.

1. Tell a story

"Those who tell stories rule society" is a quote attributed to Plato, Aristotle's teacher.

Human beings have always been captivated by good stories, by a solid narrative arc; by a beginning, a middle, and an end. As I discussed earlier, the human brain did not evolve to absorb only cold hard facts. It's hardwired for storytelling.

In fact, as Princeton University neuroscientist Uri Hasson explained in his 2016 TED Talk, our brains become "aligned" with one another's when we hear the same story. He calls it "brain-to-brain coupling." Hasson, notes Carmine Gallo in his book *Talk like TED*, used a functional magnetic resonance imaging, or fMRI, scanner in his lab to record brain scans of multiple people as they either told stories or listened to them. As Joshua Gowin, an expert on the brain, later elaborated while reviewing the results of Hasson's research:

> When the woman spoke English, the volunteers understood her story, and their brains synchronized. When she had activity in her insula, an emotional brain region, the listeners

did, too. When her frontal cortex lit up, so did theirs. By simply telling a story, the woman could plant ideas, thoughts and emotions into the listeners' brains.

How about that for serious power and influence?

For millennia, humans have been sharing stories with one another, telling multiple stories a day, often without realizing we're doing so. Evolutionary psychologist Robin Dunbar revealed, according to the *Atlantic*'s Cody C. Delistraty, that 65 percent of our daily conversations consist of sharing gossip!

Storytelling, perhaps unsurprisingly then, is a potent method of persuasion. In a 2007 study, Wharton professor of marketing and psychology Deborah Small and her two coauthors found that people ended up giving more money to charity upon hearing and seeing a story about a *single* "identifiable victim," as opposed to one that described numerous "statistical victims" in the same plight. A story about a single child, with a name and a face, in need of help, has a much bigger and more direct impact on our level of empathy than a story about *millions* of nameless and faceless people in need. That's pathos over logos in a nutshell.

And why does that happen? Stories that "are concrete (rather than abstract), personal, and narrative in form tend to evoke more emotion," Small explained to me. "Focusing on a single individual's plight checks all of these boxes." It allows us to understand and even *feel* the pain that an individual is grappling with, whereas a flood of statistics is much harder to imagine on a personal level. As Professor Hasson observed, reports NPR, a good story "lights up" the emotional regions of our brain in line with the storyteller; if the speaker talks about the fear or inspiration they felt in a moment of struggle, we "mirror" it. We feel it, too.

So next time you want to persuade an audience, tell them emotion-filled stories about specific individuals. Tell them why they should care! In 2019, for example, I spoke at a debate in London hosted

by the nonprofit Intelligence Squared, on the topic of Saudi Arabia
and its human rights abuses. I could have opened my speech making
the case for the West cutting ties with Riyadh, by quoting from long
and detailed reports by human rights groups, by citing numerous
clauses from international human rights law, or by pointing out the
sheer number of executions carried out in that country. All undeniable facts. All important evidence for my overall argument critiquing
the Saudi government.

But such an opening gambit would have been too dry, too dull,
too dense for that crowd. I knew I needed to tug at their heartstrings
from the get-go. So I kicked off by telling stories about actual Saudi citizens who have suffered tremendously at the hands of their unelected
government.

> Ladies and gentlemen, good evening. I stand before you
> tonight to make the case for the motion. And as I do, a num-
> ber of names and faces flash through my mind. People who
> are counting on me and on you to speak for them tonight,
> in this debate, to give them a voice tonight with your votes.
> Loujain al-Hathloul, for example, a young women's rights
> activist who was jailed in 2014 for trying to drive her car
> in Saudi Arabia. Upon her release, she went to live in the
> UAE, where last March, she was kidnapped on the side of
> the highway, put in handcuffs, thrown on board a private
> jet, and taken back to Saudi Arabia against her will. Today,
> aged just twenty-nine years old, she sits behind bars because
> she had the temerity to dare to call for women to be allowed
> to drive. According to her sister, as we speak tonight, Lou-
> jain is being held in solitary confinement, where she's been
> beaten, waterboarded, electrocuted, sexually harassed, and
> threatened with rape and murder.
>
> Israa al-Ghomgham is also twenty-nine years old.
> She's a young Shia human rights activist, arrested with her

husband in 2015, for carrying out peaceful protests, not for anything violent. And yet Saudi prosecutors are seeking to behead her. If they're successful, she will be the first female human rights activist that the Saudis have put to death. Executed. According to Human Rights Watch, Israa has not been charged or convicted for any acts of violence, or even anything, quote, "resembling recognizable crimes."

The blogger Raif Badawi had his thirty-fifth birthday last month, behind bars. He hasn't seen his kids in seven years. He was sentenced, for the "crime" of apostasy, to ten years in prison and a thousand lashes, fifty lashes of which he's already had to endure. His health has deteriorated in prison, and his wife doesn't think he'll survive another round of flogging. Flogging!

Amal Hussein was seven years old. A little girl in Yemen, the same age as my daughter, no threat to anyone. There she was, that harrowing photo of her, in the *New York Times* last November, her emaciated body, her sticklike arms. Within a week of that report she was dead. Literally starved to death. We in the West saw her picture, her haunting eyes! But we in the West did nothing to help her. And nor have we helped the other 1.8 million severely malnourished children in Yemen, who are suffering from a famine caused by a Saudi-imposed blockade.

And then there's Jamal Khashoggi. Jamal, who was sitting with me in the green room at Al Jazeera English last March, joking with me about whether or not he'd be safe in DC while the Saudi crown prince was in town. Less than seven months later, he was dead, brutally murdered inside the Saudi consulate in Istanbul, his body allegedly cut into pieces with a bone saw; and murdered, remember, according even to the CIA, on the direct orders of the Saudi crown prince, Mohammed bin Salman.

Ladies and gentlemen, let's not forget these people tonight—Loujain, Israa, Raif, Amal, Jamal; people who have been killed, dismembered, tortured, beaten, flogged, imprisoned, starved, sexually assaulted, at the hands of our ally, our close friend, the Kingdom of Saudi Arabia.

Names. Faces. Biographies. Which made it impossible to tune out or look away. (And in case you're wondering, we won that debate.)

It is difficult for me to *overstate* to you the power of simply sharing stories with your audience. "We are, as a species, addicted to story," writes Jonathan Gottschall, a professor of English, in his 2012 book *The Storytelling Animal*. A story, he adds, "is for a human as water is for fish." Stanford University professor of marketing Jennifer Aaker even quantified our fondness for narrative, finding that "story is up to 22 times more memorable than facts alone."

No matter how serious, no matter how technical the subject you are discussing might be, you will need to rely on good anecdotes and gripping narratives to get your point across. If you're stuck for a story, think about how the topic you are discussing—be it politics, law, religion, physics, *whatever*—impacts the lives of real people. Individuals with names and ages; friends and families; hopes and dreams. Talk about them. Tell *their* stories.

And if you're still stuck in finding a story to tell, consider sharing an event or experience from your own life. Don't be afraid to get personal.

For example, being both a Muslim and the son of Indian immigrants to the United Kingdom, I often get caught up in debates about integration, assimilation, and multiculturalism. During those arguments, I've never shied away from my own backstory or life experiences. I've never avoided making things personal in order to get my point across. In 2011, I was involved in a rather heated disagreement on the BBC's *Question Time* show about the future of multiculturalism in the UK. I could have cited multiple academic studies on the success of the multicultural model. Or I could have discussed generic migrants settling in the UK and building new lives for themselves and their children. But I wanted to use a personal story to make my point tangible to the studio audience:

> I believe I am a product of multiculturalism . . . My father came to this country in 1966. He used to write lots of letters to newspapers with his views on the stories of the day, and he used to get dog litter through his letterbox in response. That forty-five years later, in my view, his son can sit here on *Question Time* with David Dimbleby and a Conservative minister and say that I am a proud Briton, and a proud Asian, and a proud Muslim, I think is a testimony to the success of multiculturalism in this country.

You can really connect with someone listening to you, on a deep emotional level, if they feel like they can understand what *you* have been through—if they can be encouraged to imagine themselves in *your* shoes. This isn't just a folksy saying, either. It, too, is rooted in proper science. Researchers led by Kurt Gray, a psychologist and director of the Center for the Science of Moral Understanding at the University of North Carolina, conducted fifteen different experiments that found that our opponents in a debate "respect moral beliefs more when they are supported by personal experiences, not facts." Gray and his coauthors call this "the respect-inducing power of personal experiences."

So what is the first rule for connecting with other people on an emotional level? Tell them a compelling story. Maybe even your own. Keep it simple: focus on your experience and what you *felt*. And your listeners will feel it, too.

2. Choose words carefully

"Your language will be appropriate if it expresses emotion and character," writes Aristotle in *Rhetoric*. "To express emotion, you will employ the language of anger in speaking of outrage; the language of disgust and discreet reluctance to utter a word when speaking of impiety or foulness; the language of exultation for a tale of glory, and that of humiliation for a tale of pity, and so in all other cases."

To engage with people emotionally, you have to use *language* that engages with their emotions. You want to find ways to grab your audience's attention: to rouse them, inspire them, and ultimately persuade them. You're trying to change how they feel, using just your words. And every word you choose matters.

Let's say, in February 2022, you were addressing an audience on the subject of Ukraine and the illegal Russian invasion of that country. Let's say you wanted to persuade your audience to support and sympathize with the people of Ukraine.

You could say:

Ukraine was invaded by Russia.

Or you could say:

Defenseless and innocent Ukrainians are being bombed and attacked by Russian aggressors.

Both of these are statements of fact, but one is heavy with pathos, and the other isn't. The first is distant and abstract—speaking only of nations—while the second prompts us to consider the people involved and their experiences. (Of course, even the first statement was banned in Russia; Putin was so conscious of the power of word choice that within Russia, by law, the war could be referred to only as a "special military operation.")

We don't always give such consideration to the individual words we choose, but they have immense power. When you're building an argument, seek out words that invoke pathos and feeling. This is what many world leaders have done time and again throughout history—rallying nations in support of life, liberty, freedom, equality, truth, justice, and the like.

Such techniques also have a clear place on smaller stages. If you're in a debate and you believe your opponent is misleading the audience, don't just describe what they are saying as false or inaccurate—call it a *lie*! Don't just describe your own position on an issue as valid or correct—declare it the *truth*! You want capital-letter nouns, vivid adjectives, bold verbs. You need decisive language if you want to move your listeners.

Back in 1988, George H. W. Bush understood this in a way that Michael Dukakis didn't. The Democratic presidential candidate gave that lengthy answer, lacking in conviction and passion. In contrast, this is how his Republican opponent responded, when he was presented with the same question about the death penalty:

Well, a lot of what this campaign is about, it seems to me, Bernie, goes to the question of values. And here I do have, on this particular question, a big difference with my opponent. You see, I do believe that some crimes are so heinous, so brutal, so outrageous, and I'd say particularly those that result in the death of a police officer, for those real brutal crimes, I do believe in the death penalty, and I think it is a deterrent, and I believe we need it. And I'm glad that the Congress moved on this drug bill and have finally called for that related to these narcotics drug kingpins. And so we just have an honest difference of opinion: I support it and he doesn't.

Bush takes a moment. But note the invocation of "values" at the outset. Note the use of emotive language: "*so heinous, so brutal, so outrageous.*" Note the brevity of Bush's response, in contrast with Dukakis, and the decisiveness at the end: "*I support it and he doesn't.*"

The Republican candidate used pathos to let listeners know where he stood, and how he felt about the issue. Is it any wonder that Bush won that debate—and the election itself?

3. Show, don't just tell

The orator, wrote a young Winston Churchill in his 1897 essay "The Scaffolding of Rhetoric," "is the embodiment of the passions of the multitude. Before he can inspire them with any emotion he must be swayed by it himself. When he would rouse their indignation his heart is filled with anger. Before he can move their tears his own must flow. To convince them he must himself believe."

Just as facts on their own aren't enough to convince an audience, words aren't enough either. Not on their own. Often, you have to *show* your emotions; you have to *share* them with your audience.

Conventional wisdom says you should always remain cool, calm, and collected. And, as I'll explain in a later chapter, that's generally great advice. There is no value in getting flustered during an argument, or in losing control of your emotions.

But that doesn't mean suppressing your emotions altogether. You need to come across as authentic and human—and that means "showing" your emotions and not concealing them. When others see how you feel, it's easier to "connect."

So, if you're particularly passionate about an argument, it's okay to show your own enthusiasm: to raise your voice a little, to use your hands, to smile or laugh. If it's a more somber subject, do feel free to show regret or sorrow: a sadder or quieter tone of voice, longer pauses and deeper breaths.

If the situation calls for it, don't be afraid to get a little angry, even. Real people have real feelings. Is there anything more authentic than some moral outrage and righteous anger?

Back in 2013, in that debate on Islam and peace, I had arrived ready to deliver a prewritten speech. I had practiced it on the train on the way from London to Oxford earlier in the day. However, when I heard the three speakers on the opposition side make disgusting and disingenuous arguments about Islam and Muslims—as they sat right across from me, in front of hundreds of people in the Union chamber—I was furious. I ditched a lot of my prepared remarks and instead I channeled that anger. In particular, I made clear from the outset *why* I was so outraged by their bigoted drivel.

An astonishing set of speeches so far making this case tonight. A mixture of cherry-picked quotes, facts, and figures. Self-serving. Selective. A farrago of distortions, misrepresentations, misinterpretations, misquotations.

And remember how I said I ended that speech? By getting angry and getting personal:

Do you really think that? Do you really believe that to be the case?

I genuinely believe that it was by expressing my feelings, and making it personal, that I was able to win over that crowd. My opponents' argument felt outrageous and insulting, but if I'd adopted a cold or emotionless response, I couldn't have possibly captured what was so galling about the broadside. Sometimes you need a bit of "How dare you, sir?"

The lingering question, however, is when to channel that anger, and how to balance it. In an outright shouting match, no one wins. So you need to pick your moment, and be ready to back up your sentiment with substance. Where's the best moment? My own view is: do it wherever you think an emotional appeal feels genuine. But I also agree with Aristotle, who argued that the introduction and the conclusion of a speech are the two most important and memorable junctures to make that emotional appeal to your audience. Start with emotion *and* end with emotion.

On the flip side, if you are flat and emotionless throughout, be prepared to lose. We already saw that hazard with Dukakis—and it crops up surprisingly often throughout the political landscape.

One of the books that has most influenced my approach to rhetoric and debate is Drew Westen's *The Political Brain*. Westen is a professor of psychology and psychiatry at Emory University and a former consultant to congressional Democrats. Like Hasson at Princeton, Westen has used fMRI scans of the brain to study how we respond to arguments, and his central thesis is that political debates are won and lost not on the policy battlefield but on the battlefield of emotions. "The political brain," he writes, "is an emotional brain." His studies reveal, again and again, how voters are much more likely to vote for the candidate they like, rather than the candidate they agree with.

What's interesting, however, is that many politicians still don't fully realize this reality. Westen notes that Republicans often win because "they have a near-monopoly in the marketplace of emotions," while Democrats continue to naively "place their stock in the marketplace of ideas." This drives Democrats up a wall, as they cite policy propositions and figures only to lose out on inspiration. But the simple truth is that conservatives across the West know how to rile up and energize their base.

Their efforts are not always on the level. As the veteran Republican pollster and strategist Frank Luntz wrote in a now-notorious 2002 memo, outlining how conservatives should address (dodge?) the issue of climate change: "a compelling story, even if factually inaccurate, can be more emotionally compelling than a dry recitation of the truth."

Luntz is sadly right. But what's sadder is that, if Luntz's opponents don't realize that they, *too*, need pathos, then the "compelling, factually inaccurate story" is going to steal the day.

Pathos is a crucial part of the equation. You need it, if you're going to win your argument. But it's still only *part* of the winning recipe. Ultimately, a compelling story that's *backed up by facts* is much more powerful than a threadbare sob story.

In short, feelings are what help you get your facts across to your audience. They're what help listeners retain those facts. And you can ensure that you reach your audience emotionally—by telling stories, using the right language, and knowing when to show emotion yourself. But if it comes down to facts versus feelings, *beware*: feelings often win.

So, *don't* let it come down to that unfair fight. Ensure that you have the goods to reach listeners' hearts as well as their heads.

SHOW YOUR RECEIPTS

We aren't talking about translucent little slips of paper itemizing expenditures. We are talking about proof, evidence, confirmation.

—*Slate* magazine

I n 2002, ABC's Diane Sawyer secured a rare sit-down with the late pop icon Whitney Houston. The interview grabbed global headlines after Sawyer posed a rather awkward question to the award-winning singer about allegations of drug use. And, in response, Houston coined a line for the ages:

DIANE SAWYER: This says $730,000 drug habit. This is a headline.

WHITNEY HOUSTON: Come on! 730? I wish. . . . No, no way. I want to see the receipts. From the drug dealer that I bought $730,000 of drugs from. I want to see the receipts.

That line would go on to become both an internet meme and a personal philosophy of mine. If you want to convince an audience, if you want to pin down your opponent, if you want to prove that *you're* right and they're wrong, you have to be prepared. You have to show your evidence. Your proof. Your *receipts*.

FACTS ARE STUBBORN THINGS

I'll admit: it's pretty damn hard these days to make a convincing case for the reasoned, logical, evidence-based argument. For an increasing number of people, it seems that facts don't matter. Evidence is ignored. Receipts have no value. Remember former Trump adviser Kellyanne Conway's now-notorious reference to "alternative facts"? Or former Trump lawyer Rudy Giuliani's ridiculous claim that "truth isn't truth"?

In recent years, we have witnessed a full-scale and very global assault on truth, on reason, on reality itself. Back in 2018, the RAND Corporation coined the term *Truth Decay* to refer to what it called the "diminishing role of facts and analysis in American public life." Two years earlier, the phrase *post-truth* was the *Oxford English Dictionary*'s word of the year, defined as "relating to or denoting circumstances in which objective facts are less influential in shaping public opinion than appeals to emotion and personal belief."

We live in a world, wrote literary critic Michiko Kakutani, author of the 2018 bestseller *The Death of Truth*, "in which fake news and lies are pumped out in industrial volume by Russian troll factories, emitted in an endless stream from the mouth and Twitter feed of the president of the United States, and sent flying across the world through social media accounts at lightning speed."

In such an environment, it's easy to feel that evidence doesn't matter anymore—that it's impossible to build a well-founded argument that has the power to move people. But I'm not willing to give up on the importance of facts—or fact-checking. Not yet.

In 2017, a study of more than ten thousand people published in the journal *Political Behavior* found that "by and large, citizens heed factual information, even when such information challenges their ideological commitments." Presented in the right way, the facts "prevail," according to the study's authors. Or as the Pew Research Center reported in 2018, based on its own extensive survey data, we are not yet "completely detached from what is factual and what is not."

Phew. Facts (still) matter. "Facts," as U.S. Founding Father John Adams famously declaimed, "are stubborn things; and whatever may be our wishes, our inclinations, or the dictates of our passion, they cannot alter the state of facts and evidence." Adams made that remark in a courtroom, in front of a judge and jury, while defending British soldiers involved in the Boston Massacre in 1770. Even though he was a patriot—and soon to be a revolutionary—Adams was committed to the evidence, even if it went against his politics.

Judges and juries still care about facts. So do the vast majority of listeners and audiences you'll encounter. And so should you.

Confidence, charisma, eloquence, storytelling . . . they only go so far. Pathos often can trump logos, as we've seen, but emotions are quixotic. You need to have a solid factual base for what you're arguing—or you're going to get trounced by someone who can connect emotions *and* evidence. To win the argument, you'll need both: feelings *and* facts.

Antonio Damasio himself, the neuroscientist behind much of our understanding of emotions and decision-making, agrees. He does "not believe that knowledge about feelings should make us less inclined to empirical verification." As he explains in *Descartes' Error*:

> Knowing about the relevance of feelings in the processes of reason does not suggest that reason is less important than feelings, that it should take a backseat to them or that it should be less cultivated. On the contrary, taking stock of the pervasive role of feelings may give us a chance of enhancing their positive effects and reducing their potential harm.

To bring it back to Aristotle, pathos is not enough. "Think of pathos, logos, and ethos as three wheels on a tricycle," explains corporate communications consultant Paul Jones. You need all three in order to influence and move people. Pathos, in particular, writes Jones, "gets you *in* the door. But once inside, if you don't convince them, you'll be *shown* the door."

How do you convince them? With *logos*: logic, reason, and—especially—evidence.

Every culture and civilization throughout human history—going back to Aristotle and beyond!—has understood the need for reasoned discourse and evidence-based arguments. Indeed, even those of us who are people of faith, and are often dismissed as irrational, are actually taught by our religions to value the importance of corroborating our views. The Holy Quran says: "Bring your proof, if you are truthful." The Holy Bible says: "But test everything; hold fast what is good."

The importance of building a logical, evidence-based argument is universal. So the task at hand is to embrace logos, and to learn how to wield it. You'll need to know how to marshal your evidence, cite your sources, and back up your arguments.

Note that you need to go beyond just *gathering* your evidence. Doing your homework and conducting your research are crucial steps toward building any argument, and later in the book I will cover how to prepare in depth.

But it is a different animal altogether to be able to bring all those facts and figures to bear in the heat of an argument. If you're going to win, you need to have your damning factual evidence in hand—*and* you need to be able to deploy it against your opponent, *in real time.*

That's how you combine facts and feelings. And that's how you convince an audience. Your audience wants to see receipts, after all. They want to know that you can back up your claims and contentions. They want to see you do so with actual, and not "alternative," facts!

So how do you show your receipts—in a way that's clear, concise, and convincing? Here are three lessons on how to bring the evidence and best your adversary.

1. Find receipts

Let me state the obvious here: you cannot *show* receipts if you do not *possess* any receipts. Your first task is to get hold of them; to find facts, figures, and quotes that you can use to bolster your own argument while undermining your opponent's. You need to dig and discover. And, crucially, you need to keep in mind that your opponent will have ready responses to the most obvious challenges. So, the best receipts lie a little deeper in the archives.

In October 2020, while promoting his memoir on his time in the Trump White House, *The Room Where It Happened*, former national security adviser John Bolton accepted an invitation to appear on my show on NBC's streaming channel Peacock. I'll be honest: I was stunned at first that Bolton had agreed to an interview with me. Then again, the mustachioed Republican foreign policy hawk is one of those confident conservatives who seem to relish rhetorical combat and confrontation. A graduate of Yale Law School and former member of the Yale Political Union debate club, Bolton served in the administrations of Ronald Reagan, George W. Bush, and Donald Trump. He enjoys an argument—and tends to win them, especially against unprepared or uncertain interviewers.

So I spent several days preparing for my bout with Bolton. I drafted questions on the Iraq War (which he supported), the Iran nuclear deal (which he opposed), and his falling-out with Trump (which was belated, in my view). I also knew that he had been challenged on these topics a number of times before, so he would have stock responses and defenses for them.

What he wouldn't be expecting was for me to zero in on his past ties to the MEK. The *M-E-who*? The MEK, the Mujahedin-e-Khalq, an exiled Iranian opposition group that was once designated as a terrorist organization by the U.S. government. The MEK is obsessed with toppling the ayatollahs in Tehran and has spent millions lobbying and cultivating pro–regime change politicians in the West.

As part of my hunt for receipts, I found, watched, and transcribed a speech that Bolton, then a private citizen, had given to a gathering of MEK activists in Paris in the summer of 2010—when the group was still on the State Department's official list of "foreign terrorist organizations." I scoured his White House memoir for any references to the MEK. There were none. I went through recordings and transcripts of TV, radio, and print interviews that he had given in the previous days and weeks, looking for any mention of his ties to the MEK. There was nothing.

Zip. Zero. Zilch.

So I made sure I was fully prepped on this thorny issue by the time Bolton appeared on my show. And I asked whether he could explain this.

ME: How much of your antipathy toward Iran is to do with geopolitics; how much of it is to do with the fact that you have had a long association with a group called the MEK, which was once a terrorist group banned by the State Department while you worked there? You don't mention it in your book. I looked in your book. There's no mention of the MEK. I think you took tens of thousands of dollars for several speeches. Just wondering how much that influences your policy on Iran?

BOLTON: You know I took tens of thousands of dollars for speeches at liberal universities in the United States. This is really about as low as it gets. The fact is that Hillary Clinton, perhaps someone you support, took the MEK off the U.S. list of terrorist organizations. How about that?

ME: She took it off in 2012. You were speaking with them in 2010 when they were still a banned group.

BOLTON: No look, that . . . that . . . you're simply wrong on your facts on this . . .

ME: No, you were there in Paris in 2010 speaking at the MEK rally when they were still a banned terrorist group according to the State Department.

BOLTON: Nobody buys my opinion, and you can ignore that if you want . . . and we are now, sir, twenty minutes into this interview, which you said was for fifteen.

Is there a better feeling than being able to coolly respond to someone who confidently proclaims that "you're simply wrong on your facts" by demonstrating to them that you *do* actually have the facts on your side?

Bolton, for all his many sins and flaws, is a smart and self-assured operator, but there was nothing he could do when I hit him with the receipts. Unquestionable, undeniable, unbeatable receipts. They turned his trademark smugness into a hesitating defensiveness. And he demanded an end to the interview ahead of time. (I had a producer timing me in my ear and we were most definitely *not* at twenty minutes!)

Receipts don't just end interviews; they can end careers. In February 2020, Senator Elizabeth Warren arrived in Nevada for the ninth debate in the Democratic presidential primary race, ready to tear into the record of a rival who happened to be standing right next to her on the debate stage at the Paris Theater in Las Vegas.

So I'd like to talk about who we're running against, a billionaire who calls women "fat broads" and "horse-faced lesbians." And, no, I'm not talking about Donald Trump. I'm talking about Mayor Bloomberg.

Democrats are not going to win if we have a nominee who has a history of hiding his tax returns, of harassing women, and of supporting racist policies like redlining and stop-and-frisk.

Look, I'll support whoever the Democratic nominee is. But understand this: Democrats take a huge risk if we just substitute one arrogant billionaire for another.

This country has worked for the rich for a long time and left everyone else in the dirt. It is time to have a president who will be on the side of working families and be willing to get out there and fight for them. That is why I am in this race, and that is how I will beat Donald Trump.

She came prepared. She had receipts. She had quotes. She *destroyed* him.

Warren's aides were cheering and high-fiving in her green room backstage as she delivered the receipts onstage—one hugged a chair! When their boss arrived to greet them after the debate, one of them put a laptop in front of her showing an amended Wikipedia page for Michael Bloomberg: "Died: February 19th, 2020. Cause of death: Senator Elizabeth Warren."

That entire answer from Warren came in at just fifty-nine seconds but fully succeeded in recasting former New York mayor Bloomberg as an odious, Trump-like figure trying to buy his way to the Democratic presidential nomination. In the days after that debate, reported the *Guardian*, "Bloomberg, who had seen some minor polling traction in states such as Florida and Tennessee, never seemed to recover." Barely two weeks after Warren's display of receipts on the Las Vegas debate stage, Bloomberg quit the race.

To be clear: Warren didn't wing it on the night. The Massachusetts senator is a former high school debate champion from Oklahoma who went on to win a debate scholarship to George Washington University. She later taught at Harvard Law School. And, in advance of the Las Vegas primary debate, she had spent an entire week prepping intensely with her team to be able to confront Bloomberg on live TV.

That answer "was totally prepared and practiced, and perfectly executed," a Warren aide later told me. "She knew it backwards and forwards."

2. Create your own receipts

As you prepare for an argument, you'll want to gather plenty of receipts in advance. But your opportunities don't end when the debate begins. You can also create your own receipts in the midst of that argument.

What do I mean by this? Be on the lookout for moments in an argument where you can undermine your opponent's claims by citing as your receipt something *they themselves said earlier.* Listen for contradictions in their argument, and highlight any inconsistencies on their part. Doing so in real time can put them on the defensive.

Even if you've done plenty of preparation, sometimes you can spark a turning point in a debate by creating your own receipts. In 2014, in a recording of *Head to Head* for Al Jazeera English at the Oxford Union, I interviewed former Reagan administration official Otto Reich, who had been a vocal supporter of Nicaragua's vicious Contra rebels during the 1980s. "I'm sure [the Contras] murdered people," he reluctantly conceded to me, early on in the interview, adding, "In wars, those things happen." Later in the interview, however, he grew tentative when I probed into his connections to the rebels.

ME: You have already conceded yourself that some of those groups you were supporting carried out murders. Are you saying that never weighs on your conscience? Never bothers you? You're totally fine?

OTTO REICH: No, but I also told you you're drawing a false moral equivalence.

ME: It's a very simple question: Yes or no, does it bother you what the Contras did?

REICH: I told you, yes. If they committed murders . . .

Notice the "if" there? It was time for a receipt—one from only a few moments ago, that I had forced from him in front of a hall full of hundreds of people.

ME: Not "if"; you said they committed murders, Otto. There's no "if." You said it. It's on tape.

REICH: Yes, if they committed murders, it's on my conscience.

ME: Okay, good, that was real hard to get out of you.

The beauty of creating a receipt out of something your opponent has said earlier is that your audience heard them say it, too. There's no debating whether your opponent said it or not, or whether it was taken out of context. Your audience was there as witness—and they tend to nod along as you show your receipt to your opponent. Without anywhere to hide, more often than not, your opponent is left stuttering and stammering.

In March 2016, for my Al Jazeera English show *UpFront*, I interviewed the Saudi ambassador to the United Nations, Abdallah Al-Mouallimi, inside the Saudis' permanent mission at the UN. We discussed the horrific civil war in Syria and Saudi Arabia's support for anti-Assad rebels. Did the Saudis want to see an elected government in Syria if President Assad was toppled from power? "Well, yes," replied the ambassador, "that's the process that we hope will take place in Syria."

I then asked Al-Mouallimi why he was "okay with an elected government in Syria but not an elected government in Saudi Arabia." He wasn't pleased with my question and claimed the Saudi people were "happy" and "content" with their system of government.

AL-MOUALLIMI: I am saying is that if there was a way by which you could ask the common people in the street, anonymously, privately . . .

ME: There is. It's called voting.

AL-MOUALLIMI: Well, [pause] voting along the lines of Western democracy is not necessarily . . .

ME: No, along the lines of whatever you want in Syria.

AL-MOUALLIMI: Okay, well. [Pause] Even that is not the solution for [pause] a system of government.

I created a receipt. I put the ambassador on the defensive. And I produced a very unique, very watchable, very viral interview.

Oh, and I also made it out of the Saudi mission alive.

3. Time the receipts

Once you have collected your receipts, the big question is: What do you do with them? You can't just throw them at your opponent willy-nilly. That doesn't tend to work. Ideally, you want to find an opening to show those receipts, where you can catch your opponent on the back foot. In later chapters, you'll see this same rule applies to "zingers" and "booby traps," too.

Consider this exchange I had with the Slovenian philosopher and proud Marxist Slavoj Žižek, in 2016. Žižek appeared on *UpFront* to discuss his book *Refugees, Terror and Other Troubles with the Neighbors*. Žižek is often seen as a man of the left, but as I went through his book, I was disturbed to see his repeated use of far-right talking points in reference to Muslim immigrants living in the West.

I decided to challenge him on it. I brought receipts with me to the interview, and waited for the right moment.

ME: You say "refugees come from a culture that is incompatible with Western European notions of human rights."

ŽIŽEK: I wonder if I said this precisely . . .

ME: You said it precisely on page 107 of your book.

ŽIŽEK: What do I say?

ME: You say "refugees come from a culture that is incompatible with Western European notions of human rights."

Notice how I delivered this receipt. First, I simply quoted him, without an exact source. When he then questioned the quote, I followed up with his exact words and the page number on which they appeared! This is an ideal pattern—sparking your opponent's doubt or curiosity, then following up with undeniable evidence. That becomes "the right moment."

Žižek is a professional philosopher and a public intellectual; basically, he is a very well-read and supersmart guy. He's smarter than me, for sure. But I was able to put him on the back foot because I was prepared, I had receipts, and I timed them right.

Delayed gratification is often the key to deploying receipts. You might *want* to show all your evidence early on, but it's almost always better to wait for the right time, for that moment where it will have the biggest impact and undercut your opponent's argument.

In March 2021, I found myself going back and forth on Twitter with high-profile Republican congressman Dan Crenshaw of Texas on the subject of immigration and the situation at the U.S. southern border. Crenshaw was arguing that the Biden administration was responsible for a "crisis" at the border because it had reversed a series of draconian Trump administration policies.

The argument on social media turned into an argument on live TV after the GOP congressman agreed to come on my Sunday night show on MSNBC. Ahead of the show, I spoke to several immigration lawyers, activists, and policy analysts to make sure my facts were correct. My MSNBC team and I also prepped graphs and charts to put on-screen during the interview. Remember: the best receipts tend to be those that you can point to, or physically show, either in your hand or on-screen. Receipts, after all, in our daily lives tend to be physical things: pieces of paper.

Shortly after the interview began, I decided to start citing numbers and statistics to Crenshaw. "Let me just put some numbers up on-screen," I told him, as I pointed out how border apprehensions had been going up, month after month, since the start of the pandemic in early 2020. "The truth is that Joe Biden did not inherit falling numbers. He inherited nine consecutive months of increases at the border. It's right there, on the screen."

"Yeah, I'm not sure where you're getting your data from," Crenshaw responded, before going on a sixty-second diatribe in which he (falsely) accused Biden of encouraging migrants to set out for the United States from Central America, while also lamenting the repeal of Trump-era border policies.

I knew my numbers were solid. My data was from U.S. Customs and Border Protection (CBP). So I waited as he spoke for a minute, and then I showed my receipt.

"You said 'I don't know where you're getting the numbers from.' Let's just pull up the graph again," I said, adding: "Those are CBP numbers."

Crenshaw had no real response to this. He didn't dispute the numbers further, but he did try to attack me for suggesting there was no "massive increase" of migrants, or "crisis," at the border. He also referred to some vague phone call he had with "one of the former CBP chiefs"—perhaps forgetting the old saying that the plural of anecdote is not data.

The *Columbia Journalism Review* called my interview with Crenshaw a "debunking." A headline on the entertainment news website The Wrap said I "schooled" the Republican congressman. The clip has more than a million views on Twitter. And I am convinced that what made that interview stand out was that single line, that clear and crisp receipt: "Those are CBP numbers."

Another interview where I was able to both present actual receipts—in my hand, no less!—and also release them at the right moment was my exchange with former Blackwater boss Erik Prince. In an interview for Al Jazeera English at the Oxford Union in 2019, I pressed Prince, an ally of then president Donald Trump and younger brother of then education secretary Betsy DeVos, on his appearances in front of both Special Counsel Robert Mueller and the House Intelligence Committee. He had told the committee he had no "official or really unofficial role in the Trump campaign." So, during our interview in front of a live audience in Oxford, I asked Prince why he had failed to tell the House Intelligence Committee about a meeting he had attended with Donald Trump Jr. and others at Trump Tower in August 2016.

ME: How come you didn't mention that meeting to Congress, given it's so relevant to their investigation?

ERIK PRINCE: I did as part of the, part of the investigations. I certainly disclosed any meetings, the very, very few I had.

ME: Not in the congressional testimony you gave to the House. We went through it; you didn't mention anything about the August 2016 meeting in Trump Tower. They specifically asked you what contacts you have, and you didn't answer that.

PRINCE: I don't believe I was asked that question.

ME: You were asked, "Were there any formal communications or contact with the campaign?" You said, "Apart from
writing papers, putting up yard signs, no." That's what you
said. I've got the transcript of the conversation here.

At this point, the once-confident Prince began to stutter and
hesitate. He had been cornered with his own words. I had literally
printed out portions of his congressional testimony and brought
them with me to wave at him during our interview. They were my
prop—and my proof. And I also had the magic words to go with this
magic receipt: "I've got the transcript of the conversation here." How
could he dodge that, without sprinting offstage?

....

R eceipts can boost your confidence while reducing your opponent's. When you are citing hard facts at your opponent, and
you have the sources to back you up, there's no need for passion or anger, no need for a raised voice or animated tone. The facts
speak for themselves. The receipts do the heavy lifting.

Consider this exchange from an interview that I conducted with
the acclaimed Harvard experimental psychologist, public intellectual, and bestselling author Steven Pinker. In 2018, Pinker appeared
on *UpFront* to promote his book *Enlightenment Now,* which pushes
the optimistic argument that human beings are better off than ever
before, thanks to reason, science, and evidence-based thinking. It's
an argument he backs up with a bunch of social science data and
a plethora of footnotes. But I had receipts of my own to present in
response.

ME: Let's take global poverty. You have a chapter in the book
on prosperity. You want to make the case that the world is
more prosperous and less poor than ever before, and you

point to data showing the number of people living on the extreme poverty line, as defined by the World Bank today at $1.90 a day, is down from two billion in 1990 to seven hundred million in 2015. The world is becoming middle class, you say. But surely you know—I know you know, because you're a very clever, well-qualified guy—that there are numerous studies, a number of scholars who dispute that poverty measure as arbitrary, as inaccurate; that in reality, to quote from a recent academic paper by an anthropologist at the LSE, quote, "around four billion people remain in poverty today; around two billion remain hungry, more than ever before in history."

PINKER: That is completely irrelevant to which way the numbers have gone. Of course the definition of extreme poverty is going to be arbitrary. If you make it higher, then more people will be in poverty; if you make it lower, fewer people. But no matter what cutoff you set, the direction is downward.

ME: That's not true.

PINKER: Yes, it is.

ME: Actually, if you look at the work done by Jason Hickel at the LSE, if you take a poverty line of five dollars, a billion people have been added to the number of people on that poverty measure since 1981. The trend shows the exact opposite when you move it to five dollars a day.

That was Receipt Number 1 from me, citing an academic source.

PINKER: In terms of the proportion of people in absolute . . . in poverty by that criteria?

ME: No, the sheer number of people. A billion people have been added to the poverty total since 1981.

PINKER: Yes, but billions of people have been added to the world as a whole. It's relevant as the proportion.

ME: But you also use absolute numbers in your book. You say it's gone down from two billion to seven hundred million.

That was Receipt Number 2, quoting from his own book.

PINKER: I note that by at least the most widely accepted definition of extreme poverty, it's interesting that the absolute numbers have declined as well. But the main point is the proportion, because more people have been added and so anything is going to increase.

ME: You say "widely accepted," but this is my point. You don't acknowledge in the book, there's no caveats, where you say . . . for example, Professor Lant Pritchett, Harvard colleague of yours, a development economist who studies this stuff, says the poverty line shouldn't be $1.90; it should be $12, $15 a day, and when you make that simple statistical change, the entire picture of poverty changes, and the arguments in your book basically fall apart, do they not?

That was Receipt Number 3, citing another Harvard professor, an actual expert on global poverty, to this Harvard professor, who isn't.

Three arguments from Pinker. Three counterarguments from me—and each with receipts. And those receipts, in turn, brought other experts into the conversation—on my side. When you let receipts talk, you build a chorus of sources on your side, all weighing in against your opponent. And if your opponent isn't careful, their own words turn against them, too.

Steven Pinker, Slavoj Žižek, John Bolton. These are sharp and savvy interlocutors. But if you have receipts, you don't need to be intimidated by the intellect, qualifications, or confidence of an opponent. Those receipts become your unassailable weapon. And they can even become your signature weapon.

In the fall of 2019, at a live taping of my then podcast, *Deconstructed*, in front of an audience in Washington, DC, I began by asking one of my guests, Congresswoman Ilhan Omar, why she was supporting Bernie Sanders over Elizabeth Warren in the Democratic presidential primaries.

Of course, I had plenty of context to bring to the table. In an interview with me, only a year earlier, she'd been against Sanders. I asked her why. Hadn't she said that the "ship might have sailed" on a Sanders candidacy and that she had always thought of herself "as part of the Warren wing of the party"?

The congresswoman took in the question, smiled broadly, and then turned to the audience. "Mehdi always brings receipts," she said, prompting a wave of laughter.

Indeed I do. And to win every argument, you should, too.

PLAY THE BALL . . . AND THE MAN

Only an idiot would dismiss ad hominem arguments.
—Tom Whyman, philosopher

How did the wholly unqualified Donald J. Trump, a former reality TV star and failed property developer, defeat sixteen Republican rivals in the race for the 2016 GOP presidential nomination? These weren't sixteen slouches (not all of them, at least). They were major figures within the party at the time: senators, governors, business leaders, and even one candidate who was the brother of one former president and son of another former president.

Did Trump beat them by outwitting them on the debate stage? By besting them on policy? By raising more money?

Or was it . . . by taunting and diminishing them with childish nicknames?

Liddle Marco. Lyin' Ted. Low-Energy Jeb. Truly Weird Rand.

Trump's tactics were almost universally derided in political and media circles. At the time, one pundit condemned Trump for his "use of vitriolic, ad hominem attacks" and dubbed him the "schoolyard debate champion." Another said he had "honed the art of the ad hominem attack" and "insulted his way to the top of the GOP." The then presidential candidate was seen as a foul-mouthed outlier, a no-holds-barred controversialist.

Now, I'm not disputing that description of him, but what if I told you that Trump's much-maligned tactics were not that different from those deployed by one of the most respected and accomplished orators in human history?

Back in Ancient Rome, the statesman, lawyer, and rhetorician Marcus Tullius Cicero was notorious for the invective he rained down upon his rivals. He was a character assassin par excellence, with a "gift for invective," notes author Sam Leith. As the classical historian Valentina Arena has pointed out, in one famous argument, Cicero called his opponent Piso, the father-in-law of Julius Caesar, a *belua* ("monster"), *bustum rei publicae* ("funeral pyre of the commonwealth"), *carnifex* ("butcher"), *furcifer* ("scoundrel"), *maialis* ("gelded pig"), and *inhumanissimum ac foedissimum monstrum* ("most foul and inhuman monster"). Cicero, Arena added, also mocked his opponent's physical appearance, including his "hairy cheeks and discolored teeth." (Positively Trumpian!)

The Latin phrase *ad hominem* literally means "to the person"— and so the ad hominem argument is an argument that's applied to, or against, the person. The truth is, says another classical historian, that such name-calling and verbally abusive arguments were part and parcel of ancient Roman life; they were "ingrained and accepted" forms of political oratory and debate.

These days, though, such Ciceronian invective is seen as off-limits, a no-go area in both everyday argument and formal debate. Ad hominem arguments are viewed, almost universally, as bad, bad, *bad*.

In sports like soccer or basketball, players are taught to "play the ball, not the man." It's fair play to go after the ball—but as soon as you start to tackle other players in the process, it's a foul. You're penalized. In high school debate clubs and college courses around the world you'll find teachers encouraging students to do the same. Students are taught to differentiate between their opponent and their opponent's argument.

The rationale for doing so makes perfect sense. In theory, a person's merits are *irrelevant* to whether their argument makes logical sense. An argument depends on nothing more than whether its conclusion follows its premises; the speaker, you might say, is just the messenger. As academic Michael Austin, author of the bestselling textbook *Reading the World*, puts it more pithily: "If Adolph Hitler said the world was round, that would not make it flat."

So pretty much every introductory textbook on philosophy, logic, or rhetoric sequesters ad hominem arguments to the chapter on logical fallacies. That is, they are *literal mistakes in reasoning*. This is the conventional wisdom. It holds that to attack your opponent instead of their argument is (1) an example of what's known as an "informal fallacy," in which a conclusion is reached using faulty premises; (2) an implicit acknowledgment that your own argument is on shaky ground, hence the attack on your opponent; and (3) a sign of gratuitous rudeness and disrespect toward your opponent.

I don't fundamentally disagree with any of those three points. They're all valid in their own ways—all true enough. But I would simply respond by asking the question that philosopher Tom Whyman asks: "If ad hominem arguments are illegitimate, *how come they're so useful?*"

Look, yes, in theory, you should attack the merits of the argument itself and not the person making it. But, in the real world, playing the ball *and* the man can prove to be a rather effective, and often necessary, tactic. It can discredit your opponent *and* their argument at the same time. It can win over a skeptical crowd and give *you* the upper hand. And—I'll let you into a well-kept secret—it's not necessarily a fallacious argument either.

If you have a high-minded objection to calling people out, maybe skip ahead to the next chapter. If you want to win an argument by any means necessary, keep reading.

GO AFTER THEIR ETHOS

Remember ethos—the last of Aristotle's three "modes of persuasion"? As the great philosopher explained in his *Rhetoric*, "persuasion is achieved by the speaker's personal character when the speech is so spoken as to make us think him credible." He correctly pointed out that we tend to believe "good men more fully and more readily than others: this is true generally whatever the question is, and absolutely true where exact certainty is impossible and opinions are divided." It is not true, Aristotle continued, that the "personal goodness revealed by the speaker contributes nothing to his power of persuasion; on the contrary, his character may almost be called the most effective means of persuasion he possesses."

To anyone who says "play the ball, not the man," Aristotle might as well be sending a shot across the bow. If one's character and reputation are "the most effective means of persuasion," then it's dangerous to ignore them altogether. If you're unwilling to critique your opponent's credibility, you're giving them an advantage right out of the starting gate.

Think about it. If your opponent has read Aristotle's *Rhetoric* and understands the importance of the three modes of persuasion, then they will be working hard to convince the audience of their ethos, their personal credibility, as a means of bolstering their argument. Why would you *not* want to launch an attack on that ethos? How is that not *key* to your success in winning the argument?

Even Michael Austin, who wrote a bestselling introductory textbook on rhetoric, quietly agrees:

> I don't usually muddy these waters in freshman composition, but the fact is that *ad hominem* arguments are very often the best and most logical responses to another person's claims. This is true because most arguers place their

own character, expertise, or credibility at issue when they make a claim. If somebody supports an argument with a *pro hominem* argument (which we normally call an "appeal to authority") then the *ad hominem* argument becomes both a necessary and a proper response.

What does that mean? That if your opponent is halfway decent, they'll be citing their experience and expertise, sharing personal anecdotes, building trust with the audience. Meanwhile, you're doing what? Letting them go unchallenged? This isn't rocket science. You want your audience to trust and believe you—and not your opponent. And that means you can't simply let them walk away with the win. You need to establish your own credibility while challenging your opponent's.

And for that, you need to rely on ad hominem arguments—logical fallacies and politeness be damned! But how do you know when to bring out the big guns, and how do you use them without backfiring? To understand how to attack your opponent's ethos, it's best to start by understanding the basic types of the *argumentum ad hominem*—and why, in my view, they happen to be totally legit.

Here are the three most common forms of the ad hominem.

1. Ad hominem: abusive

You might call this the Trump special: an argument, as the name suggests, based on verbal abuse and name-calling. It ruthlessly highlights some character flaw, real or imagined, in your opponent and it doesn't let up.

How many times did Trump call Hillary Clinton "crooked"—without any real evidence!—during the 2016 presidential campaign? And did it or did it not stick? And now think about how Joe Biden, in the 2020 campaign, dug in to label Trump a "racist." (Though, to be fair, there was plenty of evidence for that charge!)

The critics would say that this argument is a fallacy—because whether or not Hillary is "crooked," or Trump is "racist," their arguments over tax cuts or childcare need to stand on their own merits.

They're wrong. As Bruce Thompson, a philosopher and expert on informal fallacies, has acknowledged, there is a defense of the abusive ad hominem to be made here.

People who have provided reliable and accurate information in the past are more likely to do so in the future; people who have based their arguments on unsubstantiated and inaccurate information in the past may not be worth listening to now. Where the quality of an argument rests on the accuracy and reliability of certain alleged facts, and where it is not convenient to check those facts for yourself, it is not fallacious to take into account the reputation of the person offering those facts.

The abusive ad hominem is all about the reputation of your opponent. It's all about their ethos. If an opponent is not a good or honest person, if they've been unreliable or fallacious in the past, that should affect how an audience considers their present argument. So, *say that*!

2. Ad hominem: circumstantial

This type of argument attacks your opponent by saying that their claim is driven by their own circumstances or personal situation—by some hidden bias or conflict of interest, perhaps.

Examples *abound*. What if a study suggesting that climate change isn't as bad as we thought . . . is funded by fossil fuel companies? That might raise some red flags. And if the "ordinary mom" on Fox railing against critical race theory in school turns out to be . . . a former Republican Party operative? Surprise! Maybe there's something less ordinary going on.

The critics would say that a circumstantial ad hominem argument is a fallacy because the fossil fuel funding doesn't automatically mean the study is incorrect. The mom's political affiliations don't negate the possibility that there might be a real problem with critical race theory in schools. (There isn't, but that's an argument for another book!)

The critics, though, are mistaken here—or at least being absolutist. Because the point of the circumstantial ad hominem is not to dismiss an argument out of hand but to make sure we apply extra scrutiny to the person making the argument. The point, writes philosopher David Hitchcock, is to be aware of and on guard for possible bias. To avoid being naive or getting duped.

I would also point out here that an obsession with informal fallacies ignores the reality of human nature. We human beings tend to be intuitively suspicious of conflicts of interest. In 2018, a study coauthored by Montana State University psychologist Ralph Barnes concluded that "allegations of conflict of interest may be just as influential as allegations of outright fraud" when it comes to whether or not people are willing to believe claims made by scientists. In fact, they found, raising a conflict of interest was as effective at discrediting a scientist's claim as questioning the "empirical foundation" of that claim.

3. Ad hominem: tu quoque

This type of argument is all about hypocrisy. *Tu quoque* literally means "you also." A tu quoque argument attacks your opponent by zeroing in on any of their past words or actions that contradict or cast doubt on their current claims. It highlights how they might advocate a view or position that they don't or can't adhere to themselves.

In the ongoing debate over abortion, for example, pro-choice advocates in the United States like to point to "an illustrious list of Republican men [who] are publicly anti-choice, but privately have supported women in their lives having abortions," as the *Guardian* reported in 2018.

The critics would say that those GOP lawmakers—including Tim Murphy, the pro-life Pennsylvania Republican who resigned from Congress in 2017 after it emerged that he had asked his mistress to have an abortion—may indeed be raging hypocrites. Nevertheless, the logical pedants remind us, that hypocrisy is irrelevant to any argument over whether life begins at conception, whether the fetus feels pain, or over the correct date of viability.

Again, though, the critics are missing the point. The point of the tu quoque, in this particular case, would be to challenge a Republican lawmaker to try and answer for their inconsistent behavior. Is it really unreasonable to ask a person to explain why their acts don't match their words? And who cares whether or not a conclusion was logically and deductively reached, when the purpose of the tu quoque is to look at how we act on our beliefs *in real life*. If you're demanding that others abide by rules you can't or won't follow, maybe there's a problem with those beliefs. At the very least, it's worth putting your opponent "on the spot" to make them "explain away" the inconsistency.

Put away your logic textbook. We have to treat the *argumentum ad hominem*, as the philosopher Alan Brinton has argued, "as primarily a *rhetorical* phenomenon rather than as primarily a logical one." Rhetoric is the art of persuasion, and we should view the utility of ad hominem arguments through that lens, rather than to "focus so narrowly on the relationships between premises and conclusions."

Each of the three common types of ad hominem has a useful place in a great debater's tool kit. But you'll want to apply them in the right way. If you use an ad hominem to dismiss the conclusion of an argument out of hand then it is, indeed, a fallacy. Instead, you can make them part and parcel to your larger case. If you use an ad hominem argument to question your opponent's credibility, to raise the issue of bias, or to put your opponent on the defensive, then these are legitimate and appropriate rhetorical moves that go back centuries to Ancient Greece and Rome. They're far from fallacies.

Again, this isn't that complicated. The fact that an ad hominem argument *can* be fallacious does not mean that it *must* be fallacious. And this isn't just my opinion. The Canadian philosopher David Hitchcock, a professor emeritus at McMaster University, has argued in a wide-ranging essay on the subject that "there is no such thing as an ad hominem fallacy." Why? Because sometimes calling your opponent's ethos into question is *warranted*. As Hitchcock concludes, "a move that is sometimes legitimate and sometimes mistaken is not a fallacy."

Got that? The conventional wisdom–mongers are wrong. Even top philosophers say *abusive, circumstantial*, and *tu quoque* ad hominem arguments are fine, as long as they are used in the correct way: not to go after the logos of an argument, but to challenge the ethos. Credibility is an asset in any argument, and if your opponent's isn't warranted, don't let it stand unchallenged. And don't let anyone tell you otherwise. (Notice my pro hominem argument there?)

PLAN OF ATTACK

So now we have established that ad hominems can be good arguments that get bad press for the wrong reasons. But how do we put them to work? How do you best deploy the *argumentum ad hominem* in a live debate or real-world confrontation?

For a start, in order to make an argument "to the person," you need to know everything you can about that person. You have to be willing to examine and research your opponent's background, biography, and résumé. You need to be familiar with their past statements and actions, and *especially* any scandals or controversies they may have been involved in.

Later in the book, I'll unpack the importance of doing your homework—and lay out some best practices when it comes to research and investigation. But, for this chapter, let's assume that you've done your research and know that there's legitimate grounds for an ad hominem argument.

The critical question, then, is how to carry out your attack. How do you win the battle over ethos—establishing your own authority while undermining your opponent's? The best plan, in my view, is to challenge your opponent's *three Cs*—their character, their credentials, and their claims. If all three crumble, they're going down.

1. Challenge their character

There will be many times in your life when you will be confronted with people spewing hate and bigotry. Are you supposed to just . . . give them a pass on that? In some pious, high-minded, textbook-inspired attempt to focus narrowly on the logic of their *argument*? Seriously?

Let's take an extreme example: Would you let someone you know to be a Nazi address the issue of, say, anti-Semitism in front of an audience without pointing out to that audience that that person is in fact a *Nazi*? What if that Nazi is even a smart and eloquent speaker who is able to put forward a seemingly logical and coherent argument, with facts and figures, about why fears of anti-Semitism are overblown or irrelevant? Are you going to stick to the merits of the argument, or are you going to address the elephant in the room?

Of course you'd want to address the Nazi's *Nazism* as part of your rebuttal. Maybe their arguments *do* look benign onstage; maybe they've dialed down their tone precisely to win over a general audience. But if you can show that, when your opponent steps offstage, they get *rapidly* more extreme, that's important to note! With this example, argues writer Allen Versfeld, pointing out their "history of anti-semitic statements then becomes absolutely relevant to the argument, even if this is, strictly speaking, an ad hominem attack."

Sometimes you have to "expose"—to your audience!—the bad person behind the perhaps good argument. Sometimes, as Versfeld points out, it is the person who is the problem, and therefore the argument should be *against the person*.

Don't be afraid to *identify* who your opponent really is. Don't be afraid to *define* who your opponent is. Don't be afraid to *characterize* the arguer, and not just the argument.

You don't have to launch a full-frontal assault on them, either. There are subtler and savvier ways to question an adversary's character or morals. One of my favorite debate put-downs came out of Florida in October 2018. In the televised gubernatorial debate, Democratic candidate Andrew Gillum was asked to address the issue of racism, and chose to raise the issue of his opponent Ron DeSantis's racist campaign in the following way:

> First of all, he has got neo-Nazis helping him out in this state. He has spoken at racist conferences. He has accepted a contribution, and would not return it, from someone who referred to the former president of the United States as a "Muslim [N-word]." When asked to return that money, he said "No" . . . I'm not calling Mr. DeSantis a racist; I'm simply saying the racists believe he is a racist.

Ouch! DeSantis may have ended up eking out a narrow victory in the governor's race, but he has never been able to shake off that— very legitimate and relevant!—character attack from Gillum.

2. Challenge their credentials

In any debate, of any stripe, any speaker who's read a page of Aristotle will know that their credentials matter—their expertise, their authority, their qualifications. And they will make their appeal to ethos early.

But, interestingly enough, if the opposing side decides to *attack* those bona fides, it's often dubbed a fallacy—the "credentials fallacy" to be exact. The thinking goes that the logic behind an argument doesn't ultimately *rely* on a set of credentials or qualifications, so it's fallacious to dismiss an argument simply because the person making it lacks the appropriate credentials.

That's true enough, if someone relies only on concrete evidence, facts, and stats to make their case. But *as soon* as your opponent asks the audience to rely on his or her credentials—they're fair game for attack.

Michael Austin, the academic and rhetoric expert, breaks down the boundary between fallacy and fair play:

> It is not a fallacy to directly rebut claims that have actually been made. If somebody makes an abstract statistical argument about the effectiveness of a certain medical procedure, then their evidence must stand by itself. However, when somebody says, "trust me, I'm a doctor," then both their integrity and their medical school history become completely relevant to the question at hand.

Whether we like it or not, audiences almost always connect a speaker's credibility to their credentials. There is a reason why doctors and scientists saturated the airwaves during the pandemic; why retired generals dominated cable news panels during the Russian invasion of Ukraine; why lawyers and especially former prosecutors were being interviewed and quoted all over the media during the two Trump impeachment trials. These people are (correctly) seen as experts in their fields, experts on the topic at hand, and the viewers at home are more likely to trust *their* judgment than that of a (random) reporter or pundit.

But if their credentials fall flat, challenge them. How good are those qualifications to begin with? How relevant are they to the discussion at hand? Are they overstretching, or even misrepresenting themselves?

You can make these objections politely, too. No need to even name-call or belittle. Pose a string of questions to establish, in front of your audience, that your opponent shouldn't be taken seriously: *What exactly do you know about this issue? When did you become an expert on this topic? What actual qualifications do you have to pass judgment on it?* If they can't answer them, then your audience will start to doubt the real merit behind all those credentials.

In fact, what did I do when confronted with three rabidly anti-Islam opponents in a debate on Islam and peace at the Oxford Union in 2013? Simple. I questioned their credentials:

> What I find so amusing tonight is that we're having a debate about Islam and the opposition tonight have come forward: we have a graduate in law, a graduate in modern history, a graduate in chemistry. I admire all of their intellects and their abilities, but we don't have anyone who is actually an expert on Islam, a scholar of Islam, a historian of Islam, a speaker of Arabic, even a terrorism expert or a security expert, or a pollster to talk about what Muslims believe or think. Instead, we have people coming here, putting forward these views, these sweeping opinions.

As I said this, my opponents—activist Anne Marie Waters, journalist Daniel Johnson, and scientist Peter Atkins—sat expressionless, in silence, across from me. They literally had no response!

3. Challenge their claims

What do I mean by the third of the three C's, *challenge their claims*? I'm not referring to the *substance* of your opponent's claims. That wouldn't be an ad hominem argument. I'm referring here to challenging their *record* of past claims.

As the COVID-19 pandemic progressed, for instance, plenty of well-credentialed experts made some *awful* calls—and not once, but twice, thrice, multiple times. In February 2022, I interviewed Dr. Monica Gandhi, an infectious disease physician at University of California, San Francisco, on my nightly show on Peacock. By that point in the pandemic, Gandhi had earned the ire and opprobrium of many of her fellow doctors and epidemiologists as a result of her long history of overoptimistic predictions about the "end" of the pandemic—to the point where she had laughingly dismissed COVID variants as "variants, schmariants" only weeks before the arrival of Delta in the United States. But she was still attracting an audience by appealing to her MD degree and making wishful projections. So I decided to challenge all of her overoptimistic, faulty, and false claims in one single epic question:

> Dr. Gandhi, one of the big criticisms of you is that you make these sweeping and very optimistic predictions, and they just don't pan out. I just want to run through some of them, so bear with me, and then I'll have you respond.
>
> You said last February, a month before India's horrific second wave began, killing hundreds of thousands, if not millions, quote, "India . . . now has herd immunity."
>
> Last March, pre-Delta and Omicron here in the U.S., you said, "I genuinely with all my heart apologize for anyone who continues to try to scare you about variants."
>
> In May, you gave not one but seven reasons why we won't need boosters.
>
> Also in May, you said by June fifteenth, California, your state, would "get to herd immunity."
>
> In June itself, you said not to have "doom" about Delta,

and in July you said, "What we know about the Delta variant is reassuring."

You said in September, "I truly think we are in the endgame . . . by mid-October we will be in a manageable place."

And you said in December, "Omicron won't swamp hospitals in vaccinated areas." It did.

At what point, Dr. Gandhi, do you say, "Maybe I should stop making predictions about a pandemic that I keep getting dangerously wrong?"

Gandhi tried to defend her record but ended up conceding: "Yeah, I guess it depends on . . . yeah . . . I apologize. I will try not to make any more predictions." That was a big concession! But, spoiler alert: she has since carried on making predictions about the pandemic.

There are scads of experts and commentators who have made massive misjudgments, on matters of global importance, with massively bad consequences. And many of them are still at it, without facing any consequences, still making the same appeals to their expertise. Why should we give them a pass? Why should we ignore their horrific track records and focus only on the supposed *logic* of each individual argument? At a certain point, a trend is a trend, and it's foolish to pretend otherwise.

So, use your opponent's past claims against them. They have a past, a record, a history—which shows how their judgment stands up to reality. If it's a record full of failures and misjudgments—of one abysmal prediction or contention after the next—then call them out!

I've even employed this tactic against an entire *publication*. In October 2013, I appeared on *Question Time* the week after the *Daily Mail* newspaper in the UK had run a hit piece on the late father of the Labour Party leader Ed Miliband, a Jewish refugee from Belgium. "The Man Who Hated Britain," was the headline. It was a grotesque smear, with a "whiff of anti-Jewish prejudice," to quote my friend Jonathan Freedland of the *Guardian*.

Also on the *Question Time* panel that night in Birmingham was Quentin Letts, a long-standing columnist for the *Daily Mail*. He, of course, was keen to offer an on-air defense of his employer and the hit piece in question. "Was it really completely out of order?" Letts asked. "I'm not sure it was." But when it was my turn to speak, I didn't leave anything out of order. I turned to the studio audience and said:

> Let me ask you this question: When you talk about who hates Britain, or who has an evil legacy, who do *you* think has an evil legacy? A man who sucked up to Nazis, who made friends with Joseph Goebbels and praised Hitler in the run-up to World War II—the owner and founder of the *Daily Mail*, Lord Rothermere? Or a man who served in the Royal Navy, risked his life for his adopted homeland, Ralph Miliband? Who do you think hated Britain more? And this isn't just about Ralph Miliband actually. This has opened up a whole debate about the *Daily Mail*.

Letts tried to interrupt me at this point, but I was just getting into my stride.

> Quentin, let me finish, and then you can come back in. This is a paper that in recent years said that there was nothing natural about the death of the gay pop star Stephen Gately, who said that the French people should vote for Marine Le Pen and the National Front, who attacked Danny Boyle for having a mixed-race couple in his Olympics opening ceremony, who called Mo Farah a "plastic Brit." So let's have this debate about "who hates Britain" more. Because it isn't a dead Jewish refugee from Belgium who served in the Royal

Navy. It's the immigrant-bashing, woman-hating, Muslim-smearing, NHS-undermining, gay-baiting *Daily Mail*.

The audience roared with approval as the camera cut to a silent, stony-faced Letts sitting across from me. Note that to achieve that standout reaction, I didn't *just* rely on a narrow attack. I played the ball *and* the man—I laid out my reasons for why the *Daily Mail* was wrong about Ralph Miliband and *then* I laid out what's wrong with the *Daily Mail* itself.

This is what allows an ad hominem argument to work to its fullest. You want to dismantle your opponent's appeals to claims of authority—ethos—while *also* delivering an argument on the merits—logos. The combination is so punishing that the pathos practically takes care of itself.

Aristotle, of course, called for all three appeals, working in harmony, and for good reason. Logos and pathos often get top billing, but ethos is always ticking away, quietly serving as the "most effective means of persuasion." You should feel free to boost your own ethos to your audience, but how do you find an edge over your opponent in that third, crucial realm? *Argumentum ad hominem.*

BEWARE THE COUNTERATTACK

I won't pretend that the ad hominem argument isn't a risky strategy. If you're going to dish it out, you have to take it, too. Because Jesus was right: people who live by the sword often die by the sword. If you are going to attack your opponent's character, (lack of) credentials, or history of bad claims, you have to be ready for them to counterattack *you*.

For example, I knew after my appearance on *Question Time* that the *Daily Mail* would come for me. It was inevitable. It was the *Daily Mail* after all! Sure enough, the very next day, the paper leaked an extract of a letter that I had written to them three years earlier asking for an opportunity to write in the *Mail*.

Look, Hasan the hypocrite!

When the flames blow back at you, how *should* you handle it? How should you prepare for the heat?

There are multiple ways you can address an attack on your own character or record. First, you can appeal to the old conventional wisdom and point out that your opponent is using an ad hominem argument! You can go as far as to dismiss it is a logical fallacy or a low blow if you choose. That *itself* might sound like a low blow, after I've spent so many pages defending ad hominem attacks. But it's a technique you can use for your defense if you're in a bind. And the fact is that not all ad hominems *are* relevant. In the case at hand, the fact that I once asked to write for the *Daily Mail* doesn't change any of the facts about the *Mail* that I outlined on-air on *Question Time* in front of an audience of millions.

Second, you can own it. You can own whatever attack on your character or record that comes your way. If you said something bad, dumb, or contradictory in the past, accept it, apologize for it, and move forward. Back in 2013, I was quick to acknowledge how "embarrassed" I was by the "sycophantic" letter I had written to the *Mail* three years earlier, as a young and very ambitious print journalist. It's a fair cop!

Third, you can attack back with your own ad hominem argument, and call it self-defense. That's what Cicero used to do: frame his invective against his opponents as a reluctant retaliation against an unfair attack. The master orator knew all too well: attack is the best form of defense.

....

To conclude: the ad hominem argument is a high-risk/high-reward argument. Get it wrong and your attack could backfire on you. Get it right and your opponent will be on the ropes— maybe even on the mat. The power of the ad hominem attack—and one of the main reasons why it annoys and angers so many people!—is that it is difficult to come back from.

The *argumentum ad hominem*, though, is a supplement to, not a substitute for, a substantive argument on the merits. It's not one or the other—you need to play the ball *and* the man. Cicero, for instance, may well have been a master of vitriol and abuse. But that's not ultimately *why* we remember him as being great. He was also a debater par excellence, who put in the time and effort to reason, persuade, and convince his audiences. So should you.

One final important point: everything I have outlined and advocated for in this chapter relates to arguments we have in the real world. But beware: if you are in a philosophy seminar or a class on pure logic, then your reliance on an ad hominem argument *will* be criticized and potentially rejected. The same applies in a college or high school debate, with strict rules and regulations on what you can and can't say. So please do not "attack the person" if you're in any of those settings!

Still, real life *isn't* a philosophy seminar and *isn't* a high school debate. In real life, the personal credibility of your opponent is crucial to the success of their argument. So don't hesitate to go ad hom to defeat your opponent—and, by extension, their argument.

LISTEN, DON'T (JUST) SPEAK

> When people talk, listen completely. Most people never listen.
>
> —Ernest Hemingway

It was October 15, 1992. George H. W. Bush, Bill Clinton, Ross Perot, and a live audience had gathered at the University of Richmond in Virginia for the second presidential debate. The elder Bush was the sitting Republican president, running for reelection, while Clinton was the fresh-faced governor of Arkansas, a rising star within the Democratic Party.

This night marked the first "town hall" in the history of televised U.S. presidential debates. Clinton had suggested the format, proud of his preternatural ability to charm and connect with live audiences. And the Bush campaign reportedly agreed to it after assuming that "undecided voters" in "conservative Richmond" would go easy on the president.

Midway through the debate, moderator Carole Simpson of ABC News called on a twenty-five-year-old audience member, Marissa Hall, to deliver her question to the presidential candidates.

HALL: How has the national debt personally affected each of your lives? And if it hasn't, how can you honestly find a cure for the economic problems of the common people if you have no experience in what's ailing them?

It wasn't a terribly long question, but as Hall was speaking, President Bush took a look at his wristwatch. Not a peek or a glance. He stared that thing down. And tens of millions of Americans, watching the debate live on television, saw him do it. The president wasn't paying attention! He didn't seem to want to be there!

Perot, the billionaire businessman and third-party candidate, offered the first response to Hall's question: "It caused me to disrupt my private life and my business to get involved in this activity. That's how much I care about it!" A milquetoast answer from the wannabe politician. Next, it was Bush's turn to respond.

"Well, I think the national debt affects everybody, obviously," Bush began.

Everybody? Hall had asked how it affected each of the candidates "personally." She tried again.

HALL: You personally.

Bush still wasn't listening. He began talking about interest rates, prompting Simpson, the moderator, to interrupt.

SIMPSON: She's saying, "you personally."

HALL: You, on a personal basis—how has it affected you?

SIMPSON: Has it affected you personally?

BUSH: I'm sure it has. I love my grandchildren—

HALL: How?

BUSH: I want to think that they're going to be able to afford an education. I think that that's an important part of being a parent. If the question—maybe I—get it wrong. Are you suggesting that if somebody has means that the national debt doesn't affect them?

HALL: What I'm saying is—

BUSH: I'm not sure I get—help me with the question and I'll try to answer it.

It only went downhill from there, notes one commentator, as Bush rambled on about a visit to a Black church and then raised the issue of teenage pregnancies. Why on earth he thought the questioner wanted to hear any of that remains a mystery.

Finally, it was Clinton's turn to respond. The Democratic candidate got off his stool, walked over toward Hall—something neither of the other two candidates did—and he looked her right in the eyes.

CLINTON: Tell me how it's affected you again.

HALL: Um—

CLINTON: You know people who've lost their jobs and lost their homes?

HALL: Well, yeah, uh-huh.

CLINTON: Well, I've been governor of a small state for twelve years. I'll tell you how it's affected me. Every year Congress and the president sign laws that make us do more things and gives us less money to do it with. I see people in my state, middle-class people—their taxes have gone up in Washington and their services have gone down while the wealthy have gotten tax cuts. I have seen what's happened in this last four years when—in my state, when people lose their jobs there's a good chance I'll know them by their names. When a factory closes, I know the people who ran it. When the businesses go bankrupt, I know them.

Spot the difference? Clinton had listened to the question. He had understood where the questioner was coming from. And then he engaged with her by showing empathy: "Tell me how it's affected *you*."

Clinton, for all his many flaws and sins, is not only a great public speaker but also a great listener; in fact, he is a great speaker partly *because* he is a great listener. "The Man from Hope" is a master of empathy, of forming emotional bonds with regular Americans. That night in Richmond, the Republican president ended up admonishing Marissa Hall while his Democratic opponent felt her pain.

After the debate, a CNN/USA Today poll found that 58 percent of Americans declared Clinton the winner of that town hall, compared to 16 percent who said Bush won (and 15 percent who said Perot). Guess who went on to win the presidency?

It may be one of the best-kept secrets when it comes to rhetoric: winning a debate or argument isn't just about speaking well, it's about *listening* well, too. In fact, as the old saying goes, given you're often only talking half the time, listening well is half the battle.

To be honest, though, when I told my wife I was writing a chapter on the importance of listening, she laughed out loud. Then she paused and stared at me. "Are you serious? *You* are writing about the need to be a good listener?"

She has a point. I've never been the greatest of listeners. To be fair (to me!), few of us are. We often don't realize it, but when someone else is talking, many of us don't pay attention. We get distracted, we start planning what we're going to say, or, worse, we cut them off and rant away. We *think* we're good listeners but we're not.

In an age of smartphones, the problem has only gotten worse. How can we listen to those around us when the shiny gadget in our pockets is constantly chirping for attention? One recent survey, reported *Insider*, found that iPhone users unlock their devices an average of eighty times *per day*. That amounts to six or seven times per waking hour, or once every ten minutes.

Yet still our denialism about our listening abilities persists.

CAN YOU HEAR THE DIFFERENCE?

Be honest: When people speak, do you *listen* to them? Or do you just hear them?

Hearing is a physical process. Without going too deep into the science, the experts say hearing is basically what happens when sound waves hit your eardrums and cause them to vibrate, sending electrical impulses from your ear to your brain. Hearing is something billions of people do every day without even trying. It is a passive and "unconscious" process. Think about it: if you're walking down a street, you automatically *hear* noises around you—cars, dogs, people. But you're probably not *listening* to them.

Listening requires absorbing, processing, and comprehending what you've just heard. You're consciously and actively engaged in the process. When you're walking down that same street, imagine you hear a car in the distance accelerating quickly, heading fast in your direction. Now you're listening. You turn around and you react, listening for cues about whether the driver has lost control. Are the tires squealing? Is the driver swerving? Do you need to race to the other side, are you safe here on the sidewalk? You're acutely aware of each sound and the potential danger it poses. All of *that* is listening.

In a crisis, we listen, we react, we pay attention. But when it comes to communicating with people in ordinary settings, many of us phone it in. We aren't good listeners. We prefer to be the ones doing the talking. This might even be *more* true when it comes to debates. We're not listening to what the other side has to say, we're simply waiting for *our* turn to speak. That's what we've prepared for, after all, the opportunity to make *our* argument, uninterrupted and unimpeded.

And yet, as the old saying goes, "Open your ears before you open your mouth." If you skip step one at the height of a debate or an argument, you're going to run into serious problems. If you're not listening to what your opponent is saying, how are you going to respond to them in a substantive way? How are you going to react, reject, rebut? If you're not listening to what they are saying, you're going to end up responding to what you *assume* their arguments are or, worse, what you *wanted* them to be. And that way lies defeat.

This may sound like advice from the Department of the Bleeding Obvious. "Listen to what your opponents have to say? Well, duh!" Yet you would not believe how many people I have seen turn up to a debate or a panel discussion or a live TV interview and just recite their preprepared points or arguments. They fail to adapt or respond to new critiques or comments because they were not listening to what their fellow speakers had to say.

Why would you ever want to do the same? Becoming a good listener is part and parcel of becoming a good speaker and, above all else, an effective communicator. But to *be* a good listener—when you're stressed and frenzied? It's harder than it sounds.

CRITICAL LISTENING

The experts say there are multiple "types" of listening—but the two I want to focus on in this chapter, for our purposes, are *critical* listening and *empathetic* listening.

Critical listening is about going beyond hearing to mentally engage with what's being said. It's a very dynamic process, where you're consciously absorbing, comprehending, and evaluating the information given to you by a speaker in real time. "Is it true or false?" "Does it make sense or not?" "Can I trust or believe what I am hearing?"

You need to be a critical listener when your teacher is giving you feedback on an essay you wrote. You need to be a critical listener when your boss is going through what was wrong in a report you wrote. And you need to be a critical listener when your opponent in an argument is making their case.

It's not easy. A lot of us default into taking the information and even opinions that we hear at face value. If someone tells you that they saw your cousin at the football game, why would you not believe them? We tend instinctively to trust what we hear. But you can't—or at least, shouldn't—do that in a debate. You have to be critically assessing the truth, veracity, and internal logic of everything an opponent is saying—in *real time*. But what exactly are you listening for, and how do you turn critical listening into a tactical advantage?

There are three core missteps you should look out for—three ways in which critical listening will help you win an argument:

1. **False claims:** One of the easiest and most obvious ways to defeat an opponent in a debate is to point out a falsehood or inaccuracy in their argument. If they say something that isn't true, and you point it out, then their credibility, and the credibility of their argument, is instantly undermined. And it's critical listening that enables you to keep track of the various claims and contentions that your opponent is making, and then highlight any glaring (or not-so-glaring!) mistakes or fabrications in their presentation. I cannot tell you how many times I have caught a lie or half-truth in a live debate, that no one else on the stage or panel clocked, because no one else was paying as close attention to what was being said as I was. The issue then becomes: Are you ready with your own list of facts? Ready to rebut and debunk?

2. **Fallacious arguments:** Critical listening can help you poke holes in the (supposed) facts and claims of your opponent; it can help you spot logical fallacies and contradictions within the scope of their argument. You should always be on guard for a flaw in your opponent's arguments. You can try to keep a mental outline of their key points, and then pounce on any that seem inconsistent. "Did I just hear them say something in their closing remarks that contradicts what they said moments earlier in their opening remarks?" Listen critically, and mentally evaluate what is being said by your opponent. Then, when it's your turn to speak, you'll be ready to go on the offensive.

3. **Concessions:** Critical listening can also help you out of a tight spot. If you've recognized that your opponent has a fair point, or a strong argument, one that you maybe don't have a rebuttal for, then throw them off-balance with what I'll explain later in the book is a "judo move": concede that point. It's a terrific strategy if your opponent isn't prepared. However, you cannot concede a point if you weren't *listening* when it was made in the first place! You have to be paying close attention to your opponent's claims, points, and arguments whenever they're speaking—for defensive as well as offensive purposes.

Critical listening is a crucial tool to have at your disposal in an argument, but it isn't easy and doesn't come naturally to a lot of us. You have to work at it, like any skill. So here are my top three ways to improve your ability to listen critically.

1. Keep an open mind

When you're arguing against an opponent, do not automatically assume that everything they're saying is wrong, silly, or dumb. Don't dismiss anything out of hand. Listen for valid points or clever lines that you'll then need to address or concede in your own remarks. You should be confident in your own arguments, yes, but also remain open-minded enough to see where an opponent is strong or where you may have fallen short.

2. Clear your mind

Put down your smartphone and switch off your laptop when you're listening. Don't daydream or, worse, snooze as others around you are speaking and advocating. Pay attention to whoever has the mic. For one thing, it damages your credibility and standing with an audience to be seen behaving in a rude or dismissive way—you don't want to be George H. W. Bush staring at his watch. And, just as importantly, you don't want to miss out on what's being said. How else will you know what needs to be addressed?

So, don't let yourself get distracted. Don't try to multitask. Don't let your mind get cluttered with junk, argues author Maria Konnikova. Focus laser-like on the task at hand: by listening critically to your opponent and being ready to catch fallacious or false claims, you can prepare zinger-like responses, and win your argument.

Konnikova quotes Sherlock Holmes from *A Study in Scarlet*, the first of Arthur Conan Doyle's stories about the detective:

I consider that a man's brain originally is like a little empty attic, and you have to stock it with such furniture as you choose. A fool takes in all the lumber of every sort that he comes across, so that the knowledge which might be useful to him gets crowded out, or at best is jumbled up with a lot of other things, so that he has difficulty laying his hands upon it. Now the skillful workman is very careful indeed as to what he takes into his brain-attic. He will have nothing but the tools which may help him in doing his work, but of these he has a large assortment, and all in the most perfect order. It is a mistake to think that that little room has elastic walls and can distend to any extent. Depend upon it there comes a time when for every addition of knowledge you forget something that you knew before. It is of the highest importance, therefore, not to have useless facts elbowing out the useful ones.

3. Take notes

Critical listening benefits from a sharp mind and a good memory—but both can be bolstered by good old-fashioned note-taking. Some of the most successful people on the planet are fastidious notetakers. The U.S. entrepreneur and lifestyle guru Tim Ferriss has joked that he "takes notes like some people take drugs."

British billionaire Richard Branson, who says he goes through dozens of notebooks a year, wrote about a conference in London where he shared the stage with American billionaire Bill Gates. According to Branson, reported CNBC, as Gates "made a closing speech . . . he pulled some pieces of paper out of his pocket."

"I was delighted to see Bill's notes were scribbled on some crumbled paper he had been carrying in his jacket pocket," recalled Branson, adding: "despite being renowned for his computer genius, [Gates] is not above the humble pen and paper."

Nor should you be. It's important that you take notes when listening to other speakers. Make sure you jot down anything they've said that seems important—or perhaps, what they've *missed*, which you can then raise in your own remarks.

Numerous studies of students in school suggest that those who take notes when the teacher is speaking experience increased attention spans and higher concentration in class. Their listening skills radically improve! The method of note-taking matters, too. One 2014 study of sixty-seven Princeton students, from psychologists Daniel Oppenheimer and Pam Mueller, concluded that "the pen is mightier than the keyboard": taking notes longhand, on paper, is a more effective way of documenting and processing information than taking notes on your smartphone or laptop.

Back in 2013, during the Oxford Union debate on Islam and peace, I remember feeling as if I was losing my mind, listening to so many false and fraudulent arguments from the anti-Islam opposition. Before it was my turn to speak, I grabbed a pen from the person next to me and began scribbling down each of their ridiculous claims on the back of my own prewritten, printed-out speech. For example, Anne Marie Waters, the first speaker for the opposition, had declared during her speech that Saudi Arabia was the birthplace of Islam and, therefore, that the Saudis' austere and often brutal version of Islam was an authentic representation of the faith. But as I listened to her rant and rave, I wrote down two numbers on the paper in front of me: 610 and 1932. When it was my turn to speak, I ignored my prepared remarks and looked down at the scrap of paper in front of me:

> Just on a factual point . . . you said that Islam was born in Saudi Arabia. Islam was born in 610 AD. Saudi Arabia was born in 1932 AD. So you were only 1,322 years off! Not bad.

The crowd inside the Oxford Union chamber roared with approval, while Waters looked (suitably) deflated. I hadn't prepared that line in advance, but it became one of the most memorable moments of the debate. Critical listening is what made it possible.

It takes attention, effort, and hard work to hone your critical listening skills. But the more practiced you are, the more formidable you become as a speaker and debater.

EMPATHETIC LISTENING

There's a second essential listening style that any good debater needs to master. Critical listening is what you should be doing when your *opponent* is speaking. But empathetic listening is what you should be doing when an *audience member* is speaking.

Empathetic listening is about connecting with the speaker and trying to see the world through that person's eyes. The goal of empathetic listening is to focus on the speaker's views and to understand where that person is coming from. It requires you to give your "full attention" to the other person, writes listening expert Ximena Vengoechea, and to show empathy (*obviously!*) as well as humility.

In his bestselling book *The 7 Habits of Highly Effective People*, the legendary American author and businessman Stephen R. Covey called empathetic listening the "highest form" of listening. "In empathic listening," wrote Covey, "you listen with your ears, but you also, and more importantly, listen with your eyes and with your heart."

George H. W. Bush was the exact opposite of an empathetic listener at the presidential town hall in Richmond in 1992. Did he sound like he understood or appreciated questioner Marissa Hall's concerns? No. Was he using his eyes or his heart, as well as his ears? He wasn't even looking at her when she asked her question.

In fact, the elder Bush later conceded that he had stared at his watch that night in Virginia because he so desperately wanted the town hall event to be over. "Only ten more minutes of this crap," as he put it to *PBS NewsHour* anchor Jim Lehrer in 1999. "Was I glad when the damn thing was over?" the former president said to Lehrer. "Yeah."

Bush may have been glad when the town hall was over, but the end of the debate also marked the end of his presidential campaign. The then president of the United States was mocked and lambasted after that second presidential debate. He'd come across as "bored," above it all, and "out of touch," as one report later noted. The empathetic Clinton, meanwhile, continued to climb in the polls.

Don't make the same mistake—whether you're in high school or in the Oval Office. Don't check your watch, or your iPhone, in the midst of a speech or debate—especially when someone is speaking *to you*. Don't make it look like you want to be somewhere else. Don't talk down to audience members. That way lies total defeat, and maybe even Bush-style humiliation, too.

And to be clear: it's not just about *looking* like you're paying attention. You really do have to try and empathize with the person who's speaking to, or questioning, you. They want to see that you understand their concerns and emotions—and that you're likable and relatable. And *you* want to fully understand what they're telling you, not just in their words but also in their tone, delivery, and body language.

Now, I know this idea of listening empathetically sounds like a no-brainer, but in my experience, so many people—so many smart people!—just don't know how to listen like that. Worse, they don't even recognize the importance of empathetic listening. Instead, they say or do things that make them look distracted, impatient, bored . . . as if they *heard* what was said but they didn't really *listen*.

Clinton's response to Marissa Hall in 1992, as CBS correspondent John Dickerson later noted, was a near-perfect example of "showing not telling." If you haven't seen it, I encourage you to search down the video. You can see it and hear it in Clinton's presentation. As Dickerson said, "That was Bill Clinton *showing* that he understood her, empathized with her, had answers for her."

The empathetic listener is always "fully present," says author Melody Wilding. They offer their undivided attention and are ready to put themselves in the shoes of others.

Take Nelson Mandela. The late South African president and Nobel Peace Prize laureate gave what is considered to be one of the most consequential addresses of the twentieth century: the "I Am Prepared to Die" speech, a three-hour antiapartheid address he made as a co-defendant at the Rivonia Trial in 1964. Yet those who knew him best are convinced he was an even better listener than he was a speaker.

I asked Richard Stengel, the former *Time* magazine editor who collaborated with Mandela on the latter's acclaimed autobiography,

Long Walk to Freedom, about the late revolutionary's proficiency as an empathetic listener.

"He was an especially good listener to those who disagreed with him," Stengel told me. "He really wanted to hear the argument." For example, when Mandela was in prison, he was so keen to speak with his guards, and hear their views, that he taught himself their language, Afrikaans, and urged other Black prisoners to learn it as well. "He once said to me that to really touch someone's heart, you need to speak to him in his own language," Stengel recalled. Those white guards on Robben Island knew that their Black prisoner was truly listening to them.

Mandela showed empathy as a listener not merely out of the goodness of his heart but also because he understood how effective it was as a tool of persuasion. "It is wise to persuade people to do things and make them think it was their own idea," he pointed out.

During his childhood, Mandela's father was an adviser to Jongintaba, the king of the Thembu. After his father died, Mandela became a ward of the king, and he was a keen observer of everything that Jongintaba did. He later recounted to Stengel and others how the king would hold meetings of his court, with all his advisers "gathered in a circle," and would always wait until the last adviser had spoken before he himself weighed in.

This became Mandela's own habit with his close comrades in the African National Congress and, in later years, with the members of his cabinet. "I sometimes saw his close colleagues raise their voices with him, but he never reacted—he just listened, and then replied," said Stengel. "He thought the leader's role was to speak last, summarize what had been said before, and try to find consensus."

Remember: you need not empathetically listen to your opponent in a debate—though even in this setting it can offer insights, especially if you're considering a judo move like conceding a point. In every other setting, however, it is probably in your own interest to listen empathetically. It's the only way to understand deeply, and to be able to learn when you're wrong or need to change tack.

Of course, it's not always easy to get out of your own way. I speak from experience. So here are the three strategies that I've found most useful for practicing empathetic listening:

1. **"Stay present"**: Make it clear to the other speaker, and the rest of those watching and listening, that *you* are focused on the other speaker. "Quiet your inner monologue, set your device aside, and draw your attention to the other person," says Ximena Vengoechea, author of *Listen Like You Mean It: Reclaiming the Lost Art of True Connection*. Make sure your attention is 100 percent *not* on yourself.

2. **Make eye contact:** I cannot overstate how important eye contact is as a means of showing empathy and building deep emotional ties. It shows that you're interested in what the speaker has to say, that you're paying attention, that you *care*. When you're looking directly at them and they're looking directly at you, it doesn't matter how many other people are in the room. And research supports the importance of eye contact. One study of doctors and patients found that eye contact was "significantly related to patient perceptions of clinician empathy." Another study of public speakers found "participants were more likely to believe statements by a speaker looking at them directly, compared to a speaker with averted gaze." Surprise!

3. **Ask the right questions:** Pose questions to your inter-locutors that allow *them* to "drive the conversation," and then ask follow-up questions that show you were listening to their answers. When doing so, adds Vengoechea, opt

for open-ended rather than close-ended questions, and questions that require personal and considered responses rather than one-word "yes" or "no" answers. Remember how Clinton responded to that questioner in the Richmond town hall? "Tell me how it's affected you again." That had power, after the other two candidates had delivered their spiels. It helped Clinton refocus *and* it helped Marissa Hall know that she was being heard.

Do these three things and you will be well on your way to winning over an audience. You'll also simply be a better listener for friends, family, loved ones, you name it. (You can tell them to thank Mehdi.)

PERSUADE WITH YOUR EARS

I am guessing many of you picked up this book because you wanted to learn how to build your confidence as a *speaker*, or how to craft a speech, or how to construct a bulletproof argument. You probably didn't pick it up because you wanted Mehdi Hasan to teach you to be a better listener.

Nevertheless, the truth is that whether you're speaking in a big public debate, or presenting to a few people at the office, or in school or college, study after study shows that your audience—that *real people*—will connect with you and be more open to your ideas and arguments if they feel *they* are being listened to.

To be a good listener—of the critical or empathetic variety—requires a mix of patience, concentration, and self-discipline. As Stephen Covey once observed, "The one who listens does the most work, not the one who speaks." And if you're more used to running your mouth, as I am, then it might take some *extra* practice. But it pays off. Just look at how differently Bush and Clinton came across to that audience in Virginia; you could argue that *listening* swung the race. And look at the lengths that Mandela went to, in order to connect with his own prison guards!

To debunk and defeat your opponent's arguments, learn to be a critical listener. And if you want to connect with your audience, learn to be an empathetic listener. After all, as U.S. secretary of state Dean Rusk once said: "One of the best ways to persuade others is *with your ears*, by listening to them."

MAKE THEM LAUGH

Once you get people laughing, they're listening and you
can tell them almost anything.

—Herb Gardner, playwright

There is no bigger current affairs show on British television than the BBC's *Question Time*. For more than forty years, millions of Britons have tuned in week after week to watch the country's leading politicians and pundits argue and debate the news in front of a live studio audience.

In January 2015, I was invited to join the *Question Time* panel. It was the week after the *Charlie Hebdo* terror attack, in which two French Muslim brothers had murdered twelve people at the offices of the satirical newspaper in Paris. In the weeks and months running up to the attack, offensive and racist cartoons of the Prophet Muhammad published by *Charlie Hebdo* had caused outrage and protests across Muslim-majority countries.

I knew the show's producers were keen to have a Muslim voice on the panel—and, to be honest, I was keen to be that voice. In fact, I was beyond grateful to have access to such a huge media platform from which to try and push back against the usual Islamophobia that is unleashed in the wake of every ISIS- or al-Qaeda–linked terror attack. But I knew it wouldn't be easy, and I knew I had to do it with a light touch.

That night, the opening question from the audience was about the violence in Paris and the *Charlie Hebdo* cartoons: "Free speech is good, but where do you draw the line before it becomes harmful and offensive?" And, for the opening response, host David Dimbleby handed the stage over to me. (Surprise!)

I began by making clear that I was appalled—by the massacre in Paris, by homicidal maniacs abusing my religion to justify their crimes.

> As a Muslim, I'm not going to pretend that depictions of the Prophet Muhammad in a very racialized, sexualized, even terroristic way don't offend me. Clearly, they do. Why wouldn't they? But as a Muslim, I also have to say, what offends me, what outrages me much, much more is the spilling of innocent blood in the name of Islam, in the name of my religion, and in the name of my Prophet.

Then I pivoted to the broader issue of free speech and the right to offend. Much of the debate in the news at the time concerned whether other media organizations in the West, including in the UK, should also be publishing offensive cartoons of the Prophet, in the name of "free speech" and in "solidarity" with *Charlie Hebdo*. I thought it was a bizarre argument. Why should we be offending the world's Muslims again and again to score a point against a bunch of dead terrorists? But it was a sensitive subject, innocents had been killed, and I decided to use humor to try and push back against that line of argument.

> On the specific question of free speech . . . we do have limits on free speech. Some people have been acting over the last week as if there is an absolute, untrammeled right to say whatever you like, whenever you like. That's not true. There are legal limits and there are moral limits. Forget things we

ban. There are things we just don't say out of taste, out of decency. Sorry to be crude, but you have the right to fart in a crowded lift; you just don't do it, though, do you? And when you do it, and if somebody attacks you for it, that attack is outrageous, but you don't expect everybody else in the lift to fart in solidarity with you.

I admit, it was a risky joke to make. But the audience erupted in laughter and applause. I believe I may in fact have been the first person—and probably also the last!—to say "fart" on-air in the history of *Question Time*. But that lighthearted analogy, first coined by journalist Gary Younge, allowed me to make a key point about limits on free speech—and it became a moment that everyone would remember in an otherwise very serious discussion that night.

Laughter, as the old saying goes, is the best medicine. But it's also one of the best ways to win an argument, one of the crucial ingredients of a good speech, and one of the few rhetorical strategies that an audience will always appreciate.

So make them laugh. Try some humor. And don't be afraid to lighten the mood.

THE PSYCHOLOGY OF LAUGHTER

"Laughter is a universal language," to quote from a *Daily Telegraph* headline—one that all humans speak. The science is clear about just how pervasive humor is, showing up in every human culture. One study by researchers at University College London, conducted with people from Britain and Namibia, concluded that our basic emotions—especially amusement—are shared by all human beings.

Wherever in the world you plan to speak, debate, or argue, know this: your audience will appreciate and enjoy some humor.

Then there's the science on the *benefits* of laughter, writes speech coach John Zimmer, which range from "improved memory and cognitive function" to increased attention and engagement. Stanford lecturer (and professionally trained comedian) Naomi Bagdonas, coauthor of *Humor, Seriously: Why Humor Is a Secret Weapon in Business and Life*, told podcaster Matt Abrahams that laughter helps with engagement because, when we laugh, "the reward center of our brains is flooded with the neurotransmitter dopamine," which "engenders deeper focus and better long-term retention." According to Bagdonas, "using humor not only can make our content more engaging in the moment, but it also makes it more memorable after the fact."

Laughter provides your audience with "social glue," too. Researchers at the University of North Carolina at Chapel Hill found that *shared* laughter brings people together—in ways that can help *you* as the person making them laugh. "For people who are laughing together," says social psychologist and study coauthor Sara Algoe, "shared laughter signals that they see the world in the same way, and it momentarily boosts their sense of connection. Perceived similarity ends up being an important part of the story of relationships."

Got that? Make your audience laugh and they'll like you, identify with you, and remember what you say to them. In 2011, noted Bagdonas, Obama added this crack about bureaucracy, regulation, and salmon to his State of the Union speech—a forum not generally known for its laugh lines.

The Interior Department is in charge of salmon while they're in fresh water, but the Commerce Department handles them when they're in salt water. I hear it gets even more complicated once they're smoked.

Not only did that last line draw big laughs from the lawmakers in the audience on Capitol Hill that night, but when NPR asked its listeners to describe the sixty-minute speech in three words, the word that listeners most frequently cited was . . . *salmon*! Regardless of their partisan identity, but thanks to a brief and simple gag from the president the day before, they had salmon on the brain.

THE ANCIENTS DID IT BETTER

As ever, when it comes to the art of public speaking, the ancient Greeks and Romans were ahead of their time. One of the earliest known quotes on the importance of wit and humor for rhetoric, writes academic Steve Sherwood, comes from Gorgias of Leontini, the famous Greek philosopher and educator of the fourth century BCE. "The orator should defeat his opponents' seriousness with laughter," he advised, "and their laughter with seriousness."

His point was that humor can play a hugely consequential role in speech and debate—but it should be used strategically. The point of being funny is not just to entertain or to pass the time—it's to get your audience's attention, to keep them on board with your remarks, and to surprise them at just the right moment. Plus, as a bonus, if you're in a formal debate setting, humor can be used to get the upper hand on your opponent, to get laughs *at their expense* (or at least at the expense of their arguments).

As Cambridge University classicist Mary Beard has written, "Ridicule was a standard weapon in the ancient courtroom, as it is only rarely in our own. Cicero, antiquity's greatest orator, was also by repute its greatest joker; far too funny for his own good, some sober citizens thought." But Cicero knew what he was doing. He himself said that "by making our enemy small, inferior, despicable, or comic, we achieve in a roundabout way the enjoyment of overcoming him." And the legendary Roman consul and orator practiced what he preached. More than two thousand years ago, this is how he dunked on one of his rivals: "Memmius thinks he's such a towering figure that when he comes into the Forum, he has to duck under the Fabian arch."

According to Michael Fontaine, a Cornell University professor of classics and translator of Cicero's treatise on comedy, the Roman statesman used jokes as "weapons of war" and as a source of rhetorical power over others. "His enemies said, 'This guy's a total buffoon. He's a clown. He's telling jokes, he breaks protocol,'" according to Fontaine. "And yet he keeps winning and winning and winning."

....

In my experience, humor serves three main purposes in a speech or in a debate:

1. Punch lines build rapport

"If I can get you to laugh with me," the British comedian and actor John Cleese once remarked, "you like me better, which makes you more open to my ideas."

Being funny is one of the "best ways to connect" with, and win over, an audience. When you're making people laugh, you're making a connection with them—regardless of whether they share your age or gender . . . or even your politics! It helps you "build rapport," writes SpeakerHub's Esther Snippe.

A laughing audience—whether it's a few people or a few hundred people—is also a *relaxed* audience. It's an audience that's not just paying attention but much more willing to hear you out and also take your side. Think about it: if they're laughing and enjoying what you're saying, they can't also be annoyed by you and disagreeing with what you're saying.

Remember: the audience *wants* to see you have a sense of humor, a lighter side, a human side, because that's how they connect with you. Humor, writes Zimmer, "bonds" you with your audience.

Plus, here's one other point to consider, says media trainer TJ

Walker: if they're laughing or smiling it also means they're not bored or snoozing; they're not on their phones or checking their email. They're sitting up, they're "paying attention," they're engaged.

By you.

2. Levity lightens the mood

Yes, I know it may sound odd: Why would you use humor to deal with serious stuff? Isn't humor only for lighter topics? Well, no, not necessarily. Sometimes, if you do it right, as I did on *Question Time* in 2015, then humor can help you make your point even in the midst of the most somber, weighty, and important settings.

There are times when you'll have to give a speech on or debate an issue that requires you to present contentious or provocative ideas to your audience. Sometimes your audience will come in with a less-than-open mind. How do you go about *opening* their minds? Using wit and humor allows you to present contentious ideas in a way that doesn't come across as threatening or jarring. A good joke is like a key; it can open a mind that's deadbolted shut, prompting people to consider ideas that they'd never have considered if they were delivered more somberly.

Using humor, says academic Jennifer Aaker, can help release or defuse the tension in the room. One of my favorite quotes, often attributed to Oscar Wilde, says: "If you want to tell people the truth, make them laugh, otherwise they'll kill you." Laughter can help deflect or disarm tough questions from your opponent—and even from the crowd. And, yes, it can help you get your (very serious) argument across in a way that really resonates.

Back in 2009, Bill Gates gave what would become a much-watched and much-discussed TED Talk on mosquitoes and malaria. He was discussing a life-and-death issue and giving a weighty speech filled with facts, figures, and graphs. And yet he was still able to give the audience a breather, and make them laugh a bit, while making his point.

Because the disease is only in the poorer countries, it doesn't get much investment. For example, there's more money put into baldness drugs than are put into malaria. Now, baldness, it's a terrible thing. And rich men are afflicted. And so that's why that priority has been set.

The crowd began to laugh. Gates continued:

But, malaria—even the million deaths a year caused by malaria greatly understate its impact. Over two hundred million people at any one time are suffering from it. It means that you can't get the economies in these areas going because it just holds things back so much. Now, malaria is of course transmitted by mosquitos. I brought some here, just so you could experience this. We'll let those roam around the auditorium a little bit. There's no reason only poor people should have the experience.

Gates paused on this punch line, even as mosquitos indeed flew around the auditorium. Then, with true comic timing, he deadpanned: "Those mosquitos are not infected." As the tension released, the audience laughed out loud, even as they also suddenly felt the weight of Gates's topic. Who knew the (then) richest man in the world had a sense of humor? And that he knew how to use it to make a serious topic like malaria in the developing world *feel* just as serious as it was?

3. Laughter hurts like nothing else

Don't be afraid to make fun of your opponent or their arguments. I did it at the very start of my speech during that Oxford Union debate on Islam and peace in 2013, when I went after Anne Marie Waters, the lead speaker, or should I say lead *Islam-basher*, for the opposition side. Waters was trying to get selected as a Labour Party parliamentary candidate in the forthcoming UK elections, and yet here she was, in front of me and hundreds of people in the audience, arguing for a very anti-Islam motion in a very far-right way. So, I couldn't resist a bit of spontaneous light mocking of her politics as I began my rebuttal—saying that she might be a better fit for two far-right British political parties.

I believe you're trying to stand for the Labour Party to become an MP in Brighton. If you do, and you make these comments, I'm guessing you'll have the whip withdrawn from you. But then again, UKIP's on the rise, they'll take you. The BNP might have something to say about your views.

It was a spur-of-the-moment joke and got a big laugh from the crowd, but guess what? Waters went on to join the UK Independence Party the following year, in 2014, and then allied with a former British National Party activist to found a new far-right, anti-Muslim party, For Britain, in 2018. (Jokes can be prescient, too!)

From the outset, and with the aid of an off-the-cuff joke, I had severely undermined the credibility of the opposition's lead speaker. Almost immediately, the audience started taking her less seriously; *she* was put on the defensive and in fact began trying to desperately interrupt and heckle me. (Thank you, Gorgias and Cicero!)

In 2020, I did the same to the hard-right British newspaper columnist Melanie Phillips, who has been accused of making homophobic remarks throughout her career (which she, of course, denies). In an Intelligence Squared debate in London with me on Zionism and anti-Semitism, Phillips—the archconservative, the champion of "family values"—tried to defend Israel from criticism by bragging about how pro-gay that country is.

Oh, the chutzpah! So here's how I began my remarks in London that night.

Ladies and gentlemen, we have been witnessing tonight a deeply cynical proposition deliver a farrago of strawmen, distortions, deflections, false accusations, and of course straight-up pro-Israel propaganda. Then again, hearing Melanie Phillips come here and champion the rights of gays in Israel in order to defend Zionism was well worth the entry ticket in and of itself.

It got a good laugh—but it also served as a powerful reminder to the audience in the hall just how shameless and hypocritical the other side was.

To be clear: you have to be careful in such situations. You must be absolutely sure that your joke at the other person's expense will be effective. If it isn't, then *you* are the one who could end up looking ridiculous!

Still, in my view, it is often worth the risk because, in my experience, a good gag about your opponent is worth its weight in gold. You have to deliver it with confidence, though. Most professional stand-up comedians would agree that the combination of confident delivery and stage presence helps them get laughs in a way that lesser mortals might struggle to do. (I'll have much more to say about building confidence later in the book.)

....

To sum things up, these are the three ways in which humor can help you: to build a rapport with the audience, to tackle a serious subject, and to take down an opponent. You have to be careful, however, and you have to be prepared. As the ancient Roman rhetorician and educator Quintilian once put it, "Humor is risky, since wit is so close to twit."

So, if we now know that humor *can* make all the difference, how do you find the right balance? How do you ensure that you'll be making a fool of your opponent, and not of yourself? Humor that doesn't land backfires, so you need to know what you're doing. To that end, I've assembled my own list of dos and don'ts, inspired in part by the work of several top speech coaches and experts on rhetoric.

THE DOS OF DEBATE HUMOR

1. Do be self-deprecating

Make fun of yourself. It *always* goes down well. You won't come across as some grand, or distant, or boring figure; instead you'll come across as relatable, says Hrideep Barot. I often joke at the start of my own set-piece speeches that God gave me no skills or talents in life other than a big mouth, so I decided to monetize it. It's a line that tends to be well received by a new crowd—and it also has the advantage of being true. (I really don't have any other skills. Sorry, this is it!)

Throughout his political career, Ronald Reagan used self-deprecating humor masterfully, both to undermine his opponents and to deflect from criticisms. During the second presidential debate of the 1984 election campaign, facing off against fifty-six-year-old Democratic candidate Walter Mondale, the seventy-three-year-old Reagan had to deal with the growing concerns over his age. How could he nullify the nearly two-decade gap between him and Mondale? All it took was the right quip, in an exchange between the sitting Republican president and debate moderator Henry Trewhitt of the *Baltimore Sun*:

TREWHITT: You already are the oldest president in history. And some of your staff say you were tired after your most recent [debating] encounter with Mr. Mondale. I recall yet that President [John F.] Kennedy had to go for days on end with very little sleep during the Cuban missile crisis. Is there any doubt in your mind that you would be able to function in such circumstances?

REAGAN: Not at all, Mr. Trewhitt, and I want you to know that also I will not make age an issue of this campaign. I am not going to exploit, for political purposes, my opponent's youth and inexperience.

It was *the* sound bite of the night—perhaps of the entire 1984 presidential campaign. The crowd inside the Municipal Auditorium in Kansas City, Missouri, including Mondale himself, laughed out loud. The Democratic candidate later conceded that Reagan "got the audience with that," and he wasn't able to win them back.

2. Do be spontaneous

It's great if you have some preprepared one-liners, or a few funny stories you tried out on friends or colleagues beforehand. But it's even *better* if you can react in real time to what's been said or done—to think and joke "on your feet," says TJ Walker. The best humor is the humor that comes naturally, spontaneously, off the cuff. Don't try and force it or squeeze a preplanned joke into a place where it only half fits. Allow your wit to be a reflection of your own personality.

When I interviewed retired lieutenant general Michael Flynn prior to the 2016 presidential election on my Al Jazeera English show, I had no idea he would go on to be national security adviser to President Trump a few months later, or eventually accused of endorsing QAnon conspiracies and promoting martial law! I did know at the time that he was a purveyor of far-right Islamophobic tropes and that he had tweeted that "fear of Muslims is rational."

So I wanted to challenge him on his anti-Muslim remarks and, to be honest, I did not plan on making a joke about them. It was spontaneous and in the moment—but it worked.

ME: So clarify for our viewers: You're not afraid of Muslims? In general?

FLYNN: No. No, otherwise you and I'd be wrestling right now.

ME: That's what I was confused about. And you'd probably win. [Pause] Which is why I should be afraid of you.

Like Reagan with Mondale, I even got a laugh out of Flynn that day. My joke was both spontaneous and self-deprecating—and it put the viewers watching at home firmly in my camp.

3. Do be expressive

Visual cues matter a great deal when it comes to public speaking in general, and to humorous public speaking in particular. So use this as license to *act out* your humor, your gag, your funny anecdote. Don't be afraid to use your facial expressions, your hand gestures, or your body language to convey your humor to the crowd. Sometimes a raised eyebrow or a rolled eye can get your audience giggling. If you're telling a story about someone else, you might be able to pull off a fun impression of them, maybe do their voice. (Though, on second thought, you might want to practice this in front of friends or family beforehand, otherwise it could all go very wrong!) So what other physical expressions are you able to use to signify to your audience that this isn't the most serious part of your speech? That they are okay to chill and relax, to laugh even? Maybe it's something as simple and silent as a smile.

Or even just a pause.

A comic pause.

THE DON'TS OF DEBATE HUMOR

1. Don't be offensive

Don't tell jokes about controversial, divisive, or sensitive topics, say both Barot and Snippe. It's just not worth it. You are not Ricky Gervais hosting the Golden Globes. You're not Dave Chappelle doing a Netflix special. You are not there to push the limits of comedy or take some sort of spirited stand against "political correctness."

Your goal is to win over an audience. So make sure your humor is appropriate for that audience, and don't unnecessarily annoy or gratuitously offend them with your jokes. You're in a public forum trying to make a larger point—so don't let a *bad* joke be the only thing people remember.

Of course, even some of the great rhetoricians have messed up on this front: in 2009, Barack Obama appeared on Jay Leno's late-night comedy show. "I imagine the bowling alley [in the White House] has just been just burned and closed down," Leno quipped, referring to the new president's lack of bowling skills. "No, no. I have been practicing," a perhaps overly relaxed Obama responded. "I bowled a 129. It's like—it was like Special Olympics, or something." It was an unnecessary dig that simply wasn't fitting for someone who represents all Americans. The president later called the chairman of the Special Olympics to issue a "very moving" apology and invited Special Olympics athletes to the White House.

2. Don't go over the top

Don't tell lots of jokes, back to back. You are *not* supposed to be a stand-up comedian. That is not what people are expecting to see or hear from you and . . . let's be honest with each other here . . . *this is*

a safe space, right? . . . it's probably not what you're good at either. Go
for a gag here, a one-liner there. But less is more.

In fact, my advice would be to only make jokes related to your
topic, or in response to what's been said by others before you. "Don't
use humor just for the sake of using humor," writes John Zimmer.
The best jokes are those that help you make your argument. And
again, remember, your audience doesn't want you to be a comedian.
They want to hear what you have to say about the topic; they want
you to inform them, persuade them, maybe even inspire them.

3. Don't be wooden

I agree with media trainer TJ Walker: Do not ever start a sentence
with the words "I'm gonna tell you a funny story now."

Do. Not. Do. That.

There is no need for a wooden or awkward introductory line.
That's where comedy goes to die. If you have what you think is a
funny story, just tell it and let the audience decide if it's funny. You'll
know pretty fast if they don't think it is.

In fact, writes Zimmer, maybe consider testing out what you
think are your funny one-liners or anecdotes beforehand, on people you know and trust, to see if they think they're as funny as you
do. Practice your jokes and go-to stories. Know them inside and out.
And be able to tell them off the cuff, at slightly different lengths and
with different wording. Because there is no fun or humor in watching a speaker read in monotone, argues Barot, and without looking
up from their notes or papers! You can see what might have once
been a witty or lighthearted anecdote harden into concrete before
your eyes—and then land with an absolute thud.

One of the best ways to avoid being wooden, of course, is to be
spontaneous with your humor. If it's just occurring to you, then it
can't sound rehearsed! But if you are going to prepare jokes or a story,
you need to hit the sweet spot—where you've practiced enough to

know your story down cold but haven't etched it into a robotic, recited script.

. . . .

S o those are *my* dos and don'ts when it comes to using humor. While there's clear science behind the power of laughter, there's obviously no science about what makes any of us laugh. It's very subjective, and everyone has a different way of being funny. Work out what's yours. You want to be authentically you, and you want your audience to be smiling and laughing so that they can connect with you.

Perhaps above all else, when deploying humor in a speech or argument or debate, you always want your audience laughing *with* you, not *at* you. If it's the former, you've probably won. If it's the latter, you've lost for sure.

The legendary American humorist Art Buchwald once remarked: "I learned at an early age that when I made people laugh, they liked me. This is a lesson I never forgot."

It is a lesson *you* should never forget either.

Part Two

———

TRICKS OF THE TRADE

THE RULE OF THREE

Mr. Bond, they have a saying in Chicago: "Once is happenstance. Twice is coincidence. The third time it's enemy action."

   —Auric Goldfinger, in Ian Fleming's *Goldfinger*

There are plenty of tried-and-tested rules to rhetoric, but one of the most important rules, one that you should never forget, is the Rule of Three.

Why?

Because three, to quote *Schoolhouse Rock!*, is the magic number. It covers it all: from birth, life, and death, to past, present, and future. And, once you master it, the Rule of Three will have you winning debates left, right, and center.

....

I happen to be obsessed with the Rule of Three. My family, friends, and colleagues all make fun of me. I can't have any conversation with them, make any argument, or offer any explanation, without citing three reasons for what I am saying. No matter how mundane or trivial the issue.

Ask me why I want to eat Ben & Jerry's Chocolate Therapy instead of Baskin-Robbins's World Class Chocolate, and I'll give you three reasons: 1, 2, 3.

Ask me why I prefer movies from the Marvel Cinematic Universe (MCU) to the DC Extended Universe (DCEU), and I'll give you three reasons: a, b, c.

Ask me why I parked my car in a particular spot. Yep. You got me. Three reasons: first, second, third.

I can't help myself. It's always three this or three that. There is a clarity to it. A neatness, a form, an order, to the number three.

And it isn't just me. Do you remember how Steve Jobs launched the iPhone in 2007? "Today," he told his audience, "we're introducing three revolutionary products," repeatedly referring to an iPod, a phone, and an internet communications device, before doing his big reveal. "These are not three separate devices, this is one device, and we are calling it iPhone."

Jobs, as speech coach Carmine Gallo has noted, saw magic in the number three. Two years earlier, speaking to graduating students at Stanford University in what has since become the most-watched commencement speech in history, the Apple CEO and cofounder began his address by telling the crowd he wanted to tell them "three stories from my life. That's it. No big deal. Just three stories."

There's an old Latin phrase: *Omne trium perfectum*. Everything that comes in threes is perfect. Since the era of Aristotle, good public speakers—and especially good debaters—have sworn by this principle, the Rule of Three. It says that ideas or arguments put forward in three words or three parts, in a trio of some shape or form, in the words of speech coach Dave Linehan, are "more interesting, more enjoyable, and more memorable for your audience."

LISTEN TO THE KING

By all accounts, Cicero was the ancients' equivalent of Lincoln, Churchill, and Obama rolled into one. Cicero was so scathingly critical of the Roman general Mark Antony in a series of fiery speeches called the *Philippics* that Antony had him beheaded—and Antony's wife, Fulvia, writes historian Barry Strauss, is said to have taken Cicero's head, "pulled out" his tongue, and "stabbed it" with her hairpin.

During his lifetime, in the first century BCE, Cicero was a pioneer when it came to the use of triads and deployed the Rule of Three to devastating effect—whether it was on the floor of Rome's senate or in court in front of a judge. His weapon of choice was the Greek *tricolon*—a group of three words or phrases that build in parallel toward a common point. It comes from the Greek words *tri* ("three") and *colon* ("clauses").

Ideally, each section of the tricolon, explains classicist T. N. Mitchell in his commentary on Cicero's speeches, "should be longer than the preceding, or the third one . . . should be longer than the rest, embracing, as it were, the others. The thought should also rise in force, building to a climax."

The tricolon has an uncanny way of finding itself at the center of world history. It didn't just put Cicero on the map (and off it). American presidents since the country's founding have often relied on tricola to get their points across—as John Zimmer, the renowned speech coach and founder of the *Manner of Speaking* blog, has documented. Here is Abraham Lincoln, per Zimmer, in his Gettysburg Address in 1863.

> But, in a larger sense, *we can not dedicate—we can not consecrate—we can not hallow*—this ground . . . It is rather for us to be here dedicated to the great task remaining before us—that from these honored dead we take increased devotion to that cause for which they gave the last full measure of devotion—that we here highly resolve that these dead shall not have died in vain—that this nation, under God, shall have a new birth of freedom—and that *government of the people, by the people, for the people* shall not perish from the earth.

Here is Dwight Eisenhower in his "Chance for Peace" speech in 1953.

Every gun that is made, every warship launched, every rocket fired signifies, in the final sense, a theft from those who hunger and are not fed, those who are cold and are not clothed. This world in arms is not spending money alone. It is spending *the sweat of its laborers, the genius of its scientists, the hopes of its children.*

Here is Barack Obama at the memorial for Nelson Mandela—whose clan name was "Madiba"—in 2013.

After this great liberator is laid to rest, and when we have returned to our cities and villages and rejoined our daily routines, let us search for his strength. Let us search for his largeness of spirit somewhere inside of ourselves. And *when the night grows dark, when injustice weighs heavy on our hearts, when our best-laid plans seem beyond our reach,* let us think of Madiba and the words that brought him comfort within the four walls of his cell: "It matters not how strait the gate, how charged [with punishments] the scroll, I am the master of my fate: I am the captain of my soul."

The tricolon is only one form of triad. There is also the *hendiatris,* in which three words in a row are used to communicate one main point. Think "liberté, égalité, fraternité"—the French national motto. Or "life, liberty, and the pursuit of happiness," from the U.S. Declaration of Independence. And what was it that Julius Caesar, Cicero's contemporary, is said to have bragged on the battlefield? "Veni, vidi, vici." I came, I saw, I conquered.

Three! Three! Three!

So if you want to win an argument, convince a crowd, get your points across . . . use triads.

Don't take my word for it. Dr. Martin Luther King Jr. was another loyal adherent to the Rule of Three; he was a brilliant exponent, in fact, of putting things together in triads for maximum rhetorical impact.

Remember his legendary "I Have a Dream" speech on the steps of the Lincoln Memorial in August 1963? Writing for *Forbes*, speech coach Nick Morgan reminds us how he ended it:

> When we let freedom ring, when we let it ring from every village and every hamlet, from every state and every city, we will be able to speed up that day when all of God's children, black men and white men, Jews and Gentiles, Protestants and Catholics . . .

Did you catch that? "Black men and white men, Jews and Gentiles, Protestants and Catholics."

Three groups!

Back to Dr. King:

> . . . will be able to join hands and sing in the words of the old Negro spiritual, "Free at last! Free at last! Thank God Almighty, we are free at last!"

Three times!

HERE COMES THE SCIENCE BIT

We've seen triplets and tricola and triads and *hendiatris*—but what's so special about *three*? Back in 1956, Harvard University cognitive psychologist George Miller laid the groundwork for modern theories on human memory, arguing that our "short-term memory" could only hold between five and nine "chunks of information," with a chunk referring to a digit or word or any "meaningful unit." The title of his landmark paper on the subject? "The Magical Number Seven, Plus or Minus Two."

In recent years, however, cognitive psychologists such as Professor Nelson Cowan of the University of Missouri, who says he is "interested in what the human mind can do and does do," have suggested the number of chunks is much smaller, while also distinguishing between "short-term memory" (our mind's capacity for simply holding on to a "small amount" of data or information for a short duration of time) and "working memory" (our mind's capacity for both holding *and processing* a small amount of information over a short "period of time").

Multiple studies of our working memory "converge on the notion that, reliably, people can remember up to three basic units or chunks or ideas at once," Cowan told me. "Three is a good rule of thumb."

Cowan conducts "running span" experiments, where participants are offered a list of items, but the list ends very abruptly. Participants are then asked to recall the last few items, and, as Cowan told me, "people can only usually remember about three items."

In fact, he said, this doesn't seem to be limited only to humans: "There is some research on honeybees suggesting they can count up to about three or four . . . but not beyond."

Again and again, the science comes back with three. In a 2010 paper, Cowan noted how "mathematical simulations suggest that, under certain simple assumptions, searches through information are most efficient when the groups to be searched include about 3.5 items on average."

Patterns also play a role here, because patterns are often how we process information. Again, the science is clear: people gravitate toward groups of three because our brains are always looking for patterns. And three, say the experts, happens to be the smallest number that allows us to see a pattern.

If something happens once, it's just a one-off. Twice? It's a coincidence. But when it happens three times, we tend to see a pattern—and a pattern makes us think, "Oh, something predictable is actually going on." It gives us a sense of order and comfort—and understanding.

CLAPTRAPS

Those of you who have watched the "I Have a Dream" speech will be aware, of course, of the wave of applause that comes rushing in at the end, even before King has finished speaking.

That's because there's something else the Rule of Three does when you deploy it in front of a crowd: it makes the audience clap at the end of the triad. It actually primes them to want to applaud.

There's even a name for it. In his book on speeches, called *Our Masters' Voices*, the academic and speech coach Max Atkinson unpacks how the best speakers use triads to try and "catch" applause from the audience in what he calls "claptraps."

How does it work? You hit a crowd with your three words, three lines, three phrases: boom, boom, boom.

The feelings rise with each part of the sequence, and they're ready to hit you back at the climax . . . with applause.

And it's not just the good guys who make use of this rhetorical device for maximum impact.

In January 1963, eight months before King's "I Have a Dream" speech, Governor George Wallace, the arch-segregationist and white supremacist from Alabama, the *anti*-MLK if you will, gave his inaugural address.

He delivered this line, penned by his speechwriter, Asa Carter, a Ku Klux Klansman.

In the name of the greatest people that have ever trod this earth, I draw the line in the dust and toss the gauntlet before the feet of tyranny . . . and I say . . . segregation today . . . segregation tomorrow . . . segregation forever.

There was huge applause—sadly!—for Wallace as he got to the end of this particular racist rant. The power, again, of three.

Compare and contrast two UK Labour Party leaders speaking to the Labour Party annual conference, a decade and a half apart.

In 1996, Tony Blair, in his last party conference speech before he became prime minister, delivered this iconic line: "Ask me my three main priorities for government and I tell you: education, education and education."

It was met with rapturous applause from the audience inside the hall in Blackpool. "In the context of political speeches, the three-part list may signal to the audience not when to start talking but when to applaud," writes the psychologist and communications expert Peter Bull. "In this example, the word 'and' coming before the third and final mention of 'education' acts as a signal that Blair is about to reach a completion point; the audience then responded with tumultuous applause."

Fifteen years later, however, UK Labour Party leader Ed Miliband addressed the party faithful in Liverpool. He tried to borrow Blair's rhetorical device: "Ask me the three most important things I've done this year and I'll tell you; being at the birth of my second son, Sam . . ." There was a pause—but the audience in the hall did not applaud their leader. "Presumably," wrote Bull, "the audience was still waiting for items two and three, because Miliband said 'Ask me the three most important things.'" It would require a head nod from the then Labour leader to get them to clap.

As Homer Simpson might say: "D'oh!"

BEGINNING, MIDDLE, END

The Rule of Three is much more than a rhetorical device. It is also an organizing principle for our thoughts—and our arguments. According to Cowan, the cognitive psychologist, three gives you a "stable structure"; it gives you "a beginning, a middle, and an end."

As ever, the ancients were far ahead of the science. It was Aristotle, in his *Poetics*, who said "a whole [story] is what has a beginning and middle and end." Three parts! In our own era, the Poynter Institute's Roy Peter Clark expands upon this in his book *Writing Tools: 50 Essential Strategies for Every Writer.*

"Use one for power," Clark says. "Use two for comparison, contrast. Use three for completeness, wholeness, roundness."

You can use that same logic with your speeches, presentations, and arguments. You want your audience to feel like your presentation is whole and complete, so apply the Rule of Three when you're structuring your remarks.

If, as researchers such as Cowan suggest, your audience is only going to remember three things you tell them, what do you want them to be?

Make sure that *you* know, so that they leave with the message you intend. The worst thing you can do when you're presenting your arguments in public is to lack a structure, to ramble, or to be all over the place. Who wants to listen to someone who's rambling? Would *you* want to listen to that person? Of course not. So don't *be* that person.

Here's what you should do, say the experts. Separate your speech, presentation, or argument into:

1. Introduction
2. Body
3. Conclusion

In the Body, make sure you present three main arguments. In the Conclusion, make sure you summarize and repeat those three main arguments.

Now, you might already be aware that having a structure for your argument is vital. (And if you didn't, now you do!) The Rule of Three, though, offers the perfect structure.

In fact, tell your audience or interlocutors in advance that you plan to deploy the Rule of Three. Don't be afraid to say: "I've got three reasons why you should listen to me." It gets people's attention because, as we discussed, most of us have been hardwired to recognize patterns of three, and by saying it out loud, it's like giving your audience driving directions. They know where they're about to go and they'll have an easier time following along.

Plus, as we've discussed, we all have a short-term working memory that can only really store and process, at best, three or maybe four pieces of new information at any one time. Sticking to the Rule of Three will mean your audience can easily keep track of what you're saying.

Andrew Dlugan, the founder and editor of the public speaking and presentation skills website Six Minutes, has usefully summarized a variety of ways in which the Rule of Three can be deployed to structure your speech or argument.

There's the most basic approach, which I mentioned: Introduction, Body, Conclusion.

Or: Three Main Points.

Or: Three Stories.

Or: Pros, Cons, Recommendation.

Or there's my own personal favorite: making a Political, an Economic, and a Moral argument for or against something. In my experience, that always seems to hit the spot.

Three arguments. Three items. Three points. As Dlugan puts it, "Limit yourself to your best three points. Any fewer, and your message won't be compelling. Any more, and your message risks becoming tedious."

Therefore, to conclude this chapter: if you want to win an argument, use the Rule of Three. Use it to signpost your arguments; use it for rhetorical effect; use it to be memorable. You'll be unstoppable.

JUDO MOVES

Where I come from is judo, where the principles are
"maximum efficiency, minimum effort."
　　　　—Ronda Rousey, WWE wrestler and movie star

In 1870s Japan, a teenage Kanō Jigorō kept getting bullied in
school. At five foot two and ninety pounds, he was an easy target
for the much bigger kids who pulled him out of school and gave
him regular beatings. Desperate to learn how to defend himself, and
over objections from his father, Jigorō enrolled in *jūjutsu* and dedi-
cated himself to mastering the key elements of the martial arts.

By 1882, at the age of twenty-one, he had founded his own school
of martial arts, called Kodokan Judo, in a small dojo with only twelve
tatami mats.

By 1909, at the age of forty-eight, Jigorō had become the first
Asian to be elected to the International Olympic Committee.

In 1964, twenty-six years after Jigorō's death at the age of seventy-
seven, judo was formally introduced as an Olympic sport at the Tokyo
Olympics.

Today, more than forty million people around the world practice
judo. To be clear: I'm not one of them. I have never taken a single
lesson in my life. So why am I telling you about the history and philosophy of judo in a book about . . . arguing?

. . . .

I'm not one for physical combat. I mean, have you seen a picture of me?

Like Jigorō, I used to get picked on by the bigger kids in school. Unlike the founder of judo, I never had the guts to learn self-defense.

Still—as you may have figured out by now—I found another way to fight back. There's nothing like a verbal joust. Debating, in my view, is very much a *rhetorical* martial art, complete with judo moves.

In fact, "judo" itself is derived from the Japanese word meaning "flexible" or "yielding." One of the essential principles of judo is *kuzushi*. This noun, per Wikipedia, comes from the verb *kuzusu*, meaning to "level, pull down, destroy or demolish." *Kuzushi* moves involve throwing your opponent to the ground—taking them down not through kicks or punches but by unbalancing them and putting them in a position where regaining their balance becomes impossible. In the right position, you don't need to strike out; you can let your opponent crumple under their own weight.

So how do we apply these principles to argument and debate? We often think that the key to winning an argument is to not back down. To double down, even, when confronted with an awkward rebuttal or powerful counterpoint. Nothing could be further from the truth.

To win in a debate or gain the upper hand in an argument, you often have to be both flexible and willing to yield, judo-style. It's not enough to go on the attack, bring your receipts, and deploy your humor. Sometimes you have to yield to a debate opponent—not because you're losing, but because doing so will actually help you win.

"The philosophy of judo . . . is if someone takes a punch at you, you don't punch back," says Stephen Llano, an expert on rhetoric and debate at St. John's University in New York. "You use the energy from that punch to flip them on their back, and incapacitate them."

Good debaters deploy similar techniques. They try to throw their opponents off-balance; knock them down when they least expect it. This is the path of "maximum efficiency, minimum effort" described by Ronda Rousey, who, prior to becoming a world-famous WWE champion and Hollywood actor, won a bronze medal in judo at the 2008 Summer Olympics in Beijing—the first American woman to secure an Olympic medal in the sport.

But how do you translate these principles from the mat to the debate hall? I've been honing my take-down moves for decades, and there are three fundamental "judo moves" you can try in any argument:

1. Concession

There is one thing that I can guarantee will happen during any heated debate or argument: your opponent will attack you, your arguments, or both. The way debates normally go, you each make your points and you each critique the other person's points. Both of you likely predict and prepare for this. You expect it of each other.

But here's why you should think like a judo fighter.

Your opponent is going to be unveiling their prescribed, preprepared arguments, getting passionate and energized, trying to get the audience riled up. So, what should you do to throw them "off-balance"? You can use their energy against them by actually conceding one or more of their points, says Jay Heinrichs, author of *Thank You for Arguing*. Llano suggests that you can concede an argument here or there, and then say "there's one argument here that just doesn't make much sense to me and I want to attack that." Don't be afraid to say to your audience, "Here's where my opponent is right," because that then gives you the opening to say: "And here's where they're wrong."

This will throw them off—flip them on their back, metaphorically speaking. You'll diffuse their passion and energy with your curveball concession. To an audience, you then come across as more reasonable and rational, which is how you want to present yourself prior to making your own bespoke counterarguments (and counterattacks!).

We often see making a concession as a sign of weakness. It isn't. It is a sign of strength and confidence. It shows your audience how open-minded you are. It reveals to them that you're not an inflexible ideologue. *Your opponent* might be, but you most certainly are not! Conceding certain points makes you look "honest and scrupulous," says author Sam Leith, and has the added benefit of disarming, disorienting, and throwing off your opponent at the same time.

There is, of course, a technical Greek term for this rhetorical technique: *synchoresis.* The *Collins English Dictionary* defines it as "the act or an instance of conceding an argument in order to make a stronger one."

Cicero was a master of synchoresis. Here he is defending his client Flaccus, a Roman governor accused of extortion, against testimony from Greek witnesses.

> But I say this of the whole race of Greeks; I allow them learning, I allow them a knowledge of many arts; I do not deny them wit in conversation, acuteness of talents, and fluency in speaking; even if they claim praise for other sorts of ability, I will not make any objection; but a scrupulous regard to truth in giving their evidence is not a virtue that that nation has ever cultivated; they are utterly ignorant what is the meaning of that quality, they know nothing of its authority or of its weight.

Note how Cicero concedes that the Greeks are funny, smart, eloquent, all of which are irrelevant to their testimony in court, before damning them as dishonest and unscrupulous witnesses—which is very relevant! Note also the contrast in his tone: the concession is delivered in a simple and conversational manner, while the declaration off the back of it has "strength and firmness."

Inspired by Cicero, and in my own effort at rhetorical judo, I kicked off my own speech in London in 2019 at the Intelligence Squared debate on anti-Zionism and anti-Semitism with these concessions.

Let's be clear about what this motion is tonight. Because it is the motion you all have to vote on, in good conscience. The motion says, quote, "Anti-Zionism is anti-Semitism." It doesn't say, "Some anti-Zionists are anti-Semites," which is true. It doesn't say, "Anti-Zionism can sometimes turn into anti-Semitism," which is true. It doesn't say that "anti-Semites often use anti-Zionism as cover, as an excuse, for their bigotry and racism," which is true. I wouldn't oppose any of that.

See? I made a series of good-faith concessions from the get-go. And then, the floor was mine.

But that's not what the motion says. The motion says, ridiculously, sweepingly, offensively, ahistorically, that "anti-Zionism is anti-Semitism." That merely being opposed to Zionism, a political ideology, remember, is—inherently, by definition, ipso facto—anti-Semitic, which is absurd.

That's judo!

2. Preemption

It is often assumed that having the last word in an argument or debate is more important than anything else.

It isn't.

In fact, in any debate or argument involving multiple speakers, I often prefer to go first and not last. That's not to say it isn't important to leave a lasting impression on both your opponent and your audience, but going first allows you both to set the terms of debate and to unbalance your opponent *before* they even start speaking.

Imagine this: your opponent in a debate has come prepared to make a powerful, seemingly irrefutable argument, building from one premise to the next to their ineluctable conclusion. However, what if you use your remarks to address, debunk, and dismiss all of their points before they have even made them? What will they do now? You have undermined their position before they have said a word. You've completely stolen their thunder and—in judo terms—knocked them to the floor.

Preempting your opponent's arguments is one of the most powerful moves you can make in a debate. You should also consider this flexible technique whenever or wherever you plan on giving a speech or presentation in which you are trying to convince people to agree with you.

In fact, you've probably even heard speakers use phrases like:

"I know what you might be thinking . . ."
"You've probably heard others say . . ."
"Critics argue . . ."

A word of warning, however, about the risks involved in a strategy of preemption, or what the ancient Greeks called *procatalepsis* (from the Greek word for "anticipation"). As George A. Kennedy, a scholar of classical rhetoric, has pointed out, if this technique is not used both sparingly and carefully, it may "throw the orator on the defensive and undermine his credibility, especially if he seems to acknowledge strong arguments against him and does not answer them with absolute conviction."

Nevertheless, if done right and with confidence, it can be a devastating judo move. Why wait to rebut, when you can prebut?

In 2019, I was the opening speaker for the proposition side in another debate for Intelligence Squared, entitled "The West Should Cut Ties with Saudi Arabia." Preemption was a big part of my strategy— identifying, anticipating, and undercutting the opposition side's key arguments before they were able to make them.

Now I'm guessing we'll hear a lot of whataboutism tonight from the opposition. A lot of excuse-making from the opposition. "What about Qatar, what about Turkey, what about Iran," defenders of Saudi Arabia often say. And those countries, yes, have major human rights abuses. Trust me, I know. I've interviewed the leaders of all of them, including the Qataris, and asked them about those human rights issues. But let's be clear: tonight's debate is about Saudi Arabia. Don't allow yourself to be distracted by the opposition.

Such preemption is the rhetorical equivalent of pulling the rug from under your opponents' feet. It's *kuzushi!*

3. Reframing

Those of us who debate like to pretend our arguments revolve *only* around cold, hard logic. But the reality is that the success of many of our arguments depends on the language, metaphors, and narratives that we deploy.

Humans don't make decisions, or conclusions, based on facts alone. We interpret those facts, and doing so requires context and background; our conclusions depend on how we "frame" a particular situation. Frames, say experts, are the "filters" our brains use to try and process and interpret information in any given setting. Do we frame abortion as an attack on the right to life for the unborn child, or as a woman's right to choose what she does with her own body? We could start off in either direction using the same set of facts. It all depends on the frame we choose to rely on, argues Heinrichs.

So, the judo move here is to help your audience draw conclusions based on a framing of the facts and information that suits your side of the argument. It unbalances your opponent, who may not be expecting such an approach. In a formal debate, the motion might be so much in your favor that you can easily use it to advance your case.

Or it might be so tough for you to argue that you have to work out how to neutralize or discard it early on.

If you think the motion works in your favor, then stick to it, narrowly, rigorously, religiously. You should also ensure the other side knows you plan to hold them to it, every single word of it.

However, if the motion does not work in your favor, you should try and reframe it, "redefine" it, broaden its meaning and message. That's exactly what I did in the Intelligence Squared debate, where the rather sweeping and tricky motion I had to argue in favor of was "The West should cut ties with Saudi Arabia." Here is what I said:

> Let's also be clear about the wording of this admittedly awkwardly phrased motion: "cut ties" doesn't mean blockade them or bomb them; it doesn't mean we treat Saudi Arabia the way they've treated Yemen. We're not calling for regime change either. But what it does mean is that we no longer treat them as our BFF in the Middle East, we no longer supply them with bombs that they then use with our assistance to flatten schools, hospitals, markets, and flour mills across the poorest country in the Arab world; it means we no longer cover for them at the United Nations or help get them a seat on the UN Human Rights Council, as David Cameron so shamefully did; it means we do not call for our government to roll out the red carpet for the Saudis every time they come to town . . . That's what we mean by cutting ties tonight, that's what we're arguing for tonight, and that's what we want you to vote for tonight.

I reframed the debate; I made the motion mean what I wanted and needed it to mean. You can reframe or redefine the motion as you want, especially if you are the one proposing it—as I was in that debate on Saudi Arabia and the West.

On the other side, you can also question the premise behind a motion. If it says, "The occupation is undermining liberal democracy in Israel," you could add: "Well, who said Israel was a liberal democracy in the first place?" If a motion says, "Should the West intervene in Syria?" you could argue: "Well, why do we assume the West isn't *already* intervening in Syria?" It is a useful way of getting yourself out of a hole, of turning an awkward debate on its head, and knocking your opponent off-balance: to question everything, not just their facts, figures, and arguments, but the premise and framing of the debate itself!

This same technique applies to questions that you may get asked, too. Many of the guests I interview on TV try to duck and dodge my questions by questioning the premise behind them. It can be a very effective tactic for those who want to reframe an argument they're losing. Back in 2019, at the Oxford Union, I hosted an edition of the Al Jazeera English show *Head to Head* that was focused on China and the misdeeds of the Chinese Communist Party. During a segment in which I was discussing the plight of persecuted Uighur Muslims in China, I asked panelist Victor Gao, a high-profile defender of the Chinese government, about the brutal treatment of those Uighurs in detention camps across Xinjiang Province.

ME: Victor, how long do these camps stay open?

VICTOR GAO: First of all, I do not agree with the premise of your question. There are more mosques being built as we speak than probably any other religious establishment in China.

To be honest, questioning the premise of a question, the assumption it's based on, and the frame it is using, is a good trick. I've done the same myself when I've been invited as a guest on other people's TV shows.

In 2020, I appeared on *Cuomo Prime Time*, on CNN, and I was asked a question by host Chris Cuomo about a story in the news that was framed in a way that I didn't think was fair. The story centered on the Democratic presidential primaries, when candidate Bernie Sanders was demanding that candidate Joe Biden disown and apologize for a proxy's offensive remarks. Cuomo was arguing that the proxy, Hilary Rosen, was not formally employed by the Biden campaign and therefore Biden was under no obligation to throw her under the bus,

So, what did I do in response? I challenged the premise behind his line of questioning; I turned it around and reframed our discussion.

CUOMO: And today, he tweeted that Biden has to apologize—

ME: Well—

CUOMO:—for what was said here. By the way, Hilary Rosen—

ME: But that's understandable, Chris.

CUOMO:—doesn't work for the campaign. She endorses him.

ME: Oh, but come on, hold on, hold on, Chris.

CUOMO: But she doesn't work for the campaign.

ME: Come on!

CUOMO: Yes.

ME: A lot of the "Bernie Bros" who are rightly accused of being toxic, or using bad language, they don't work for Bernie either. But the media and a lot of the Democrat candidates insisted Bernie take responsibility for them. So, I'm not sure why there's a double standard in play here. I think we need to be very clear. Let's be consistent. She may not work for the Biden campaign. But I think everyone needs to denounce bad things when they happen in this race, especially on a high-profile prime-time show, like yours.

CUOMO: You are exactly right. Well argued, as expected.

DON'T OVERDO IT

I agree with author Jay Heinrichs: Throwing your opponent off-balance is one of the most effective ways of winning an argument.

Nevertheless, whether it is conceding, preempting, or reframing, all of these rhetorical judo moves should be used conservatively. Don't overdo them, and don't force them, or they become obvious and they lose value.

So be selective about where and when you want to try this technique. If you use these moves only when you need to, at the right place and time, you'll be unbeatable. Because, remember, the philosophy of judo itself is not about responding to force with more force, but responding in a more flexible, yielding, and subtle way.

To quote Kanō Jigorō: "Resisting a more powerful opponent will result in your defeat, whilst adjusting to and evading your opponent's attack will cause him to lose his balance, his power will be reduced, and you will defeat him."

In other words, don't be afraid to adjust or evade—even against a powerful opponent. In fact, do so *especially* against a powerful opponent. By conceding, by preempting, by reframing the motion or argument, you can lure them off-balance and then triumph.

THE ART OF THE ZINGER

Unless there is the zinger or the kind of the cute line or
whatever, the quotable moment, there's no victor, in a
sense.

—George W. Bush

In the summer of 1988, George H. W. Bush surprised his party,
the press, and the public by picking Dan Quayle to be his vice
presidential running mate.

Dan *who*? The *Los Angeles Times* called Quayle "a relatively
unknown 41-year-old junior senator from Indiana." For the *New York
Times*, he was "a wealthy, 41-year-old conservative with scant national
reputation."

Upon his selection as the GOP vice presidential nominee, Quayle
was immediately engulfed by questions about his lack of experience.
Defensively, he began comparing his own political career to that of
John F. Kennedy, pointing out to interviewers and audiences that JFK
had served fourteen years in Congress prior to running for president,
while he himself had served twelve years in the House and Senate.

Quayle's counterpart on the Democratic side of the aisle was the
polar opposite. The Dems' vice presidential nominee, Lloyd Bentsen,
was a three-term Texas senator who first entered Congress, via the
House of Representatives, in 1948—the year after Quayle was born.

Bentsen had experience in spades, but the question now was whether his time had passed.

As the two nominees headed into the vice presidential debate, held on October 5, 1988, at the Civic Auditorium in Omaha, Nebraska, Dan Quayle was the favorite. "Bentsen, then 67, was born before the era of television," recalled the *Los Angeles Times* in 2016. "His timing was off. He did not respond well to the lighting."

Still, there was the thorn in Quayle's side—how he addressed the question of his experience, or lack thereof. During debate prep, he was repeatedly told by his own aides that his much-favored JFK analogy might come back to bite him. He ignored their warnings, preferring to be bold.

But, sure enough, in Omaha, co-moderator Tom Brokaw of NBC News asked again about Quayle's lack of experience. The Republican senator responded just as he'd planned:

> I will be prepared not only because of my service in the Congress, but because of my ability to communicate and to lead. It is not just age; it's accomplishments, it's experience. I have far more experience than many others that sought the office of vice president of this country. I have as much experience in the Congress as Jack Kennedy did when he sought the presidency. I will be prepared to deal with the people in the Bush administration, if that unfortunate event would ever occur.

The same old "Jack Kennedy" reference didn't come across as bold or original, however. It felt canned. And an indignant Bentsen pounced, delivering a now-legendary riposte.

> Senator, I served with Jack Kennedy, I knew Jack Kennedy, Jack Kennedy was a friend of mine. Senator, you are no Jack Kennedy.

Boom! To get a sense of the reaction in the hall, this is how the official transcript from the Commission on Presidential Debates describes it: "Prolonged shouts and applause." Quayle's own reaction? As one columnist for the *Washington Post* put it, the senator from Indiana "looked like a man who knew he has just had his teeth knocked down his throat."

As he waited for the clapping and cheering to die down, Quayle could only offer this weak and halfhearted response to Bentsen: "That was really uncalled for, Senator."

The line "Senator, you're no Jack Kennedy" is widely considered to be, in the words of the *Los Angeles Times*, "the biggest VP debate moment in history." It not only has its own Wikipedia entry but also has been parodied and echoed in popular culture, from movies like Disney's *George of the Jungle* to TV shows like *30 Rock* and *Ugly Betty*. In the late 1980s, *Saturday Night Live* had a child actor play Quayle, to better capture the moment.

Quayle had leaned into his very weakness compared to Bentsen— until it took just a single line to make his shortcomings abundantly clear. Bentsen nailed it. And, more than a decade after that debate, even Quayle grudgingly admitted in an interview that the zinger was a "good line."

....

So what is a zinger? The term originated in baseball slang, reports the *Christian Science Monitor*, where it was used in the 1950s to describe the fastball that a pitcher throws to catch a hitter "off guard." By the 1970s, it had entered the American political lexicon as a sharp and witty remark, a "barbed quip" that catches the *listener* off guard. And by 2020, when Pauline Bickford-Duane wrote a book on the subject—*The Little Book of Zingers: History's Finest One-Liners, Comebacks, Jests, and Mic-Droppers*—we'd developed a whole lexicon of terms to capture the effect of a great one-liner. Bickford-Duane offers a rather expansive definition of the zinger: an "insult, quip, burn, comeback, clapback, rant, critique, rude comment, critical observation, devastating remark, or (metaphorical) slap in the face."

Zingers are used to undermine an opponent or their argument— to leave them red-faced and speechless, like Quayle. They are often retorts, according to psychologist Mardy Grothe, a word that derives "from the Latin word *retortus*, meaning 'to turn back.' And this, of course, is exactly what a perfectly executed retort does: it turns back a personal attack, turning a momentary threat into a personal triumph."

Zingers might be fun and lighthearted, but they are often . . . cruel. *A weapon.* "It can be both a bludgeon to injure an opponent and a shield to deflect an opponent's attacks," writes journalism professor Chris Lamb in *The Art of the Political Putdown.* "But, perhaps most importantly, it can establish one's superiority over a rival."

This is what we remember, the highlight reel moment where one person suddenly flips around and pins their opponent to the mat. It's why Bentsen's zinger still lands with kinetic force over thirty years later. In a PBS special in 2008, looking back on the history of TV debates, then president George W. Bush highlighted the importance of zingers for political candidates running for public office. "Ronald Reagan in 1980 came up with some zingers, and that became, you know, the measure of success, to a certain extent," said Bush. "Unless there is the zinger or the kind of the cute line or . . . the quotable moment, there's no victor, in a sense."

I hate agreeing with George W. Bush, but the former president has a point.

THE ANCIENTS DID IT BEST

"Zingers are as old as humankind," writes Bickford-Duane in *The Little Book of Zingers.* And it should come as no surprise that the ancient Greeks and Romans loved a great one-liner. Remember Cicero? "By making our enemy small, inferior, despicable, or comic, we achieve in a roundabout way the enjoyment of overcoming him."

Before Cicero, there was Diogenes the Cynic, the Greek philosopher—and notorious troublemaker—who lived in the fourth century BCE. He, too, happened to be an early master of the zinger. When Alexander the Great once visited him and asked Diogenes to make a request of him, promising to grant him any wish or favor, the latter responded by asking the legendary Macedonian king . . . to move and stop standing in the way of the sunlight.

Diogenes was also a long-standing and very sarcastic critic of Plato. He would often disrupt Plato's public lectures, says one writer, by heckling the great philosopher from the audience. On one occasion, it is said that Plato was lecturing on his theory of ideas, using the example of a cup and a table and arguing that the "idea" of a cup or a table came before every actual cup and table in the world.

"I see a table and a cup," interrupted Diogenes, "but I see no table*ness* or cup*ness*."

Plato, fed up with Diogenes' constant interjections, tried out a rare zinger of his own. "That is natural enough, for you have eyes, by which a cup and a table are contemplated, but you have not intellect," tapping the side of his head, "by which tableness and cupness are seen."

Still, Diogenes had the last laugh. Walking over to the table with a cup on it and peering inside, he asked if the cup was empty. When Plato nodded, Diogenes asked: "Where is the 'emptiness' which precedes this empty cup?" As Plato was trying to think of an answer, Diogenes leaned over and, tapping Plato on his head, said, "I think you will find here is the 'emptiness.'"

Ouch.

. . . .

As Bickford-Duane writes in her book—and as Diogenes proved!—a zinger can be "a spine tingling arrangement of words that makes the recipient suck in their breath—or perhaps fashion an equally crushing retort."

So what are the best ways to invent and unleash zingers of your own?

In his book, Chris Lamb writes that the best comebacks require "a good ear, a nimble brain, a sharp wit, and a comic's timing." He's right; there's a certain amount of quick thinking necessary to come out on top. But delivering a good zinger, or a devastating comeback, can also be taught.

There are three guidelines you'll need to know and follow, if you want to master the art of the zinger:

1. Be prepared

Bentsen's now-celebrated zinger didn't come out of nowhere. Dennis Eckart, a Democratic congressman from Ohio, was tasked with prepping his party's vice presidential nominee for the clash with Quayle in 1988. The *Los Angeles Times* revealed how Eckart spent weeks watching videotapes of Quayle's public appearances and spotted the Republican candidate's constant invocation of John F. Kennedy. "Quayle thinks he's JFK!" Eckart wrote on his yellow legal pad.

Eckart then even played the part of Quayle in the mock debates with Bentsen. According to the *Los Angeles Times*, "when it came time for the mock debates, Eckart repeated the comparison to Bentsen." Funnily enough, the Texas senator became increasingly irritated with Eckart in those mock debates. He reminded Eckart and his other advisers that he had known and worked with Kennedy and, at one point, he exploded: "There is no way he can compare himself to Kennedy."

That was it. *That* was the line his team urged him to hone, practice, and deploy while looking directly at Quayle.

So "you're no Jack Kennedy" was by no means as ad-libbed as it looked or sounded. Even a politician as seasoned as Bentsen had to work on it. But that gives hope for the rest of us. We can work at it; we can hone our craft to get the line just right. Even when the great orators make it look like magic, there's more going on. To quote Winston Churchill, who was renowned for his own caustic wit and scathing put-downs: "All the best off-the-cuff remarks are prepared days beforehand."

For that matter, you can even rely on history's most prominent orators to help you with your zingers. Don't be afraid to use, or *re-use*, what has been tried and tested by other quick-witted debaters. Invest in books of quotations or one-liners, like Grothe's or Lamb's or Bickford-Duane's. Check out websites like BrainyQuote or ThinkExist, which collate one-liners and put-downs from across history and across the globe. You can create your own "commonplace books"—that is, take a blank notebook, divide it into sections and topics, and start jotting down—and then messing around with—any fun or famous quotes you come across. These notebooks trace back to the era of Cicero, Quintilian, and Seneca, who used the analogy of a bee in one of his *Epistles* to drive home the point about borrowing, aggregating, and synthesizing from others:

> We should follow, men say, the example of the bees, who flit about and cull the flowers that are suitable for producing honey, and then arrange and assort in their cells all that they have brought in.

There are countless examples of zingers that have been used, re-used, and adapted across centuries, reappearing in debates and arguments to devastating effect each time. Take the line "In the name of God, go." It was originally delivered, during the English Civil War era, by Oliver Cromwell in the House of Commons. In 1653, while using a group of armed men to shut down the so-called Long Parliament, Cromwell declared:

> You have sat too long here for any good you have been doing. Depart, I say, and let us have done with you. In the name of God, go!

Nearly three centuries later, in May 1940, that phrase again echoed through the House of Commons chamber. It was in the midst of the famous Norway Debate over the conduct of the British war effort against the Nazis. The backbench Conservative member of Parliament Leo Amery laid into Prime Minister Neville Chamberlain over his lackluster policies, before closing his speech with the following familiar lines:

> This is what Cromwell said to the Long Parliament when he thought it was no longer fit to conduct the affairs of the nation: "You have sat too long here for any good you have been doing. Depart, I say, and let us have done with you. In the name of God, go."

Amery said those last six words, Cromwell's words, in a hushed tone and sat down. He didn't need to say more. Within three days, writes historian Martyn Bennett, Chamberlain resigned as prime minister and was replaced by Winston Churchill.

More recently, in January 2022, then prime minister Boris Johnson was facing calls from the media and the opposition to resign over a series of parties allegedly held in Downing Street in violation of COVID lockdown rules. In a debate in Parliament, David Davis, a backbench Conservative MP and former government minister, gave a withering speech. And how did he end it?

> I will remind him of a quotation altogether too familiar to him of Leo Amery to Neville Chamberlain, "You have sat there too long for all the good you have done. In the name of God, go."

MPs across the Commons chamber roared and cheered. A defensive and mumbling Johnson, who happens to be a biographer of Churchill, pretended to be unaware of the origins of Davis's zinger.

I don't know what he's talking about. I don't know what quotation he is alluding to.

The clip of Davis in Parliament quoting Amery (who was quoting Cromwell!) grabbed news headlines in the UK and around the world. It added to the crescendo of voices calling on Boris Johnson to resign from office. Six months later, Johnson announced he was quitting.

2. Keep 'em short

If you google "best debate zingers," these are some of the quotations from U.S. presidential debates that tend to pop up again and again in various online listicles:

- "There you go again."—Ronald Reagan to Jimmy Carter in 1980, suggesting that his Democratic opponent had a history of not being truthful with Americans.
- "Where's the beef?"—Walter Mondale to Gary Hart, during a 1984 Democratic primary debate, dismissing the policy-lite platform of his opponent by invoking the famous slogan from a TV commercial for Wendy's, in which an elderly woman angrily questioned the size of a fictitious rival's burger patty.
- "It's fuzzy math."—George W. Bush to Al Gore in 2000, suggesting his Democratic opponent was using misleading statistics to criticize Bush's plans for Medicare.
- "You're likable enough, Hillary."—Barack Obama to Hillary Clinton, during a 2008 Democratic primary debate, when she tried to sound self-deprecating by joking how she didn't think she was "that bad."
- "The 1980s are now calling to ask for their foreign policy back."—Barack Obama to Mitt Romney in 2012, mocking the latter during an exchange over al-Qaeda for having

earlier called Russia "without question, our No. 1 geopolitical foe."

What do these debate zingers all have in common? They're short, pithy, and to the point. There is a reason that zingers are often referred to as "one-liners." For maximum impact, writes comedian Kendall Payne, your putdown should be a single statement or sentence—it can be a bit longer, especially if you're building up to a single climactic line, as Bentsen did. But it's best not to go over ten or fifteen seconds. "Keep it short and sweet," says Payne.

The Spartans of Ancient Greece were the masters of brevity when it came to quips and comebacks—to the point where dry wit is known today as *laconic* humor (after Laconia, the historical region of Greece that included the city-state of Sparta).

On one famous occasion, King Philip II of Macedon threatened to invade Laconia, sending a message to the Spartan leaders asking them if he should come as "friend or a foe." Their reply? "Neither."

A frustrated Philip sent another warning: "If once I enter into your territories, I will destroy ye all."

To which the Spartan leaders replied: "If."

The more laconic your comeback, the more damning it can feel. If your opponent has spent paragraphs upon paragraphs trying to dismantle your ideas, and you can cut them down to size in just a line, the contrast is glaring. It won't be missed by the audience, and—as the frustrated King Philip shows us—it will drive your opponent up the wall.

3. Pick your moment

When it comes to zingers, preparation is good but spontaneity is great. Even a line you've prepared needs to be delivered in a way that sounds perfectly spontaneous, and this is not always easy. Getting it right requires searching for moments, in real time, in the midst of a heated argument, to interject your verbal beatdown.

Timing matters. Remember how I was invited on BBC1's *Question Time* in 2015 to debate free speech and Islam in the wake of the awful *Charlie Hebdo* terror attack? One of the other panelists that night was David Starkey, a right-wing British historian who had previously made a bunch of bigoted and racist remarks, including blaming Pakistani culture for child sex abuse and Jamaican culture for urban riots.

That night, in his remarks on the Paris attack, Starkey referred to the Islamic faith as "backward"; he claimed "nothing important" had been written in Arabic for five hundred years; and he tried to smear me as an extremist based on a distortion of some ill-judged comments of mine from almost a decade earlier. In the midst of his rambling tirade, he also referred to me as "Ahmed."

There it was, I realized. My opening for a stinging rejoinder, which I could use to drive home the rest of my argument. When it was finally my turn to respond to his smears, my zinger was ready: "Given you can't get my name right—my name is Mehdi, not Ahmed—I would question your selective quotation of something I said a decade ago." The overwhelming applause from the *Question Time* studio audience drowned out the blustering Starkey as he tried—but failed—to continue the argument.

Of course, I couldn't have prepared in advance for Starkey's gaffe. Instead, I needed to be prepared for the opening he presented—and prepared to develop an on-the-spot put-down. It may seem like pure chance that the opportunity arose, but such openings are incredibly common in debates and arguments. What's rarer is that we're ready for them and willing to integrate them into otherwise prepared remarks. In this sense, the art of the zinger builds on many of the previous lessons we've covered. It folds in humor and spontaneity, but also the importance of active listening. As you learn each of these skills, you'll be able to pounce on each of the mistakes your opponent makes. And while you hone these skills, it also helps to listen and learn from the debaters who've done just that.

You can learn, for example, from Chris Christie, who took rival

Marco Rubio to the woodshed during a Republican presidential primary debate in Manchester, New Hampshire, in February 2016.

Rubio, the senator from Florida, was keen to keep repeating a rehearsed line about the sitting Democratic president. Early on in the debate, he declaimed: "Let's dispel once and for all with this fiction that Barack Obama doesn't know what he's doing. He knows exactly what he's doing. Barack Obama is undertaking a systematic effort to change this country, to make America more like the rest of the world."

Then, later in the debate, after attacking Christie for his record as governor of New Jersey, Rubio said: "I would add this. Let's dispel with this fiction that Barack Obama doesn't know what he's doing. He knows exactly what he's doing. He's trying to change this country."

Standing there, listening to Rubio repeat the same phrase again and again, Christie spotted an opening for a zinger. He pointed at the Florida senator and then turned to the audience in the auditorium in Manchester. "That's what Washington, DC, does," he said, still pointing at Rubio. "The drive-by shot at the beginning, with incorrect and incomplete information, and then the memorized twenty-five-second speech that is exactly what his advisers gave him."

Suddenly, the audience saw through Rubio like an X-ray. In just twelve seconds of speaking from Christie. Bang. Bang. Bang. The crowd began to cheer, and even Rubio let out an awkward laugh.

Christie followed up his zinger with a point of substance, too: "See, Marco, the thing is this: when you're president of the United States, when you're governor of a state, the memorized thirty-second speech where you talk about how great America is at the end of it doesn't solve one problem for one person."

Still, Rubio couldn't help himself. He went on to repeat his Obama line yet again, only minutes later, during another attempted critique of Christie's gubernatorial record. "Chris, your state got hit by a massive snowstorm two weeks ago and you didn't even want to go back," Rubio said. "They had to shame you into going back, and then you stayed there for thirty-six hours and then he left and came back to campaign. Those are the facts."

Okay, there was a new point to consider. But then, weirdly, the senator continued: "Here's the bottom line. This notion that Barack Obama doesn't know what he's doing is just not true. He knows exactly what he's doing."

Christie practically lit up. Hearing Rubio's rote anti-Obama line yet again, he jumped back in: "There it is! There it is, the memorized twenty-five-second speech. There it is, everybody."

Marco Rubio was destroyed that night in New Hampshire, as Chris Christie proved to be a master of the clapback, because he was listening, in real time, and willing to adjust his own remarks and cut to the point.

"One-liners are much better when they come spontaneously than when they're prepackaged," Christie later told the *New York Times*. "Most of those precanned lines don't really go over all that well. I think it's got to be spontaneous. I think it's got to be something that comes about in the context of what people are hearing."

. . . .

That's what makes the one-liner an art form. It's important to work on your zingers and to be prepared when you enter a debate. As you do so, you'll want to keep them brief and draw on the masters of the craft. But, then, when the arguments start flying, you need to let yourself slip into the moment. That might mean identifying the perfect moment to deploy your polished zinger—or it might mean changing course, and responding to the gaffes and remarks that your opponent is making in the moment.

A final word of advice, however: don't put all your debate eggs in the one-liner basket. Substance matters, too. Zingers, as George W. Bush suggested, may give you a sense of victory and triumph, but the reality is that they may not endure *beyond* the night. They work best as part of a larger strategy that involves challenging your opponent, questioning their credibility, and winning over an audience. A single killer line is not enough on its own.

So always remember: zingers can give you an upper hand, and even provide a bit of fun and levity, but they cannot be relied on to seal the deal or win the argument. After all, Quayle lost that debate to Bentsen, the Democrat, in Omaha, and Bentsen's zinger has been repeated for decades since. But, three months later, it was Quayle, the Republican, who was sworn in as vice president in front of the United States Capitol.

SETTING BOOBY TRAPS

Knowing where the trap is—that's the first step in
evading it.

—Duke Leto Atreides, in Frank Herbert's *Dune*

When I was growing up in the 1980s, I was obsessed
with the original Rambo movie trilogy. *First Blood.*
Rambo: First Blood Part II. Rambo III. I've watched and
rewatched them multiple times over the decades.

So, here's a question, and piece of movie trivia, for you: In the
first film, how many people does John J. Rambo, the eponymous
character played by Sylvester Stallone, ultimately kill?

Despite its name, *First Blood* doesn't show Rambo killing *anyone.* It isn't until the second and third movies that we see Stallone
start to stab, shoot, and blow up his dozens and dozens of enemies.

Instead, in the first movie, Rambo follows a different strategy.
When the grizzled Vietnam veteran is hiding out in the forest,
pursued by a vindictive local sheriff in the fictional town of Hope,
Washington, he chooses to fight off his attackers with a number of
(nonlethal) booby traps. There are spikes, sticks, pits, and more.
The sheriff and his men never see it coming. They just walk right in
until—*snap.*

Why am I telling you all about a schlocky old action movie?
Because one of the best ways to win an argument is John J. Rambo

style: to set rhetorical booby traps for your opponents, then sit back and wait until they race toward the spikes.

....

A booby trap is defined by *Merriam-Webster* as "a trap for the unwary or unsuspecting," a "pitfall." The word *booby* itself, in this context, has nothing to do with birds (or even human anatomy) and everything to do with the Spanish word *bobo*, meaning "stupid, daft, naive." The point of this chapter is to show you how to set pitfalls using seemingly harmless questions or comments—traps that make your opponent look daft, foolish, and—ideally—lost for words.

What makes a booby trap so unique, and so uniquely dangerous, is that the victim of the trap unwittingly triggers it themselves. In the context of a debate or argument, the effect can be unforgettable, as someone who's spent hours preparing (or hours talking nonstop) suddenly finds themselves sputtering.

So how do you set a booby trap in an argument or even a formal debate? How do you then lure your opponent to walk into the pitfall? And what kinds of rhetorical traps can you get away with setting in the course of a real-time argument?

Here are my three favorite ways to plant booby traps for your unsuspecting opponents.

1. Trap them with their own words

As I pointed out in the chapter on receipts, using your opponent's own words against them is a powerful way of discrediting both their claims and their credibility, thereby gaining an upper hand in the argument.

But the way to use your opponent's words as a booby trap is to bring them into the conversation *without identifying them as your opponent's words*.

To be honest, it's an old trick that TV interviewers like to use against politicians or public figures—especially those who have spent years giving interviews and making speeches. They tend not to remember every word they have uttered, and, so, if you can find them saying something in the past that undermines their argument in the present then . . . you can set the booby trap!

I'm not saying it's easy. You have to do the research and preparation beforehand, but in the age of social media, it's no longer just politicians who have a long backlog of past commentary. You can often find a trap-worthy quote on an opponent's Facebook page or Twitter account, and then construct a line of attack that allows you to deploy the goods without them seeing it coming. Execution is everything.

In 2015, on Al Jazeera English, I interviewed retired U.S. lieutenant general Michael Flynn, who would later go on to serve as President Donald Trump's first national security adviser for all of . . . twenty-three days. Flynn had a reputation as a hawk on Iran and a critic of then president Obama's nuclear deal with the Islamic Republic. Yet while prepping for the interview, my team of producers and I had come across testimony he had previously provided to Congress, in his former role as director of the Defense Intelligence Agency, in which Flynn had minimized the threat from Tehran.

Time to set the trap!

ME: You keep going on about the Iranian threat and you began this part by talking about Iranian bad behavior. Isn't it the case, General, that Iran, for all its bad behavior, in terms of threat levels, "is unlikely to initiate or intentionally provoke a conflict or launch a preemptive attack on the United States"?

MICHAEL FLYNN: Iran, well, I think no. I don't think that's . . .

ME: You don't agree with that statement?

FLYNN: I don't think that's a true statement. I don't think that's a true statement.

ME: That statement, General, that statement is your statement from February 2014.

Boom! There's almost nothing more gratifying than watching an opponent fail to recognize their own words quoted back to them. Except, perhaps, for the moment that comes just afterward—the embarrassed realization that dawns on their face when *you* make the big reveal. It's not something your opponent will be prepared for, and if you can plan out how to introduce your opponent's quote without them recognizing it, you will create a showstopper moment.

But even if your opponents are aware that the words are their own—the audience probably isn't! In 2019, in my debate on Saudi Arabia and the West for Intelligence Squared in London, I was up against Middle East scholar and author Mamoun Fandy. At one point, he tried to defend the Saudi government against charges of inciting extremism by going on a long tirade against the Muslim Brotherhood of Egypt while claiming it was a "myth" that Saudi Arabia was a "bedrock" of radical Islam. He even dismissed Osama bin Laden—a former Saudi citizen!—as a "very close friend of Al Jazeera network, who had the exclusive rights to all his tapes and interviews." He smirked in my direction as he said this—I was working as an anchor for Al Jazeera English at the time. Oh, the good ol' "guilt by association" trick!

But I wasn't annoyed. Why? He had actually triggered a booby trap I'd laid. I had wanted him to explicitly defend Saudi Arabia against charges of fundamentalism and extremism, and I had wanted him to come after me personally, too. So that I could then fire back with my response.

Let me make one very quick point to Mamoun. Mamoun, you talk about Islam and Mawdudi and Qutb; the *Christian Science Monitor* published a piece in the 1990s saying that Egypt shouldn't bow down to "Saudi-style Islam . . . As a student . . . I saw fundamentalist students go to Saudi Arabia . . ." come back and distribute books.

"Saudi style fundamentalism unnerves . . . Egyptians . . . Saudi influence [must] be curbed." The author of that piece was one Mamoun Fandy.

The triumphant smile was gone from Fandy's face. "Well done," he heckled sarcastically as the crowd cheered my remarks. But I got the last, killer line in that particular exchange: "Your words, Mamoun."

2. Trap them with a contradiction

Many of you will have seen the 1992 Rob Reiner movie *A Few Good Men*. Even if you haven't, you're probably familiar with the legendary courtroom exchange in the movie's climactic scene. "I want the truth!" shouts Tom Cruise's Lieutenant Daniel Kaffee, shaking his fist at the defendant on the stand. "You can't handle the truth," fires back Jack Nicholson's Colonel Nathan Jessup, taking over the scene.

It's the stuff of movie magic, but what you might not remember is the back-and-forth that leads up to that famous exchange. It's an exchange in which navy lawyer Kaffee sets a booby trap for Jessup, who he believes—but cannot prove!—ordered a "code red," or an off-the-books punishment, which caused the death of marine William Santiago.

First, Kaffee gets Jessup, who is sitting in the witness box, to state in open court that his marines never disobey orders: "We follow orders, son. We follow orders or people die. It's that simple." Then he gets Jessup to (falsely) claim that he'd approved a transfer for

Santiago, sending him off the base for his own safety, after Santiago had called out the wrongdoing of a fellow marine. At this point, the trap is about to be sprung. The lieutenant highlights the contradiction in Jessup's testimony. "You made it clear just a moment ago that your men never take matters into their own hands. Your men follow orders or people die. So Santiago shouldn't have been in any danger at all, should he have, Colonel?"

You can see from Jessup's face, and the narrowing of his eyes, that this is the moment of realization. The marine colonel has walked right into a trap; he has been caught in a clear contradiction while under oath in court. And his petulant response says it all: "You snotty little bastard." Moments later, Kaffee has gotten his "truth": it was Jessup who ordered the "code red" that killed Santiago.

I have been a fan of *A Few Good Men* since my teenage years. As a high school student in north London in the 1990s, I asked a friend in drama class to join me in performing the courtroom scene in front of our peers. On the day of our performance, he was sick and stayed home. So I stood up in front of dozens of kids and a disapproving drama teacher, and I played both Cruise's and Nicholson's roles, both Kaffee and Jessup, at the same time: standing then sitting, standing then sitting. It was . . . shall we say . . . a bizarre ten minutes.

Later in life, though, I would borrow from Lieutenant Kaffee's cross-examination technique for my own combative interviews on television. In 2015, I sat down with the renowned British economist Sir Paul Collier in front of a live audience at the Oxford Union. Despite pitching himself as a liberal and centrist, Collier has rather conservative and reactionary views on immigration and asylum. He had published a provocative book called *Exodus: How Migration Is Changing Our World*, and I noticed that, in his book, he seemed to contradict himself when talking about "indigenous" Britons—and in a rather disconcerting and even offensive way. So I made that the focus of my interview with him.

ME: You repeatedly refer in the book, almost on every other page, to indigenous Britons or indigenous members of the population, which as you know has a certain resonance to some people on the far right. How do you define an indigenous Briton? What is an indigenous Briton?

PAUL COLLIER: Well, we've gotta have some sort of concept for the nonimmigrant population.

ME: So what is it?

COLLIER: I mean, we might as well say "indigenous" for that.

ME: But what does it mean?

COLLIER: Well, if you've got a concept of immigrant, you've gotta have a concept of a nonimmigrant, haven't we.

ME: So what is the concept of a nonimmigrant?

COLLIER: What's the concept of an immigrant, Mehdi?

ME: Well, am I an indigenous Briton?

COLLIER: Were you born here?

ME: Yes.

COLLIER: Then you're a Briton, yeah.

ME: Okay, so it's people who are born here indigenous?

COLLIER: That will do, yeah.

ME: Okay. So here's my question. In your book you say that, in the 2011 census, it was revealed that the indigenous British had become a minority in their own capital. The census showed that 63 percent of the population of London is born in Britain. The only way you can get a "minority status" is if you're [looking at] white British. Then you're a minority in London. It's a phrase you've used in many interviews, many articles, in the *Daily Mail*, *New Statesman* . . .

COLLIER: You can look to the second generation.

ME: Well, I'm asking you a simple question. Is that wrong? It is wrong, isn't it? In your book you say that the indigenous British are a minority in their own capital. They're not. Sixty-three percent.

COLLIER: If you want to score a point, then . . .

ME: I'm not scoring a point. I'm asking a professor of economics, did he get a quite glaring error in his book?

COLLIER: No, I didn't.

ME: And repeated in the *Daily Mail*.

COLLIER: No, I didn't.

ME: And repeated in the *New Statesman*, and repeated in the *Economist* . . .

COLLIER: No, I did not get a glaring error. It's a perfectly meaningful statement.

ME: Explain the meaning to me.

COLLIER: The use of the word indigenous, right? There are . . . there are various definitions you can have.

ME: I asked you for one two minutes ago, and you said, "Born here."

COLLIER: Yeah, okay, and I gave you one.

ME: So that doesn't apply to this. The ones you gave me . . .

COLLIER: It certainly doesn't apply to that.

ME: So what does it apply to in this context?

COLLIER: It applies to the . . . the second generation.

ME: The second generation? I'm not indigenous now according to this sentence.

COLLIER: Um, then, absolutely. Yeah.

ME: Am I or am I not indigenous?

COLLIER: Of course you are.

The audience in the Union roared with laughter as the award-winning economist tied himself up in verbal knots. But Collier didn't laugh. He left the Union chamber that night in silence and without even a goodbye.

Note that I didn't let him wriggle away from his statement; I didn't let him wave his hand at the obvious contradiction. Instead, I made him sit with the contradiction until he could explain it—or *fail* to. That's catching your opponent in a booby trap.

3. Trap them with a question

We can apply a similar tactic with our third method of springing a trap—sticking your opponent with the straightforward question that turns out to be a trap.

How do you set a trap with just a question? It's simple. You ask your opponent a question that you know, from your preparation, they cannot or will not be able to answer. The value is not so much in the answer—or *non*answer for that matter!—but often in getting them to consider the question itself. Once they're offtrack and out of rhythm, the trap is sprung.

What do I mean?

The late Christopher Hitchens, the British American author and journalist, was a master of debate and, in particular, a master of this technique. In 1991, in the run-up to the Gulf War, CNN hosted a debate between Hitchens and the legendary actor-turned-Republican-Party-activist Charlton Heston. Live on air, Hitchens, then an outspoken opponent of war with Iraq, confronted Heston, a supporter of military action, with this booby trap of a question.

HITCHENS: Let me ask a question to Mr. Heston. Can he tell me, clockwise, what countries have frontiers and borders with Iraq, starting with Kuwait?

HESTON: Yes, indeed, I can. Those borders are going to be very flexible, I think. Iran and Iraq demonstrate that . . .

HITCHENS: You can, can you? It wouldn't take a minute.

HESTON: Let me come to your comment. Kuwait, Bahrain, Turkey, Russia, er, Iran.

HITCHENS: Exactly, you don't know where it is, in other words, do you? You have no idea where the country is on the map, and you're in favor of bombing it now rather than later, on the whim of a president.

CNN ANCHOR BOB CAIN: Mr. Hitchens, if I can interject, I'm not sure that the instantaneous command of the geography of a region . . .

HITCHENS: Oh, I don't know, if you're in favor of bombing a country, you might pay it the compliment of knowing where it is.

Hitchens had come prepared. He was both determined to set his trap (*"You can, can you?"*), and ready if Heston had sought to avoid the trap. Heston could have sidestepped, after all. He could have taken the approach of the CNN anchor, Cain, and pointed out that "the instantaneous command of the geography of a region" is not strictly relevant to the case for military action against Iraq. But then Hitchens was prepared with his one-liner: "If you're in favor of bombing a country, you might pay it the compliment of knowing where it is."

Yet the guy who played Moses in *The Ten Commandments* didn't even try to dodge the question. Heston's ego got the better of him— and he walked straight into Hitchens's booby trap. He tried to answer the question and got it wrong, making a fool of himself on live TV, in front of millions of Americans. (For the record, the correct answer to the question of which countries border Iraq is: Kuwait, Saudi Arabia, Jordan, Syria, Turkey, and Iran—and, yes, in case you're wondering, I did have to google that!)

I've used Hitchens's tactic myself, and it is perfectly potent. In 2014, I interviewed the Chinese author and academic Zhang Wei-wei, a vocal supporter of the Chinese government, on *Head to Head* at the Oxford Union. At one point in the show, an audience member raised the issue of Beijing's human rights abuses in Tibet, and I was ready and eager to follow up with a preprepared point of my own.

ME: Between half a million and over a million Tibetans are estimated to have been killed over the last sixty years.

ZHANG: One hundred percent wrong. You can check the statistics.

ME: Okay, you tell me, how many Tibetans have been killed since 1950?

ZHANG: No, no, no . . .

ME: No, you tell me. How many have been killed?

ZHANG: You can check the population in 1950. What's the population today?

ME: I am asking a simple question. The studies I've seen say between half a million and a million. You dispute that. How many do you say have died?

ZHANG: This is the wrong question . . .

At this point, the audience was laughing out loud. Zhang himself was laughing—but nervously. He paused, before conceding: "I don't know the answer." To which I could not help but respond: "Okay, if you don't know the answer, perhaps you shouldn't question the studies that have been done."

Going in, I knew that Zhang would never agree to statistics that suggested the rulers of China had the blood of between half and one million Tibetans on their hands. But the point of the booby trap was not to get him to agree with me but to expose the fact that he had no answer of his own. In fact, I *wanted* him to disagree with me so that I could set the trap: "Okay, you tell me, how many Tibetans have been killed since 1950?" Once that question landed in his lap, he was stuck.

Note that with both this question and with Hitchens's, the ask seems very straightforward on the surface. It's a question of fact, so your opponent thinks it can be easily handled. But that's where the trap lies. Because the question of fact is embedded in a topic your opponent would much rather have avoided. If Hitchens had asked, "What business do we have being in Iraq?" he would have encountered a prepared talking point. If I'd asked Zhang, "How do you respond to allegations about human rights abuses in Tibet?" he would have been ready with a vague answer and steered on to a preferred subject. But the trap questions immediately leap down to concrete details that are beyond talking points. Once the opponent pauses to take on your simple question, you've mired them deep in a subject that they would have avoided if faced with a more general question.

....

Should I feel bad for making Fandy look foolish in London? Or for tripping up Collier and Zhang in Oxford? Did Hitchens feel sorry when he outwitted Heston on CNN?

Nope. All is fair in love and war—and debating, in my view, is a rhetorical form of warfare. You have to use the oratorical weapons available to you. And, like ex–Green Beret John J. Rambo in the woods of Washington state, you have to prepare and plan in advance. Use traps that your opponents don't see coming. Deploy the element of surprise. Dangle a phrase, a quote, or a question that looks harmless. Until—*snap*. The trap is sprung and the floor is yours.

"Do we get to win this time?" Rambo famously asks his former commanding officer at the beginning of *First Blood Part II*. By unleashing booby traps against your opponents, you can win *every* time.

BEWARE OF THE GISH GALLOPER

The amount of energy needed to refute bullshit is an
order of magnitude larger than is needed to produce it.
—Alberto Brandolini, computer programmer

I t was the first televised presidential debate of the 2020 U.S. presidential election campaign. Sitting president Donald Trump was
facing off against former vice president Joe Biden in Cleveland,
with Chris Wallace as the moderator. Election day was still more
than a month away, but amid the COVID-19 pandemic, many states
were already rolling out expanded early voting options. And Trump
and his team were already sowing seeds of doubt about voter fraud
and the very legitimacy of the election itself.

So, during the final segment of the debate, Wallace raised that
issue directly. He asked the two candidates: "How confident are you
that this will be a fair election? . . . And what are you prepared to do
to reassure the American people that the next president will be the
legitimate winner of this election?"

Biden spoke first, affirming his trust in the election process and
committing to honor the results, whether or not he emerged the winner. Then it was Trump's turn. And . . . buckle up.

WALLACE: Mr. President, two minutes.

TRUMP: So when I listen to Joe talking about a transition, there has been no transition from when I won. I won that election. And if you look at crooked Hillary Clinton, if you look at all of the different people, there was no transition, because they came after me trying to do a coup. They came after me spying on my campaign. They started from the day I won, and even before I won. From the day I came down the escalator with our first lady, they were a disaster. They were a disgrace to our country, and we've caught 'em. We've caught 'em all. We've got it all on tape. We've caught 'em all. And by the way, you gave the idea for the Logan Act against General Flynn. You better take a look at that, because we caught you in a sense, and President Obama was sitting in the office.

He knew about it, too. So don't tell me about a free transition. As far as the ballots are concerned, it's a disaster. A solicited ballot, okay, solicited, is okay. You're soliciting. You're asking. They send it back. You send it back. I did that. If you have an unsolicited—they're sending millions of ballots all over the country. There's fraud. They found 'em in creeks. They found some, with the name Trump, just happened to have the name Trump, just the other day in a wastepaper basket. They're being sent all over the place. They sent two in a Democrat area. They sent out a thousand ballots. Everybody got two ballots. This is going to be a fraud like you've never seen. The other thing, it's nice. On November third, you're watching, and you see who won the election. And I think we're going to do well because people are really happy with the job we've done.

But you know what? We won't know. We might not know for months because these ballots are going to be all over. Take a look at what happened in Manhattan. Take a look at what happened in New Jersey. Take a look at what happened in Virginia and other places. They're not losing two percent, one percent, which by the way is too much. An election could be won or lost with that. They're losing thirty and forty percent. It's a fraud, and it's a shame. And can you imagine where they say, uh, "You have to have your ballot in by November tenth." November tenth. That means, that's seven days after the election, in theory, should've been announced.

WALLACE: Okay.

TRUMP: We have major states with that . . .

WALLACE: Sir. Time . . .

TRUMP: . . . all run by Democrats—

WALLACE: Sir, two minutes is two minutes.

TRUMP: All run by Democrats.

WALLACE: President Trump . . . I, I, . . .

TRUMP: It's a rigged election.

At that point, the two talked over each other until Chris Wallace finally regained the floor. But, *sheesh*! Where would you even begin, trying to rebut all the fictitious and false claims in that rambling rant from the former president, delivered on live TV in front of tens of millions of people?

Here are just some of the key factual points we should note:

- There *was* a transition after he won.
- Hillary Clinton is *not* a criminal.
- She did *not* launch a coup against him.
- There was *no* spying on his campaign.
- *No one* was caught.
- *Nothing* was on tape.
- Mail-in ballots were *not* a disaster.
- There was *no* major voter fraud.
- There were *no* ballots found in creeks.
- Everybody did *not* get two ballots.
- *Nothing* happened in Manhattan, New Jersey, or Virginia.
- No one can vote *after* election day.
- The election was *not* rigged.

A baker's dozen of lies, half-truths, and exaggerations from Trump in the space of just two minutes—or *one every nine seconds*! But do you think either Wallace or Biden had the time or ability to fact-check Trump on all or even most of them?

Not. A. Chance.

And there's a frightening power in that. Perhaps unbeknownst to himself, Trump was engaging in what has become known in debating circles as the Gish Gallop. This is a speaking method that involves, to quote the Urban Dictionary, "spewing so much bullshit in such a short span that your opponent can't address let alone counter all of it." It has one aim: to bury your adversary in a torrent of incorrect, irrelevant, or idiotic arguments.

Both Trump's critics and supporters agree that, when challenged by an opponent or interviewer, this is his technique of choice. The leftist author and essayist William Rivers Pitt, who refers to Trump as "the reigning world heavyweight champion of the Gish Gallop," describes the former president turning up to debates, interviews, and speeches to issue "dollops of galactic nonsense delivered in an avalanche of jumbled verbiage, all of which is abandoned without correction or refutation as the next avalanche comes sliding down the hill."

From the other end of the spectrum, Trump's former White House chief strategist Steve Bannon, in an interview with journalist Michael Lewis in 2018, summed up the rationale behind the then president's approach. "The Democrats don't matter," Bannon told Lewis. "The real opposition is the media. And the way to deal with them is to flood the zone with shit."

That is exactly what the Gish Gallop is designed to do in any argument: to leave you gasping for air, sunk in a flood of falsehoods and fabrications; drowned in a deluge of distortions, deflections, and distractions. All of which lands like a true load of bullshit: all at once, with a splat, in a way that's impossible to clean up without getting dirty.

The Gish Galloper, argues Carl Alviani in *Quartz*, knows full well that it takes more time and energy to "disprove" a "false claim" than to make one—time and energy that you almost certainly don't have. They then try to claim victory when you're unable to rebut *all* their points—hence the relentless barrage of falsehoods that they level in your direction to begin with. Often, by the time you've begun preparing your rebuttal of the Galloper's first lie, they've rattled off another dozen. It's what's become known as proof by verbosity—or, as another saying goes, being baffled by bullshit.

The Gish Galloper wants to trick the audience into believing that the facts and the evidence are on their side. They have so many examples after all: *Creeks! Wastepaper baskets! Virginia!* The entire technique is based on a sleight of hand, on delivery over depth, on an "illusion of authority," to quote the folks at RationalWiki.

It is a powerful, if dishonest, method of winning an argument. And while Trump may be the grand master of the Gish Gallop, he's far from its originator. So where does the Gish Gallop come from, and how do you defeat it?

MEET THE GISH BEHIND THE GALLOP

The late Duane Tolbert Gish was an evolution-denying biochemist who worked as the vice president of the Institute for Creation Research (ICR). The Dallas-based pseudoscience outfit has long wanted to mainstream "Young Earth" creationism—the Genesis-based religious worldview that says all life on Earth was created in six days by the God of the Old Testament at some point in the past ten thousand years, with evolution playing no role. In fact, as the *San Antonio Express-News* reported in 2011, the ICR "tried to force the state of Texas to allow it to offer master's degrees in science education"— from a biblical perspective, of course. But a federal judge threw out the ICR's lawsuit in 2010, rejecting it as "overly verbose, disjointed, incoherent, maundering and full of irrelevant information."

Still, while Gish's organization could not win in a Texas courtroom, Gish himself made a name for the ICR and Young Earth creationism by winning argument after argument against evolutionists in debate halls across the country.

To be clear, he wasn't winning on substance or through erudition. He was winning with speed and confidence—and humor, too. "It was perhaps his personal presentation that carried the day," noted a flattering obituary published by the ICR itself upon Gish's death in 2013. "In short, the audiences liked him." Even his critics, like the computer scientist Richard Trott—who tangled with Gish on more than one occasion—acknowledged the latter's "extraordinary charisma" and his "natural gift for a folksy and relaxed presentation."

Conspiracy theory expert John Grant explained the key to Gish's style and strategy in his book, *Debunk It! Fake News Edition: How to Stay Sane in a World of Misinformation.*

Gish would insist his opponent go first. After his opponent was finished with his or her argument, Gish would begin talking very quickly for perhaps an hour, reeling off a long string of "facts." His debating opponent, of course, didn't have the chance even to note down all those "facts," let alone work out whether or not they were correct. In his or her rebuttal, the opponent could either ignore Gish's tirade altogether, which would look like dodging the issue, or try to answer as many of the points as possible, which meant looking as if he or she were floundering. Gish's trick was a clever one, and it fooled a lot of audiences.

What was missing from those presentations? Credible evidence. Verifiable facts. Scholarly arguments. But in a real-time setting, this wasn't obvious to many audiences.

According to the ICR, Gish participated in more than three hundred debates with evolutionists over the course of his life. In 1994, after watching a disingenuous, bullshitting Gish run rings around far more eminent and qualified scholars and scientists in one formal debate after another, a frustrated Eugenie Scott, then the executive director of the National Center for Science Education, coined the term "Gish Gallop," describing it as the method by which "the creationist is allowed to run on for forty-five minutes or an hour, spewing forth torrents of error that the evolutionist hasn't a prayer of refuting in the format of a debate."

Scott pointed out that while appearing on television and radio with creationists, she herself had "been able to stop Gish, et al., and say, 'Wait a minute, if X is so, then wouldn't you expect Y?' or something similar, and show that their 'model' is faulty. But in a debate, the evolutionist has to shut up while the creationist gallops along, spewing out nonsense with every paragraph."

This is the key point that you need to take away from this chapter: the "nonsense" is a feature, not a bug, of the Gish Gallop. Gish and his creationist pals were told time and time again that their claims were false, yet they regurgitated them ad nauseam, at the same speed, in the same order, in debate after debate. As *Skeptic* magazine pointed out in 1996, "many scientists have publicly corrected Gish in his presence, but Gish has gone on to repeat the same errors in later debates and writings . . . He succeeds at this, because in the next city, with a new audience and a new scientist to debate, who's to know that his argument got shot down, with evidence, by that other evolutionist last week?"

It's the same today with the climate change deniers or the anti-vaxxers, especially in online forums—no matter the number of fact checks and corrections, they continue to relentlessly push extraordinary amounts of misinformation and disinformation into the public consciousness.

In fact, it is the deliberate repetition of "nonsense" that differentiates the Gish Gallop from similar tactics like "spreading." The latter is a debating technique—said to come from a combination of the words *speed* and *reading*—in which the debater packs as many arguments as possible into their allotted speaking time by delivering them at a furious pace. In a formal debate competition, in which every point is supposed to require a rebuttal, the aim is to defeat your opponent by making such a point-by-point rebuttal virtually impossible. However, the Gish Gallop, unlike spreading, is *all* bad faith. It's all about the BS!

Like Gish before him, Trump again and again repeats claims and arguments that have been publicly discredited and debunked. He simply doesn't care—as long as he can get away with it! It wasn't just one debate in 2020, of course. There was also the notorious ABC News town hall in September 2020, where in front of a live audience in Philadelphia, Donald Trump—shock! horror!—told lie after lie on everything from COVID to crime to health care. Over the course of the ninety-minute event, moderator George Stephanopoulos simply could not correct, dispute, or fact-check the blizzard of falsehoods that the president of the United States unleashed on the audience in the hall—and on those watching at home on TV.

In fact, after the ABC town hall was over, CNN's fact-checker Daniel Dale appeared on Don Lemon's prime-time show that night to correct Trump's litany of bogus claims and spoke uninterrupted for two minutes in rapid-fire: "He insisted he didn't praise China on the virus. He did so repeatedly . . . He claimed that Biden said in March that the pandemic was quote 'totally overexaggerated.' I can find no evidence that Biden ever said that." Eventually, Dale stopped to take a breath and looked stricken: "And Don, this is a preliminary list," he said. "I have hours of fact-checking tonight to do because there is even more than this. This was just a fire hose of lying, again, from the president."

"Do you need a drink of water?" Lemon responded. "Because that was a lot . . ."

In theory, it's exactly how you should tackle a Gish Gallop. A point-by-point rebuttal. But we're not all Daniel Dale, and we won't always have Don Lemon giving us two uninterrupted minutes. In the real world, you rarely have the opportunity to do a point-by-point rebuttal. Indeed, the best Gish Gallopers take advantage of the fact that you simply do *not* have the time, space, or resources to comprehensively counter their dizzying catalog of falsehoods in real time.

So what do you do? How do you best respond? Here is my three-step process to beating a Gish Galloper in an argument.

1. Pick your battle

Perhaps the first time I encountered a Gish Gallop in person was in 2013, during my debate on Islam and peace at the Oxford Union. As I mentioned in the earlier chapter on listening, one of my opponents during that debate was long-standing Islam-basher Anne Marie Waters. She began her remarks that night with this word salad of an attack on my faith and my coreligionists:

> Let me tell you what actually whips up fears of Islam. Let me take it from the top: 9/11; the London Underground bombings; Madrid; Mumbai; Mali; Bali; northern Nigeria; Sudan; Afghanistan; Saudi Arabia; Iran; Yemen; Pakistan; death for apostasy; death for blasphemy; death for adultery; death for

homosexuality; gender segregation; gender discrimination; unequal testimony between men and women in legal proceedings; child marriage; amputations; beheadings; imprisonment for being raped; anti-Semitism; burqas; execution for this, that, and the other; the slaughter of Theo Van Gogh on the streets of Amsterdam; death threats on the streets of London; "butcher those who insult Islam"; Muslim patrols in East London telling people they are entering "sharia-controlled" zones; polygamous marriages; marriages not requiring the consent of the bride. This is what causes fear of Islam. It is not me, it is not my colleagues on this side . . . It is the actions of Muslims that are causing fear of Islam. That is the real world. That is where we actually live. Then, we'll be told this is just the extreme fringe of Islam. Well, let me have a look at Saudi Arabia, the birthplace of Islam.

She Galloped on in this bigoted vein for several more minutes, piling one ridiculous and offensive "example" of evil Muslims upon the next, and not stopping to expand or elaborate. Mali! Bali! Polygamy!

I knew I had to take her down . . . but how? There was no way I could address *all* the supposed examples she cited to justify "fear of Islam." Count 'em: in the passage above, she lists thirty-three items in less than two minutes—or around *one every four seconds*!

It would have taken me several minutes, if not my entire speech (max time: twelve minutes!), to try and rebut each and every one of those false or misleading claims. It also would have put me on the defensive, when the key to winning any argument is to put your opponent on the back foot. So, instead, as I mentioned earlier, I chose to zero in on the most ludicrous one: her totally inaccurate and ahistorical contention that Saudi Arabia was the "birthplace of Islam." (*"You were only 1,322 years off! Not bad."*)

By mocking and debunking that particular claim, I poured doubt on the rest of them—and made her look foolish in the process.

That's one way to start: find the weak links in the chain. But the Gish Galloper, if they're smart, will say you're cherry-picking from their overall argument—"This is what Mehdi Hasan always does," Waters heckled from her seat during my rebuttal of her argument about Saudi Arabia, implying that I was picking out the weakest points and counting that as a win. But, frankly, this is an opening that the Gish Galloper brings upon themselves.

Engaging in a "single flaw" or "worst-point" rebuttal isn't always going to work, and I don't recommend it when your opponent has woven a strong, cohesive argument. But as the philosophy website Effectiviology concedes, this approach "can be reasonable" when you "explicitly acknowledge the fact that the argument that you're addressing is the worst of those presented, and explain why you're doing it; a notable valid reason for this is that the argument in question forms the core of the opposing stance, and refuting it therefore refutes the overall stance."

When facing a Gish Galloper, you need to be able to quickly point out the *weakness* of their fire hose strategy rather than attempting a point-by-point rebuttal. It's impractical, if not impossible, to go line by line. Instead, single out the weakest claim or argument made by the Galloper. Pick on that. Highlight and mock it, and present it as representative of their overall strategy. Doing so will put *them* on the defensive.

2. Don't budge

Referring to Steve Bannon's quote about "flooding the zone with shit," the writer and author Jonathan Rauch once remarked: "This is not about persuasion: This is about disorientation."

He's right. When the likes of Trump and Gish engage in the Gallop, their purpose is often not to try to win people over but to muddy the argument for everyone involved. They can bewilder and confuse while hopping from one falsehood to the next.

The best defense against this tactic is to make sure you stop them midstream. And then don't budge. Don't let them move on to the next falsehood. "Hammer away," says one writer, with a well-chosen, well-prepared rebuttal until they cannot help but concede.

For several years, Trump was able to pursue his Gish Galloping unchecked and disorient opponents and audiences alike, as unprepared, time-limited, or weak-willed interviewers and moderators failed to interject, correct, or take a pause to respond to his nonsense. That is, until August 2020, when my friend Jonathan Swan, national political correspondent for Axios, sat down with the then president for a televised interview on *Axios on HBO*. Trump wanted to spout a bunch of dodgy stats on COVID, to make it seem as if he had everything under control. But Swan wouldn't let him. Waving away other vague metrics about the pandemic, Swan cut to the chase:

SWAN: The figure I look at is death. And death is going up now.

TRUMP: Okay. No, no.

SWAN: It's a thousand a day.

TRUMP: If you look at death—

SWAN: Yeah. It's going up again.

Trump then pulled out a sheaf of papers with charts, and tried to do a real-time Gish Gallop, looking for *any* positive metric. But it was clearly not something he'd prepared for, and suddenly his game was up.

TRUMP: Take a look at some of these charts.

SWAN: I'd love to.

Trump: We're going to look.

SWAN: Let's look.

Trump: And, if you look at death per—

SWAN: Yeah. It's started to go up again.

TRUMP: Here is one. Well, right here, United States is lowest in numerous categories. We're lower than the world.

SWAN: Lower than the world?

TRUMP: We're lower than Europe.

SWAN: What does that mean? In what? In what?

TRUMP: Look. Take a look. Right there. Here is case death.

SWAN: Oh, you're doing death as a proportion of cases. I'm talking about death as a proportion of population. That's where the U.S. is really bad, much worse than South Korea, Germany, et cetera.

Trump: You can't do that.

Swan: Why can't I do that?

TRUMP: You have to go by where . . . look. Here is the United States. You have to go by the cases. The cases are there.

Again, Swan would not budge, would not allow Trump to overwhelm him with nonsense numbers.

SWAN: Oh. It's surely a relevant statistic to say, if the U.S. has

X population and X percentage of death of that population versus South Korea—

TRUMP: No. Because you have to go by the cases.

Swan: Well, look at South Korea, for example. Fifty-one million population, three hundred deaths. It's like, it's crazy compared to—

TRUMP: You don't know that.

SWAN: I do.

TRUMP: You don't know that.

SWAN: You think they're faking their statistics, South Korea? An advanced country?

TRUMP: I won't get into that because I have a very good relationship with the country.

SWAN: Yeah.

TRUMP: But you don't know that. And they have spikes. Look, here's one of—

SWAN: Germany, low nine thousand.

TRUMP: Here's one. Here's one right here, United States.

SWAN: Let me look.

TRUMP: You take the number of cases.

SWAN: Okay.

TRUMP: Now look, we're last meaning we're first.

SWAN: Last? I don't know what we're first in.

TRUMP: We have the best.

SWAN: As a what?

TRUMP: Take a look again. It's cases.

SWAN: Okay. I'll just . . . okay.

TRUMP: And we have cases because of the testing.

SWAN: I mean, a thousand Americans die a day. But I understand. I understand on the cases, it's different.

TRUMP: No, but you're not reporting it correctly, Jonathan.

SWAN: I think I am.

Notice how Swan would not let Trump dodge or evade—or move on to his next fabrication. When the president tried to imply South Korea's death rate wasn't believable, Swan didn't let it go unchecked. He pushed back. When Trump started waving a bunch of printouts of graphs and tables to try to find *something* that would bolster his false claims, Swan went through the printouts himself and debunked them in real time. Throughout, Swan gave Trump plenty of openings to speak, but he never let the president bowl him over or get up to Galloping speed. As soon as it aired, Swan's interview went viral— the rare in-person interview that revealed Trump's Gish Gallop for exactly what it was.

I asked Swan how prepared he had been for the torrent of misinformation from the then president. "The Trump interview is the hardest possible interview because of the bombardment," he told me. "Whole paragraphs [of claims] flung at you and they may be entirely false or made up."

Swan says he spent an "inordinate amount of time" workshopping the entire interview beforehand, familiarizing himself with Trump's "series of stock responses" and methodically preparing follow-up questions. "How is he going to answer? What am I going to say back?"

A year after his viral clash with Trump and his takedown of Trump's Gish Gallop, the Axios journalist deservedly won an Emmy for Outstanding Edited Interview.

3. Call them out

To borrow a line from the fictional TV anchor Will McAvoy, in the opening episode of HBO's *The Newsroom*, "The first step in solving any problem is recognizing there is one."

The Gish Gallop is an undeniable problem—and challenge. There is no simple solution to the opponent who captivates an audience with a stream of rapid-fire, impressive-sounding claims—no matter how nonsensical or fact-free they might turn out to be upon closer examination. Especially if there is no *time* for closer examination!

So, in a pinch, don't be afraid to "call out" the Gish Galloper for their Gish Gallop. Call bullshit on the bullshitter. Point out to the audience exactly what your opponent is doing—whether you're in a classroom, a boardroom, or a debating chamber. Make sure that others in that room, or watching at home, understand what you do— that the Gallop is a tactic. Don't allow an audience to be fooled into assuming your opponent has special command of the subject because of all the "facts" they've just spouted. You can call it out! And you can also pair this approach with our first technique: highlighting one of the Galloper's weaker arguments. Reveal your opponent's strategy, then zero in on one (weaker) argument from among many they've rattled off—and ask them to explain it in detail. Chances are that they've revealed only the sketchiest understanding of what they're even arguing—just as Trump revealed in his interview with Jonathan Swan.

The key here is to *expose* the overall strategy. Another devotee of the Gish Gallop is Russian president Vladimir Putin. In recent years, the former KGB agent and his acolytes in state-run media have perfected what has been dubbed "the fire hose of falsehood." Whether it is justifying the illegal invasion of Ukraine or interfering in U.S. elections, the Russian government's model of propaganda, to quote from a study by the RAND Corporation, uses "high numbers of channels and messages and a shameless willingness to disseminate partial truths or outright fictions."

But the RAND study also suggests this piece of handy advice for fighting disinformation: "Don't expect to counter Russia's fire hose of falsehood with the squirt gun of truth. Instead, put raincoats on those at whom the fire hose is aimed."

If your job in an argument with a Gish Galloper is to "put raincoats" on your audience, that begins by making your audience aware of what they're being subjected to. Point out the speed at which your opponent is speaking, and the laundry list of lies that they've just recited aloud in record time. You can even point out that your opponent is using a propagandistic move straight out of the Kremlin playbook. Or point out that your opponent is behaving in a Trumpian manner.

Remember: your audience may not have heard of Duane Tolbert Gish, but trust me, they all know Donald John Trump.

． ． ． ． ． ． ． ． ． ． ．

In 2018, in the wake of the U.S. congressional midterm elections, I interviewed Steven Rogers, a regular guest on Fox and a member of Trump's campaign advisory board in the run-up to the 2020 election.

My Al Jazeera English team and I knew that Rogers, like his boss, would try to Gish Gallop his way through the interview. He wouldn't want to defend Trump's long record of gaslighting, and based on his previous appearances on Fox that we watched closely, he would probably tell a fair few porky pies of his own! So we prepared intensely, drawing up a long list and then a short list of every major Trump lie. There were, of course, dozens upon dozens to choose from. (The fact-checkers at the *Washington Post* would later calculate that the forty-fifth president of the United States made 30,573 false claims during his four years in office—almost certainly a conservative underestimate.)

During my interview with Rogers, I decided to home in on one particular lie of Trump's that he had rattled off at a number of press briefings and business roundtables in the run-up to the midterms.

Me: [Trump] said during the campaign that there are six to seven steel facilities that are going to be opened up. U. S. Steel has not announced any facilities. Why did he say they have announced new facilities? That's a lie, isn't it?

Rogers: No, it isn't because there are a lot of companies opening up. There are steel facilities that are going to be opening up . . .

Me: Sorry, Steven, that's not what he said. I know it's difficult for you; I know you want to try and defend him.

Rogers: No, it isn't difficult for me [laughs].

Me: Well, okay, let me read the quote to you. "U. S. Steel just announced that they are building six new steel mills." That's a very specific claim. U. S. Steel have not announced six new steel mills. They have said they have not announced six new steel mills. There's no evidence of six new steel mills. He just made it up. And he repeated it. He didn't just say it once.

ROGERS: Look, I don't know of what context these statements were made. But I can tell you this: the president of the United States has been very responsive to the American people and the American people are doing well.

ME: That's fine, the American people can be doing well and the president can be a liar. There's no contradiction between those two statements.

ROGERS: I am not going to say the president of the United States is a liar.

ME: I know you're not, but I have just put to you multiple lies and you have not been able to respond to any of them.

ROGERS: I did respond to them. What didn't happen is that you didn't hear what you wanted to hear.

ME: What did I want to hear? I wanted to hear that there are no steel mills.

ROGERS: You wanted to hear me say . . . well, let's go on.

ME: You want to go on because you know it's a lie.

Did you catch the three-step process in that exchange? I picked my battle (steel mills!); I didn't budge (*"I know it's difficult for you; I know you want to try and defend him"*); and I called out the Gallop (*"You want to go on because you know it's a lie"*). And I was only able to do all this because I was superprepared, I'd done my homework, and I was confident.

The interview clip with that Trump campaign adviser went viral and has amassed—at the time of writing—more than ten million views on Twitter. Actor Mark Ruffalo (aka the Hulk) shared the clip to his seven million followers, saying: "There is such [a] thing as the truth, even today. This is how a journalist does their job to uncover it." NBC's Seth Meyers invited me on his *Late Night* show to discuss the interview, calling it "the template for talking to people within the Trump sphere."

During the interview with Meyers, I told him then what I am telling you now: "There's the same problem everywhere. Unfortunately, interviewers on U.S. television tend to have limited time, limited resources, and just want to keep moving things along. And when I interview people, I don't want to move along. I want to stick to it. I want to get an answer."

When you're faced with someone who's spouting lie after lie, exaggeration after exaggeration, this is the approach to take. You don't have to be afraid or overwhelmed by the Gish Galloper. You can be ready and waiting to ensnare them. You can even make them wallow in their own bullshit.

Part Three

———

BEHIND THE SCENES

CONFIDENCE IS EVERYTHING

> There are two types of speakers: those that are nervous
> and those that are liars.
>
> —Mark Twain

"**S**hould the Liberal Democrat voter feel betrayed that their vote is being used to prop up a Conservative government?"

It was May 2010. Exactly a week after the closest British election in a generation. Emotions were running high across the country. The right-wing Conservatives, with the aid of the center-left Liberal Democrats, were back in office for the first time in thirteen years; the UK had its first coalition government in sixty-five years.

And it was my first ever appearance on the BBC's *Question Time*, the most-watched current affairs show on British television. I was sitting on a panel alongside four veterans of the show, including Michael Heseltine, the legendary former Conservative cabinet minister, who had appeared on one of the first editions of *Question Time* when it launched in 1979—the year I was born!

That night, host David Dimbleby mischievously came to me first. "Should the Liberal Democrat voter feel betrayed?" he asked, repeating the opening question from a member of the audience. "Mehdi Hasan?"

There were several hundred people in that studio audience in

London staring at me as I scrambled to formulate my answer to that question. But that was small potatoes. There would be several *million* more watching me when the show aired later that night. I had sat on plenty of panels before. But never a *Question Time* panel. Never alongside such esteemed guests, either. And never in front of a television audience so . . . *huge.*

My stomach was churning. My heart was racing. My whole body was sweating. But here's the thing: only I knew that.

It might have been my first appearance in front of such a big audience, but I'd learned enough by then to know that I could feel completely nervous without letting it torpedo my performance. While my innards roiled, I projected *confidence*—to both the audience in the studio and the audience at home.

My first answer, delivered with passion and without hesitation, received a big round of applause. So did my second. And my third. By the end of the night, all that nervous energy had subsided. I was standing my ground against Lord Heseltine and thoroughly enjoying myself as I provoked his rage.

That first appearance on *Question Time* in 2010 did more to push me into the public eye in the UK than any other media appearance has ever done. Before the show had even finished airing on television, my email inbox had filled with hundreds of emails of support and praise. People came up to me to shake my hand on the bus and the train the next morning. As my former editor at the *New Statesman* would later proudly tell the *Columbia Journalism Review*, I "dominated" the panel that night, and "the next day, when we came into the office, we'd had a surge of subscriptions from people who had seen him."

But I couldn't have done it without confidence. Or without knowing how to summon confidence, even when I was on the edge of panic.

. . . .

W hat do most people look for in a successful speaker or communicator? It's the same thing they look for in a successful leader, says author Carmine Gallo: confidence. And when it comes to winning an argument, I simply cannot overstate how important it is to both *be* confident and *show* confidence.

Confidence is neither an ability nor an attribute. It is, as the experts say, "a belief in oneself"—the certitude that you have what it takes to succeed out in the big, bad world. And it is an attitude, crucially, that inspires both action and presence. Confidence is what allows you to look someone right in the eyes and say, "Sorry, you're wrong" (even if, in your head, you suspect they might be right). Confidence is what allows you to stand in front of hundreds, thousands, or even millions, and speak from the heart. Confidence is what allows you to get knocked down in life—and get right back up again.

"Without self-confidence," wrote novelist Virginia Woolf, "we are as babes in the cradle."

Confidence, notes Wikipedia, comes from the Latin word *fidere*, which means "to trust." So self-confidence is "having trust in one's self." Having the *ability* to accomplish your goals is one thing, but confidence is what allows you to apply that ability. It's what lets you translate ability into success. To quote billionaire tycoon Richard Branson, "confidence breeds confidence and negativity breeds negativity."

Studies even suggest that confidence "matters just as much as competence" when it comes to predicting performance. In fact, confidence is *preferred* to expertise! In 2009, *New Scientist* magazine, citing research by Don Moore of Carnegie Mellon University, found people "prefer advice from a confident source, even to the point that we are willing to forgive a poor track record."

That's a little worrying, to say the least. But for the purposes of persuasion, it underscores the bottom line: confidence is crucial to winning an argument. So, how do we make sure we have enough of it?

BUILDING CONFIDENCE

Let me be blunt: you simply cannot begin to do what I do—speaking to crowded auditoriums, presenting live on television in front of millions, picking fights with world leaders and public intellectuals—unless you have confidence in yourself.

Even as a kid, I didn't exactly lack for confidence. I was the perhaps obnoxious child who wouldn't raise their hand in class or wait for the teacher to call on them. I would just (rudely) shout out the answer. So, did some level of confidence come naturally to me? Yes. But did I have to develop, cultivate, and strengthen it over the decades? Most *definitely*.

There are myriad ways to build and bolster one's self-confidence. There are the obvious ways to prepare and practice: working on your delivery beforehand, so you have less to worry about on the big night; doing your homework in advance of a debate, so that you know the topic inside and out; testing each strength and weakness in your own arguments, so that you're ready for any rebuttal. I'll expand on these methods in the coming chapters, and they're all important and useful. But each, in its own way, is tied to developing your *ability* to argue and persuade.

For now, in this chapter, I want to focus on the mental game—because confidence might build off ability, but it's rooted in something more ethereal—in how capable we are of believing and trusting in ourselves. To that end, I'd like to suggest three perhaps less-conventional, more "outside the box" techniques for building up your confidence.

1. Visualize success

The next time you are asked to give a speech or presentation—whether it's to friends and family, or to a boardroom full of colleagues—I want you to try something out beforehand. "Find a quiet place," says the Presentation Training Institute, a few hours or even days in advance, then "close your eyes and visualize yourself giving your speech." Imagine yourself standing there in front of your audience, speaking loudly and *confidently*. "See yourself" delivering every line to perfection, covering every relevant argument crisply and coherently.

"Be as detailed as possible": pay attention to the size of the room, the type of flooring, the number of seats. Bring the scene to life: visualize your friends or colleagues laughing at your jokes, imagine the smiles on their faces. Even try to hear the "sounds of their applause" at the end.

It might sound goofy, but no one else needs to know. And if you put this exercise into practice—and repeat it until you know every turn of phrase—two things will likely happen. First, say the experts, you'll start feeling much more comfortable about giving that speech. You may even start to look forward to it. Second, you'll end up delivering a damn good speech!

"Seeing" yourself succeed gives you the confidence that success is indeed around the corner. When I went on *Question Time* that very first time, in May 2010, I had already visualized that panel and that audience as part of my preparation for the show. I had anticipated in my head the reactions to my planned zingers, booby traps, and gags. I could hear the crowd applauding and laughing . . . long before I had arrived at the venue.

Positive visualization is one of the most ingenious methods out there for developing and expanding your self-confidence. And it can ultimately improve your performance as well. When you visualize a situation beforehand in the most vivid way possible, and do it again and again, say experts, you can "trick" your mind into assuming it has *already* occurred. No, really. The science behind this is solid. "It is now a well-known fact that we stimulate the same brain regions when we visualize an action and when we actually perform that same action," wrote Harvard professor of psychiatry Srini Pillay back in 2009. "For example, when you visualize lifting your right hand, it stimulates the same part of the brain that is activated when you actually lift your right hand."

This means that visualization itself helps us to prepare for the task at hand—and there is plenty of research supporting the efficacy of such techniques. One study on "mental practice," published in the *British Journal of Surgery* and reported by the *Globe and Mail*, found that senior surgical trainees who had engaged in visualization techniques for a week prior to performing a technically challenging laparoscopy, or keyhole surgery, performed markedly better than trainees who didn't. Another study, published in the *American Journal of Clinical Hypnosis*, found "visualizations under hypnosis enabled nationally ranked Stanford male gymnasts to execute for the first time several complex tricks that they had been working on for over a year. The gymnasts were able to eliminate timing errors in the tricks, to increase flexibility, and, possibly, to concentrate strength."

In fact, some of the most successful athletes on the planet say they confidently prepare for victory by using visualization techniques. Take Michael Phelps, perhaps the greatest swimmer of all time. "There are times in my sleep when I literally dream my race from start to finish," wrote the twenty-three-time Olympic gold medal winner in his 2004 memoir, *Beneath the Surface*. "Other nights, when I'm about to fall asleep, I visualize to the point that I know exactly what I want to do: dive, glide, stroke, flip, reach the wall, hit the split time to the hundredth, then swim back again for as many times as I need to finish the race."

Two-time UFC champion and mixed martial artist Conor McGregor also swears by what he calls "the power of visualization." In one video, his coach John Kavanagh outlines how it is that McGregor always comes across as calm and assured when he walks out for a fight, no matter how big the crowd in the arena.

> He knew exactly what was going to happen [in a fight] long
> before it happened because he had done it a thousand times

in his head. He had warmed up backstage. He had heard the crowd. He had smelled the arena. He had seen the audience. He really immersed himself in the Fight Night. So by the time Fight Night came along, for a lot of people, they had maybe been training in kind of a quiet gym, for eight or twelve weeks, and then they would walk out to fifteen thousand people and get shocked. He used to walk out and go: "Yeah, this is my thousandth time doing this."

When you stand up to give a speech in front of a crowd, you want it to feel like your thousandth time doing it, too. Because that's what confidence looks and feels like. And that's what positive visualization can do for you.

2. Take risks

"You gain strength, courage, and confidence by every experience in which you really stop to look fear in the face," wrote the legendary former First Lady Eleanor Roosevelt in her book *You Learn by Living.* "You are able to say to yourself, 'I have lived through this horror. I can take the next thing that comes along' . . . You must do the thing you think you cannot do."

We can't gain confidence about what we can do until we actually try to do it—and that means "taking risks," say the experts. To work on your confidence, therefore, you have to consider your own willingness to take more risks in your everyday life. Because our self-confidence increases not just through success and achievement but through our experience of "risk and failure" as well. "Confidence comes with familiarity," writes the acclaimed executive coach Megan Bruneau. "Familiarity comes with experience." And experience comes from trying new things!

How can we apply that to building confidence when it comes to public speaking and communicating?

Volunteer to speak in front of crowds. "Seize every opportunity" to speak in front of friends or family, says speech coach Simon Trevarthen. Get used to having all eyes on you as you speak aloud to a group of people. Start small (family dinner? team meeting?) and then slowly add to the number of people in front of you (best man speech? commencement address?). It's better to crash and burn in front of five people, and learn from that, than it is to flail in front of fifty or five hundred. Making the most of smaller opportunities allows you to work your way upward. Or as cognitive scientist Sian Beilock notes in her book *Choke*: "Even practicing under *mild* levels of stress" can prevent you from choking "when *high* levels of stress come around."

Challenge a friend or colleague to an argument. Look for opportunities to debate with people around you, ideally on topics that they know more about than you do. They'll probably run rings around you. You might even make a fool of yourself trying to defeat them. But, again, it'll help in the long run, helping you get a feel for how arguments can flow together . . . and fall apart. That familiarity will help you gain confidence for higher-stakes opportunities.

Ask for a pay raise or promotion at work. It's both risky and intimidating to ask a boss for more money or responsibility, isn't it? Yet, per Eleanor Roosevelt, "you must do the thing you think you cannot do." Don't necessarily do this on a whim—the stakes are getting higher now. Instead, make your best argument and pick the right moment. Odds are you've been wanting to ask anyway. Even if they end up saying no, or that they don't have the budget, you'll show initiative. And if you can negotiate successfully with your boss on an issue as scary as a pay raise or a promotion, then you'll find yourself much more confident about winning an argument on some abstract topic.

Taking risks not only requires confidence but also helps you build more of it. All of us, says executive coach John Baldoni, can afford to stretch our comfort zones and take more risks. Myself included.

I'm used to speaking in front of crowds now—it's something that I enjoy and even look forward to. Addressing an audience of little kids, however? Not so much. A few years back, I accepted a request from the head teacher of my kid's Islamic Sunday school to address their morning assembly. I spent days fretting over it, writing and rewriting my planned remarks.

"I've never seen you like this," my wife said as she watched me nervously preparing my presentation.

Why? Because I was way, *way* outside my comfort zone. I had interviewed the British prime minister in Number 10 Downing Street. I had done countless debates on live TV, sometimes where it was only me versus two or three people on the other side of the argument. But a room full of six- and seven-year-olds? I was petrified. Nevertheless, I took a risk and I did it. And how did it work out? Well, in my defense, the kids didn't *hate* my presentation.

Self-confidence isn't a way of avoiding failure—those kids weren't exactly erupting with applause—but it is a great way of dealing with failure. Taking risks and failing lets you learn what went awry, and also that life goes on. This can create a "kind of virtuous circle," as author Claire Shipman has observed—failure helps build confidence, and confidence helps you better cope with failure.

"Paradoxically, by being more willing to fail, you'll actually succeed more—because you're not waiting for everything to be 100 percent perfect before you act," writes Barbara Markway, a clinical psychologist and author of *The Self-Confidence Workbook*. "Taking more shots will mean making more of them."

Or consider radio host Zane Lowe's words to Kanye West in an interview in 2015.

KANYE WEST: You win some games and you lose some.

ZANE LOWE: You win or you learn, right?

KANYE WEST: Yeah, you win or you learn. Bam, there's a jewel; I'll take that one with me.

I'm not sure Ye did "take that one" with him, but that's a story for another book. The bigger point is this: take risks, experience failure, learn from where you went wrong . . . and watch how your confidence grows.

3. Keep good company

I'm going to let you in on a secret: most people want you to succeed. They do. Whether it's your partner, parents, or kids—or an audience of strangers. The truth is that most people are "rooting for you," writes psychologist Lybi Ma. "Why wouldn't they?"

Of course, our minds are terrible at absorbing this idea. We remember the one person who teased us in high school better than the hundred who were casually friendly. We stew over the one frown, as the saying goes, in a sea of smiles.

So, the challenge is to surround yourself with the kind of people who end up boosting your confidence, rather than those who chip away at it. There's a saying often (mis)attributed to Albert Einstein: "Stay away from negative people. They have a problem for every solution."

I happen to have been blessed with plenty of *positive* people in my life. I have a best friend who lives in Australia, ten thousand miles Down Under, and yet is always available on the other end of the phone to cheer me up. Then there are my extended family members around the world—in particular, my cousin and his wife in London, as well as my sisters-in-law—who text me "Amazing!" "Awesome!" and "Congratulations!" after even the most minor of successes or achievements on my part. I even have a group of friends who once attended a live recording of my Al Jazeera English show, *Head to Head*, in Washington, DC, and excitedly invited me into a WhatsApp group for the occasion—calling it "Head to Head Cheer Squad."

None of that may seem like anything to write home about. But do you think that all of it doesn't affect my confidence level? In a positive way? Of course it does. Their positivity impacts my own, and their belief in me reinforces my own. (I should add that I also have a wonderful wife and two kids at home who help keep me grounded whenever I get *over*confident!)

Many of us don't realize how much the negativity of others affects us. In the next chapter, I'll talk more about our inner voice, the one that tells us we can or can't do this or that. Of course, we have to work hard to ensure that our inner voice is a positive and not a negative one—but we also have to recognize that the people around us make a huge difference. To quote University of Chicago therapist Rameya Shanmugavelayutham, "the voice in our head that tells us we are not good enough is not our authentic voice but an aggregate of all the voices of those who have criticized us in the past." We need to "talk back" to those inner critics, she says, and reject them.

Constructive criticism and feedback are one thing, but constant carping and complaining from the naysayers is another. To build your confidence, you need to counterbalance the voices of the pessimists, negativists, and defeatists in your life, the Debbie Downers and the Negative Nancys. Keep those at a distance, and bring the positive and uplifting voices close.

"Cutting negative people from my life does not mean I hate them," Marilyn Monroe is said to have once remarked. "It simply means I respect me."

FAKING CONFIDENCE

Okay, so that's Plan A. Visualize success; surround yourself with positive people; take risks, fail, learn, grow; earn your confidence the hard way. It all sounds great, but it also sounds like it might take a bit of time.

What if you have to go onstage . . . tomorrow? And your confidence levels are shaky at best. Is there a Plan B?

You've heard of the old adage "Fake it till you make it"? Well, that's the idea. But in 2012, Amy Cuddy, a social psychologist at Harvard Business School, delivered a modified version of the adage that makes the point better: "Don't fake it till you make it. Fake it till you *become* it."

Our confidence levels go up and down throughout our lives. All of us—no matter how accomplished, successful, educated, wealthy, powerful, or famous we might be—have moments where we're just not feeling it. Our self-confidence is shot—maybe because we're nervous, anxious, unprepared even. In such moments, Plan B is to fake it. You have nothing to lose and, if you persist and persevere in "faking it," everything to gain.

Consider this exchange between pop megastar Rihanna and a reporter with *E! News*.

E! NEWS: What do you do on those days where you don't feel that confident or fearless or powerful?

RIHANNA: Pretend.

E! NEWS: Fake it?

RIHANNA: Yeah.

E! NEWS: Till we make it?

RIHANNA: I mean, why not? It's either that or cry myself to sleep. Who wants to do that? You wake up with puffy eyes the next day. That's a waste of tears.

Another way to think of it is the "as if" technique. "If you want a quality," noted William James, dubbed "the father of American psychology," "act *as if* you already had it."

The beauty of this technique is, in the short run, acting "as if" you're confident convinces others to *see you* as confident, and in the long run, say experts, acting "as if" you're confident helps you "become more confident." So how do you act "as if" you're confident, even if you're not feeling it inside? There are a few simple and effective methods I know of, and that I regularly practice myself—both when I'm on my A game, and when I need to fall back on plan B.

1. Fix your body language

Sitting in a studio across from an interviewee, I can tell whether they are feeling confident before the interview has even begun. Even before they have said a word. Are they leaning forward or back? Are their arms open or crossed? Are they sitting up straight or slouching?

As the saying goes, "there are always two conversations going on": what you're saying to your audience, and what your body language is saying to your audience.

Consider this: when you're trying to change someone's feelings or attitudes, your words account for just 7 percent of your overall message. *Seven* percent. That's it. In contrast, your tone of voice accounts for 38 percent of it, and your body language accounts for a colossal 55 percent. This is the famous 7-38-55 rule, or concept, which Albert Mehrabian, a professor emeritus of psychology at the University of California, came up with in 1971 in his book *Silent Messages*.

Mehrabian's research makes literal the old adage: our actions speak louder than our words. Yet think about how much effort we put into our words compared to our nonverbal communication— even as the latter represent *93 percent* of what we're communicating.

That's why we have to be mindful of how others see us. Carmine Gallo cites research showing we make snap judgments when we see someone for the first time. These first impressions can be formed in milliseconds; they're difficult to erase; and they're based on body language and bearing. So why not learn to speak that language?

When it comes to projecting confidence, you can accomplish *a lot* simply by changing how you carry yourself. So, here are my top dos and don'ts, inspired by comms expert Lillian Glass's interview with *Insider* (and also Carmine Gallo's book *Talk Like TED*).

- *Do* "keep your chin and head up"—because confident people, says Glass, look up, not down.
- *Don't* cross your arms—you want to avoid adopting a defensive or "closed off" posture.
- *Do* "stand up straight" and keep your shoulders squared— it makes you appear both confident and in control.
- *Don't* slouch or shrug—it can convey laziness, untrust- worthiness, and a lack of self-confidence.
- *Do* "gesture with your palms" open and up—it shows you have nothing to hide.
- *Don't* fidget—you'll come across as "nervous," says Gallo, anxious, and even insecure.

Here's another key reason why body language matters so much: while it makes other people see you as confident, it also helps you feel confidence in yourself. For example, Cuddy, in her 2012 TED Talk, argued that adopting expansive postures—"power poses"— even for two minutes at a time can lead to people *feeling* more power- ful, more confident, and more willing to take risks. "Our nonverbals," said Cuddy, "do govern how we think and feel about ourselves" and also "our bodies change our minds." (Follow-up studies didn't repli- cate everything that Cuddy said about changes in our hormones, but the basic idea—that open stances, with good posture, make us feel more confident—*does* stand.)

Pay attention to the physical, then, and not just to the mental or verbal. It's a quick fix to projecting confidence—and even to *feeling* more confident.

2. Project your voice

If you want to come across as confident, you have to *sound* confident. If you want to exude power and authority, you have to use a powerful and authoritative voice. How we sound is just as important to our confidence as how we appear.

"The human voice: It's the instrument we all play," said sound consultant Julian Treasure at the start of his now-viral TED Talk in 2013. "It's the most powerful sound in the world, probably. It's the only one that can start a war or say 'I love you.'"

Yet so many of us pay so little attention to the tone or volume of our voice. We assume "it is what it is," but that's not true. Even the quietest person can learn to project their voice—and project confidence in the process.

Here are my own dos and don'ts for using your voice as an *asset*, inspired in part by the work of speech coach Justin Aquino.

- *Do* "speak from your diaphragm"—that is, breathe calmly and deeply, as if into your belly, and use that breath to propel your words with much more vigor and energy.
- *Don't* mumble or murmur. You'll come across as hesitant or fearful.
- *Do* "stand straight" when you're speaking. It will help get more air into your lungs and make your voice resonate better.
- *Don't* speak too fast—something I'm often guilty of! Your audience needs time to take onboard your arguments, and you don't want to come across as nervous.
- *Do* smile when you talk—not all the time, obviously, but when it's appropriate. You can "hear" a smile in someone's voice even over the phone, right?
- *Don't* be afraid to pause. Volume is important, but moments of silence accentuate the power of what you're saying. They

can be a powerful tool to build drama and to convey self-confidence.

One final trick comes from communications coach Aquino: When speaking to people at a distance, try to speak *past* them when you do it. It'll prompt you to raise your volume, to breathe more deeply, and to ensure that your voice carries. Basically, it's a one-stop shop for better speaking habits. "A good rule of thumb is to speak to a point three feet behind the person's head," says Aquino. "For example, if you're standing six feet away from someone, try to speak loud enough so that someone standing nine feet away could hear you clearly."

3. Make eye contact

"It's the eyes, *chico*. They never lie."

Tony Montana, aka "Scarface," was right.

Multiple studies show that our eyes play a crucial role in establishing trust, sincerity, affection, and, yes, confidence as well. Researchers at the Max Planck Institute for Human Cognitive and Brain Sciences found that "when humans observe others' faces, eyes are typically the first features that are scanned for information."

Every time I have appeared in front of an audience—whether it is on a *Question Time* panel, at an Oxford Union debate, or giving a keynote speech—I have gone out of my way to make eye contact with my audiences. Because you cannot—I repeat, *cannot!*—project confidence to another person if you avoid eye contact with them.

Whenever you look down at your notes, your phone, or the table, whenever you glance off to the side or avert your gaze, you come across as insecure and anxious. According to communications expert Lillian Glass, author of *The Body Language Advantage*, there is no better way of showing you have self-confidence than making eye contact: "When eye contact is maintained, it signifies control or power over a situation and establishes dominance."

It is difficult to overstate the power and import of making eye contact when it comes to working on our body language. Yet many of us don't do it! Based on a study of three thousand people, reported the *Wall Street Journal*, the communications-analytics company Quantified Impressions found adults on average only make eye contact "30 to 60 percent of the time." However, to create an "emotional connection" with other people, the analysts said, we should be aiming to make eye contact with them "60 to 70 percent of the time."

Confident and relatable speakers make eye contact not only when they're speaking but when they're listening, too. I always try and lean forward and look an interviewee in the eye when I am listening to them talk, as it shows I am focused. That said, don't stare; you'll make others feel uncomfortable if you look at them for *too* long. Here, the 50/70 rule is your friend: when you're speaking to people, "maintain eye contact" for at least 50 percent of the time; when you're listening to people, do it for up to 70 percent of the time. Experts say it's the right mix of "interest and confidence."

Remember: whether or not you *feel* confident, making eye contact is one of the quickest and simplest ways of *exhibiting* confidence. It can undoubtedly be uncomfortable, especially around new people or with big crowds. But it works. And, as it works, you're on your way to building that lasting sense of self-confidence.

....

"Personally I am always very nervous when I begin to speak. Every time I make a speech I feel I am submitting to judgment, not only about my ability but my character and honor. I am afraid of seeming either to promise more than I can perform, which suggests complete irresponsibility, or to perform less than I can, which suggests bad faith and indifference."

Who said it? The greatest of the great classical orators, Cicero himself. Even he was open and honest about his nervousness when the time came to speak.

Lacking confidence is not unique to you, nor is it a vice or a shortcoming. It's part of life. And it affects the best of us. Indeed, confidence is incredibly *rare* when it comes to public speaking. If you're nervous at the prospect of going onstage, that's a feeling you probably share with billions of people across the planet.

The question is: What are *you* willing to do to address it? How far are you willing to go?

Confidence isn't innate. It can be taught, learned, and developed. And it's well worth developing. Because even though Cicero might have grappled with nerves like all of us, he also understood the importance of possessing self-confidence. And, above all, he knew the crucial role that confidence plays in winning an argument and triumphing in public.

So visualize your successes and spend time with the right people. Take risks and learn from your failures. And, if your confidence levels are still taking a hit, then *act* as if you have it: project confidence through your body language, your tone of voice, your eyes.

The "confidence coach" Jo Emerson compares confidence to a muscle in the body. You need to work on it, she told the *Guardian*, like you would work on any other muscle. Doing so allows you to maintain, grow, and strengthen it. And, over time, you'll build a lasting confidence—through perseverance and effort, success and failure.

"Confidence is like respect," writes comedian and actor Mindy Kaling in her book *Why Not Me?* "You have to earn it." Of course, even then, like Rihanna, or Cicero, or anyone in the millennia between, you'll have to fake it sometimes.

KEEP CALM AND CARRY ON

Be like a duck. Calm on the surface, but always pad-
dling like the dickens underneath.

—Michael Caine

I was freezing cold. It was the winter of 2010 and I was part of a panel at Merton College, Oxford, in front of a drafty room full of both undergraduate and postgraduate students. The event had been organized by the Orwell Foundation and the title was: "What Can't You Speak about in the Twenty-First Century?"

The author Douglas Murray was addressing the room, and I was listening to him and smiling. Why was I smiling? More on that in a moment.

Murray is a smooth-talking right-wing polemicist. He is on record saying things like "conditions for Muslims in Europe must be made harder across the board"; Britain needs "less Islam" to avoid terrorist attacks; and "London has become a foreign country" because of the declining number of *white* British residents. Charming, right?

During the early 2010s, when I lived in the UK, I often agreed to debate him on television—something I now look back on with quite a bit of regret and embarrassment. Whether it was *Question Time*, *Daily Politics*, or *Sunday Morning Live*, you name it, we debated on it. British TV producers, it seems, enjoyed seeing sparks fly between us live on-air.

That night in Oxford, I was on a panel with him, listening intently as Murray went on and on about the danger that Islam and Muslims posed to free speech in the West. Murray called the Prophet of Islam a "madman, or a lunatic, or a fraudster," and even accused him of child rape.

Believe it or not, that was the exact moment when I smiled. In fact, while writing this chapter, I went back and rewatched a video of the event on YouTube. And there it is. There's me smiling as Murray makes those grotesque, inflammatory, and false charges about the founder of my faith.

A Muslim friend of mine who watched the event online later asked me why on earth I had been smiling as Murray smeared our beloved Holy Prophet. "Didn't you want to interrupt him and shout at him?"

My response? It's precisely *because* I wanted to lose my rag at him that I bit my tongue instead and smiled awkwardly.

Let's be clear: Murray was baiting me. I was sitting right next to him, less than two feet away, when he made his remarks. He *wanted* me, his Muslim co-panelist at a public event about the importance of free speech, to get visibly angry and offended, to try and shout him down. He wanted to playact as the measured defender of free speech who was attacked in a fit of rage by an angry partisan.

I couldn't afford to take that bait. I had to stay calm. And, I'll be honest, as a Muslim who loves and reveres the Holy Prophet, it was tough. Painfully tough. Nevertheless, when it was my turn to speak, I was able to use my own remarks to coolly push back against his Islamophobic fearmongering, while citing actual facts and data.

So, the moral of this story? If I can stay calm, so can you.

COOL, CALM, COLLECTED

If you lose your cool during an argument, odds are you'll lose that argument. It's really that simple. In order to make your point, sound convincing, and win over an audience, you have to be calm and collected. Now, as we have discussed in earlier chapters, there is certainly a role and a place for righteous anger, for passion and energy and emotion. But at no point can you lose control of your feelings.

Why is it so, *so* important to stay calm?

For a start, getting stressed-out or losing your temper undermines your ability to get your point across. You will struggle to coherently explain your position if you're worked up, agitated, or flustered. When you see red, you lose focus—of both your own argument and your opponent's.

Any half-decent opponent of yours will know this. They will see they're getting under your skin, winding you up, knocking you off-balance—and they'll keep doing what they're doing. They will sense weakness. Make provocative or offensive remarks. Interrupt you. Go ad hominem perhaps!

Next, there's your audience. If you lose your cool, you'll lose them, too. They'll see you as defensive. A loose cannon. Maybe even an oddball.

None of the fundamentals of debate—be it storytelling, bringing receipts, critical listening, connecting with an audience—can be achieved if you aren't calm. If you're agitated or stressed—or worse, if you've worked yourself up into an uncontrollable rage—then all the skills you've built slip out of your grasp.

So, when planning a major speech, a big argument, or an interview, you should also make a plan for staying cool, calm, and collected.

How do you do that? How do you stay stress-free in a stressful situation?

Different people have different methods. Alastair Campbell, the infamously hotheaded communications director for Prime Minister Tony Blair during the latter's early years in Downing Street, liked to surreptitiously poke his hand with a sharp object to remind himself to calm down in public and not shout at those around him. As the

Observer reported, while giving evidence during a libel trial involving then Labour MP George Galloway, Campbell used the sharp beak of his daughter's toy duck. When being grilled by MPs on the UK Parliament's Foreign Affairs Select Committee over the invasion of Iraq, he jabbed himself in the hand with a pin. "When colleagues took back the briefing notes Tony Blair's communications director had used," revealed the *Observer* in 2003, "they were sprinkled with spots of blood."

Personally, I prefer to avoid spilling blood, and I'd recommend you do the same. At the very least, it makes for easier cleanup. Here are my top three tips for staying calm in an argument or debate, no sharp objects necessary!

1. Breathing

"When the breath wanders the mind is unsteady, but when the breath is calmed, the mind too will be still." Those words of wisdom come from the Hatha Yoga Pradipika, a fifteenth-century yogic text authored by Swami Svātmārāma. Today, more than five hundred years later, the scientists have caught up with the swami. They've discovered that breathing helps control how we feel.

In 2017, in a paper published in *Science* and reported on by *Time* magazine, researchers led by Stanford biochemist Mark Krasnow studied a group of "three thousand neurons in the brain stems" of mice. This chunk of gray matter controlled how the mice breathed, whether fast or slow, and the researchers found that it had a direct biological link to "the locus coeruleus, a brain center implicated in attention, arousal, and panic that projects throughout the brain."

"This liaison to the rest of the brain means that if we can slow breathing down, as we can do by deep breathing or slow controlled breaths, the idea would be that these neurons then don't signal the arousal center, and don't hyperactivate the brain. So you can calm your breathing and also calm your mind," Krasnow told *Time*.

"Take a deep breath." It's a cliché we've all heard time and again, from the very first tantrum we threw as a child. But it's a cliché backed by hard science. To breathe deeply—whether you are being interviewed on live TV, giving a speech in front of hundreds in a hall, or in the midst of an argument with your partner in private—is to send a message to your brain, as the old saying goes, "to chill out." A "message," the experts say, the "brain then sends . . . to your body."

Something as simple as taking a couple of deep breaths can calm your nerves, slow your racing heart, and send some blood back to your brain. It helps, as they say, with both the mind and the body.

Every Sunday evening, as I am about to go live on MSNBC hosting my weekly show, I'm hyperaware of the fact that hundreds of thousands of viewers across North America are about to see and hear me speak. I take a single deep breath, and then I'm ready. For the next hour, I'm racing through commentary and coverage—facing interviews with my guests that might be friendly or combative. That one deep breath locks me in.

Now, you might want to go further than ad hoc breathing and engage in a number of formal breathing exercises—or even actual yoga itself. There are a lot of methods to choose from. You could try the 4–7–8 technique, also known as "relaxed breathing," which involves switching up your inhaling and exhaling via periods of four, seven, and eight seconds. You could try the SKY method, or Sudarshan Kriya Yoga, which is based on a sequence of five different breathing exercises. You could try "pursed lip breathing," which is all about taking slower and more efficient breaths, and requires much more regulation. Try them out, look up the various options, and figure out what works for you.

In *The Karate Kid II*, when our hero Daniel is stressed, what does his mentor and sensei Mr. Miyagi say to him? "When you feel life out of focus, always return to basic of life . . . Breathing. No breathe, no life."

One of my personal mottos? Always listen to Mr. Miyagi.

2. Laughing

We've already seen how laughter can help you win over an audience and disarm your opponent. But it can also help *you* to stay calm and steady over the course of a roller-coaster debate.

"Humor is the shock absorber of life," wrote Peggy Noonan, the acclaimed former speechwriter to President Reagan. "It helps us take the blows."

How so? Again, the science is clear: endorphins and "feel good" neurotransmitters like dopamine and serotonin help keep us calm and in a superpositive mood. Cortisol, on the other hand, is the body's main stress hormone. Laughter has been shown to help boost endorphins, as well as dopamine and serotonin, while reducing cortisol levels in the blood. So it has a calming and de-stressing effect.

Consider this: in a laboratory study published back in 1990, subjects were told they would get an electric shock after twelve minutes. That was a lie, but as they prepared to get shocked, they were divided into three groups, each of which "listened to either a humorous tape, a nonhumorous tape, or no tape." While anxiety increased across all groups as the twelve minutes elapsed, the study found that "subjects from the humor condition consistently rated themselves as less anxious and reported less increase in stress as the shock approached."

Laughter can work as a technique to calm the mind and body. However, in most fraught settings, you won't have a funny recording to listen to. You have to therefore find humor in your situation.

That's what I did that night in Oxford with Murray in 2010. I thought about how ridiculous it was for my opponent to be spewing hateful remarks left and right, in the hopes of getting *me* to lash out and look like the irrational one. He was going for optics, but his words were digging him into a pit he couldn't get out of.

You had to laugh! And this points to a second calming benefit of humor. It's giving us a rush of endorphins while also helping us improve our perspective. As the famous psychologist Rollo May put it, the use of humor is about "preserving the self ... It is the healthy way of feeling a 'distance' between one's self and the problem, a way of standing off and looking at one's problem with perspective." Which can give us, as bestselling author Andie Kramer writes, "a sense of power over the frightening situations we are facing."

If you can smile and laugh, you can turn a stressful situation into a ridiculous one. And you can relax. I guarantee it. Abraham Lincoln was a leader and a speaker who understood this aspect of humor. On September 22, 1862, the president gathered his cabinet together. In the midst of the brutal Civil War, he wanted their approval for his preliminary Emancipation Proclamation, which aimed to free millions of enslaved people across the Confederacy. The meeting came five days after the bloody Battle of Antietam, the deadliest one-day battle in American history, and Lincoln knew that his cabinet secretaries were on edge.

The president needed to calm their nerves and lighten the mood in the room, prior to raising the very serious issue of the proclamation. So Lincoln began the meeting by reading aloud from a book of humorous stories, writes historian Merrill D. Peterson, pausing to laugh loudly at the end. Then, he put the book to one side and asked the members of his cabinet: "Gentlemen, why don't you laugh? With the fearful strain that is upon me night and day, if I did not laugh I should die, and you need this medicine as much as I do."

3. Self-talking

Without warning, the scar on his forehead seared with pain again and his stomach churned horribly.

"Cut it out," he said firmly, rubbing the scar as the pain receded again.

"First sign of madness, talking to your own head," said a sly voice from the empty picture on the wall.

—*Harry Potter and the Order of the Phoenix*

Talking to yourself gets a bad rap—but Harry Potter happens to be right. It isn't the "first sign of madness" but rather an effective technique for keeping calm in a tense situation.

The truth is that many of us have an inner voice that we listen to in moments of crisis or calamity. At one point or another in our lives, most of us engage in an internal monologue. The question is: How do we ensure that our inner voice acts as a force for calm—and not alarm? How do we use it to keep composed in an argument, when our heart is pounding?

"Self-talk" is what psychologists call the personal commentary that goes on inside almost all of our brains as we offer ourselves advice and reflect on our thoughts, emotions, hopes, and fears. It's happening constantly and can swing from the positive ("I'm doing great!") to the negative ("I suck!") in a flash.

But one of the most effective ways we can channel self-talk to our benefit is to make a small but key change: Get rid of the "I." Instead of silently talking to ourselves in the first person, it's more effective to do so in *the third person*, by using our own names.

Yes, it sounds a bit crazy. But it isn't. In a paper published in 2017, a group of psychologists from Michigan State University and the University of Michigan confirmed "that third-person self-talk leads people to think about the self similar to how they think about others," which allows them the "psychological distance" to keep their own emotions under control. They conclude that "third-person self-talk may constitute a relatively effortless form of self-control."

I know what you must be wondering right now. Does anyone actually do this? Does *Mehdi* actually talk to himself in that way?

Yeah, I do. Next time you watch me on television clashing with a guest in a live interview, do so with the full knowledge that, even as I'm sparring with them out loud, I'm also silently coaching myself to stay calm and on track. *"Focus, Mehdi!" "Don't take the bait!" "You got this!"*

WHAT *YOU* CAN CONTROL

"You can't always control what goes on outside," the renowned author and motivational speaker Wayne Dyer likes to say. "But you can always control what goes on inside."

The key to staying calm in any situation is to remind yourself that you are in control. These are *your* emotions—and you can master them.

As for what "goes on outside"—even if you can't control the external situation itself, you can put it in context. You can take a step back and see the bigger picture. It's rarely ever as bad as you think it is.

Messed up a one-liner you wanted to deliver perfectly? No biggie. There'll be other lines.

Lost all your notes and can't remember exactly what you wanted to say? Be self-deprecating and make a joke out of it.

Your opponent just humiliated you in front of an audience with a killer put-down? Roll with it and see if you still have time to land a rhetorical counterpunch.

Speaking of punches, I inadvertently engineered a perfect practice scenario for all my zen techniques back in 2016, when I interviewed three-time heavyweight boxing champion of the world Vitali Klitschko.

Klitschko had been elected mayor of Kyiv two years earlier, and the purpose of the interview was to talk about Ukrainian domestic politics and his government's ongoing conflict with Russian-backed separatists in the east of the country. Before the interview began, the six-foot-seven, 250-pound Klitschko, nicknamed Dr. Iron Fist, asked me to speak slowly when we talked. "My English not so good," he told me as he settled his huge frame into the tiny chair in front of me. "Sure," I said, and kicked off the interview sounding like the stereotypical British tourist on holiday in continental Europe, talking both superslowly and superloudly to the locals ("CAN . . . YOU . . . SHOW . . . ME . . . THE . . . WAY . . . TO . . . THE . . . COL-OSSEUM?").

Over the course of the eleven-minute prerecorded interview, however, my talking speed reverted to its normal *fast* pace, and I completely failed to notice him becoming irritated. It didn't help matters when I asked Klitschko about his alleged ties to a Ukrainian mafia boss—which he denied. Finally, as the interview came to a close, the former boxing champion stood up from his chair, his face red with anger. He towered over me and, in his Ivan Dragoesque accent, boomed: "You said you would speak *slowly!*"

How do you remain calm in a moment like that? I'll be honest: i was terrified. Klitschko's arms looked like they were the size of my entire body! I mumbled an apology, but in my head I was thinking: "If he hits me right now, I'll die." Then another part of me thought, "But if he hits me, the clip of it will go viral!"

I'll admit, it was a rather ridiculous thing to think in that moment. Then again, it did make me smile inside, helped keep me calm, and prevented me and my big mouth from escalating the situation any further.

Looking back now, it's clear how I kept my composure: I silently addressed myself in the heat of the moment (*self-talking!*); I found humor in that bizarre situation (*laughing!*); and I also probably inhaled and exhaled a fair few times along the way (*breathing!*).

. . . AND CARRY ON

The now-legendary World War II propaganda poster published and distributed by the British government in 1939—"Keep Calm and Carry On"—has since become an internet meme. For me, those last three words—"and carry on"—are as crucial as the first two. Employing a tool kit of calming techniques can certainly go a long way. But sometimes you simply have to plow on, no matter how bad you feel or how badly things around you seem to be going. That way, believe it or not, lies (eventual) victory.

I often consider the sage advice that Armand Goldman (played by Robin Williams) offers to his oft-hysterical partner Albert (played by Nathan Lane) in the acclaimed 1996 comedy *The Birdcage*.

ALBERT GOLDMAN: Oh God, I pierced the toast!

ARMAND GOLDMAN: So what? The important thing to remember is not to go to pieces when that happens. You have to react like a man, calmly. You have to say to yourself, "Albert, you pierced the toast, so what? It's not the end of your life." Try another one.

ALBERT GOLDMAN: "Albert, you pierced the toast, so what?" You're right. There's no need to get hysterical. All I have to remember is: I can always get more toast.

The pressure might mount, tempers might flare, disaster might loom. But when you keep calm and carry on, you can still carry the day—and the argument. Oh, and you can always get more toast.

PRACTICE MAKES PERFECT

The more you practice, the better you get, and slowly
the fear goes away. Reps, reps, reps.

—Arnold Schwarzenegger

Meet Demosthenes. Orphaned at the age of seven and raised by guardians who then embezzled from his inheritance, he made his name in ancient Athens at the age of twenty when he sued those guardians in court. Within a matter of years, he had become famous as a logographer, or professional speechwriter, and then began giving impassioned public speeches himself. He became a lawyer and statesman of legend, to the point where he has been cited for centuries since, inspiring everyone from the ancient Romans to the U.S. Founding Fathers to the French Resistance during World War II.

The Roman poet Juvenal dubbed Demosthenes *largus et exundans ingenii fons* ("a large and overflowing fountain of genius"), the Roman educator Quintilian praised him as *paene lex orandi* ("*the* standard for oratorical excellence"), and the Roman statesman Cicero, no rhetorical slouch himself, called Demosthenes "the perfect orator."

You get the drift, right? As a public speaker, Demosthenes was basically badass.

But guess what? Demosthenes started off as an awful, *awful* orator. In *Parallel Lives*, the Greek historian Plutarch says the young Demosthenes suffered from a speech impediment and was mocked for his "weakness of voice" and "shortness of breath." He only improved because he was committed to it. And do you want to know *how* committed Demosthenes was?

Plutarch writes that the young Demosthenes built a "subterranean study" into which he would "descend every day without exception in order to form his action and cultivate his voice, and he would often remain there even for two or three months." He went so far as to shave one half of his head to ensure he would be too ashamed and embarrassed to leave his underground cavern and go "abroad." And when it came to his speech impediment, what Plutarch called "an inarticulate and stammering pronunciation," do you have any idea how Demosthenes overcame it? By putting pebbles in his mouth while practicing his speeches. Yeah, literal stones! His shortness of breath was easy pickings after that. According to Plutarch, the orator improved his stamina by running uphill while "reciting speeches or verses at a single breath."

By his early thirties, Demosthenes was delivering passionate public tirades, now known as *The Philippics*, against the invading Philip II of Macedon, father of Alexander the Great. His speeches were rousing and so inspiring, notes writer Steven John, that Athenians literally took up arms and prepared to fight their Macedonian invaders upon hearing him speak. John quotes Demosthenes in his now-legendary Third Philippic:

> You are in your present plight because you do not do any part of your duty, small or great; for of course, if you were doing all that you should do, and were still in this evil case, you could not even hope for any improvement. As it is, Philip has conquered your indolence and your indifference; but he has not conquered Athens. You have not been vanquished, you have never even stirred.

It is difficult to overstate both how brilliant an orator Demosthenes was *and* how much work he put into becoming such a brilliant orator. Demosthenes, in my view, is perhaps the best proof that this stuff can be taught—and that, if you're committed, you can make incredible progress.

These days, there is a widely held assumption that public speaking is a skill you either have or *don't* have. Many people watch those of us who regularly appear onstage or on TV and assume that we're winging it, delivering zingers and mic drops off the cuff. It all comes so naturally to us, the thinking goes; no need for practice, training, or preparation.

Oh, how I wish that were true! But it just isn't. When I deliver a ten- or fifteen-minute address at an event, that's all the audience sees or thinks about. But what they won't see is how much time went into that speech in the days, weeks, or months prior. Not just to research and write it but also to prepare and practice it, in my head and out loud. As Mark Twain once quipped: "It usually takes more than three weeks to prepare a good impromptu speech."

The truth is that no good speaker or debater tries to make it up as they go along. There are of course moments where you may need to improvise, or be spontaneous. But to quote the CEO and communications consultant Somers White, "90 percent of how well the talk will go is determined before the speaker steps on the platform." To succeed, you need to be prepared to talk about the topic at hand *and* you also need to have practiced talking about it.

You want it to seem natural—which requires a great deal of work. Still, that's good news for you. Because it means you can *learn* how to get it right—over the long term, like Demosthenes, and also in the run-up to a speech you have on the horizon. This is one of the most important pieces of advice I can give you when it comes to public speaking: Do. Not. Wing. It.

Prepare. Practice. Know that it takes time. But also know that you can get it right.

IT WASN'T JUST DEMOSTHENES

We assume everyone who is a good or great speaker is a *natural-born* speaker.

They aren't.

Take two of the greatest English-speaking orators of the past hundred years: Winston Churchill and Martin Luther King Jr.

Believe it or not, both of them had to do serious work to become the iconic orators we now know them to be.

1. "Fight on the beaches"

Let's start with Churchill. As a child he had a stutter and a stammer, he often spoke with a lisp, and he was shy. Even by the time he had entered politics in his twenties, he still had issues with his speech. As one early observer noted: "Mr. Churchill and oratory are not neighbors yet. Nor do I think it likely they ever will be."

In 1904, at age twenty-nine, Churchill stood in the House of Commons to deliver a speech. It began well, full of bombast and energy, and he went along without the aid of notes, speaking purely from memory. But as he reached the climax of his address, writes one of his biographers, the young Conservative MP suddenly lost his way.

"And it rests with those who . . ." he started to say, but then stopped midsentence.

He tried again.

"It rests with those who . . ." and, yet again, his voice trailed off, note the writers Brett and Kate McKay.

For three entire minutes—three minutes that must have felt like an eternity for the young Churchill!—he tried to find the right words but couldn't. MPs in the Commons chamber began to "heckle" him, say the McKays. "I thank the House for having listened to me," he said, red-faced, as he sat down and put his head in his hands.

Yet, come 1940, that same Churchill would rally millions of

Britons with talk of "blood, toil, tears, and sweat" and the need to fight Nazis "on the beaches." He was in no danger of losing his train of thought then. And, in 1953, he was awarded the Nobel Prize in Literature "for his mastery of historical and biographical description *as well as for brilliant oratory* [emphasis added]."

How did he become a "brilliant," award-winning, nation-inspiring orator? Through practice and preparation. One of his many biographers, former prime minister Boris Johnson, says Churchill's speeches "were a triumph of effort, and preparation, in which phrases were revised and licked into shape as a she-bear licks her cubs."

Churchill himself resolved never again to behave like those orators who "before they get up, do not know what they are going to say; when they are speaking, do not know what they are saying; and when they have sat down, do not know what they have said." As Johnson writes, referring to the 1904 incident in Parliament:

> He never made that mistake again. He kept his sheaf of typewritten notes, pinned together, and had no shame in peering down at them through his black horn-rims. Churchill's speeches were Ciceronian in their essentially literary nature: they were declamations of text.

Churchill wrote out his speeches in full; he would even write out every planned pause. But he did not read them out. In fact, as another of his biographers, William Manchester, has pointed out, Churchill put so much time into rehearsing his speeches that when he did deliver them, he took only the odd glance at his notes—and his audiences were none the wiser.

And what of his stutter and lisp? While walking around outdoors, Churchill would try to tackle his issue with words that started with *s* by repeating aloud ridiculous sentences such as "The Spanish ships I cannot see since they are not in sight." Later, he would proudly declaim: "My impediment is no hindrance."

He would also practice his speeches wherever and whenever he could. His valet Norman McGowan tells the story of how he once heard his boss murmuring in the bathtub. "Do you want me?" the anxious valet called out. "I wasn't talking to you, Norman," came the reply from Churchill. "I was addressing the House of Commons."

2. "I have a dream"

Even the most acclaimed piece of oratory in modern American history is a testimony to practice and preparation: Dr. Martin Luther King Jr.'s "I Have a Dream" speech.

MLK may have been a fourth-generation Baptist preacher with a flair for improvisation that Churchill lacked, but it would be a mistake to assume that his political speeches, in particular, came naturally or spontaneously to him, or that he didn't spend hours and hours planning and writing them. "I think one of the misconceptions people have about King was that all of his material was spontaneous and did not repeat," says Stacey Zwald Costello, who served stant editor at the King Papers Project at Stanford University's Luther King, Jr. Research and Education Institute. "However, site is true—he spent a lot of time preparing his speeches a recycled material, using it in different places and ways in get his point across."

well known that King delivered most of the 'I Have a Dream' ithout any notes and that he improvised much of it on the otes author and executive coach Scott Eblin. "What's not as w. .nown is that he had been working with much of the content of that speech in other addresses he gave months and years before the March on Washington. He took the time and opportunity to get very comfortable with his content and experimented with what worked and did it work in venues that weren't as prominent as the National Mall."

He put the hours in! Yet, even so, the night before he delivered his most famous speech on the steps of the Lincoln Memorial to over 250,000 people, King was reportedly awake till 4:00 a.m., writing and rewriting it.

Think about it: the greatest of orators, people like Demosthenes and MLK, had to work on their oratorical skills, *they* had to practice and prepare their speeches—their style, content, tone, delivery, and the rest. So guess what? So do you. So. Do. You.

Sorry, there's no debate about that.

. . . .

How should you practice and prepare for public speaking, though? In my experience, it works best to start with the basics of public performance: how you look, how you sound, and how you time each moment of your speech. Each of these elements will benefit from feeling confident and calm, as we covered in the previous chapters. They'll also need to be combined with substance and research, as we'll see in the next chapter.

But confidence and knowledge aren't enough on their own. You need a certain stage presence—that performative magic that has the potential to hold an audience rapt. "If your voice, gestures, and body language are incongruent with your words, your listeners will distrust your message," writes communications coach Carmine Gallo in his book *Talk Like TED*. "It's the equivalent of having a Ferrari (a magnificent story) without knowing how to drive (delivery)."

So let's learn how to drive. Here are my own top three suggestions on how to practice and prepare your delivery.

1. Practice how you "look"

Remember Demosthenes? He would rehearse his speeches in front of a mirror, and so should you.

Stand in front of a mirror. It might sound weird but you need to try having a conversation with *yourself*. See how you look and how you come across as you speak in front of your own reflection.

Examine your posture and make sure you're not slouching, swaying, or bobbing when you speak.

Check your facial expressions, too. What "look" do you have on your face when you're speaking? How expressive is it, and is it the correct expression deployed at the correct time? Does it match what you're saying or are you, to borrow a line, smiling while delivering the bad news and frowning while delivering the good?

You'll want a smartphone, as well. A couple thousand years means we can one-up Demosthenes.

Film yourself speaking aloud. Then you can see and hear what others see and hear when *you* speak to *them*. Try watching the videos without volume, CEO Jen Glantz has suggested, so you can concentrate solely on your facial expressions and body language and see if they're helping or hindering your delivery. "Simply seeing yourself in action makes you more conscious of how you come across," writes Gallo in *Talk Like TED*, "making you better equipped to eliminate useless movements and gestures."

(An added bonus: I can guarantee that once you become comfortable watching and hearing yourself speak on video, you will find yourself much more comfortable with *others* watching and hearing you speak, too.)

Let me make an admission here: If you're feeling awkward and overwhelmed as you start to watch yourself, know that you are far from alone. I have long had issues with my own facial expressions. I have what I call RAMF—or "Resting Angry Muslim Face." My default look is one of anger and intenseness, and being an adult Muslim male, looking angry and intense comes with all sorts of unwanted (and unfair!) connotations and assumptions. It's something I have had to work hard on prior to TV appearances and public presentations: to *not* permanently look like I want to bite someone's head off!

It's not just your face, either. Watch your hands as well. Do you use them too much? Too little? Are you making strange motions with them that you may not have even realized? It's incredibly common once you start looking for it. I'm certainly guilty of this. A TV producer I used to work with once told me he wanted to strap my hands to my side when I spoke on camera!

I managed to avoid that fate, but it's still something I've had to work on and practice over time. When you're talking to yourself, whether on camera or in front of the mirror, act as if it is a conversation you might be having with a friend or family member. Gesture only when you need to emphasize something and otherwise try and keep your hands by your side. If you find that to be a forced or unnatural pose, then try holding the sides of the lectern with your hands, writes rhetoric expert Sam Leith, or "clasping" them together in front of you (my own preferred option). The point is not to avoid gesturing—but to do so with purpose, rather than erratically or haphazardly.

2. Practice how you "sound"

> I did not know before I got married that every single day of my life . . . I would be discussing the tone in my voice. I didn't know this. I was not aware that I spoke in so many different tones. I have since learned not only do I speak in many different tones, I am often speaking in the incorrect tone. I thought it was a marriage; apparently it's a musical . . . My actual speaking voice that I am using right now to communicate with you is not welcome in my house. Oh no! That's why I'm out here talking to you.

That's the legendary Jerry Seinfeld in one of his early stand-up routines, riffing on a truth that every public speaker needs to keep in mind: how you sound changes how people listen—or even *whether* they're willing to listen. As the German philosopher Friedrich Nietzsche is said to have observed, "We often refuse to accept an idea merely because the tone of voice in which it has been expressed is unsympathetic to us."

Are you aware of how your voice sounds and comes across to others? Are you aware of how it changes when you are giving a speech to a crowd? Perhaps you have volume or tone issues that, like Seinfeld, a friend or spouse has kindly flagged for you already. So here's what you need to know to start working on them.

There are four basic aspects to vocal delivery, says speech coach Helen von Dadelszen, known as the 4 Ps: pitch, power, pace, and pause.

Pitch is your tone of voice.

Power is how "loudly or quietly" you speak.

Pace is how fast or slow you speak.

Pauses are the breaks you leave between sentences or declamations.

The 4 Ps require polishing and perfecting. And here, again, a smartphone is your friend. First, record yourself speaking. Listen out for your volume, for your *power*. DO YOU SOUND LIKE YOU'RE SHOUTING? Do you sound too quiet? It's really important to make sure people can hear you, but at the same time, it is important to sound relaxed and easy to listen to. You may want to vary your volume, writes Von Dadelszen, depending on whether you're trying to project joy and humor or sadness and fear. You'll also want to get louder or quieter depending on where you are in your speech—be it a personal anecdote or a sweeping proclamation.

Likewise, your dynamics should change depending on where you are, physically. Are you in a cavernous auditorium, or a cramped conference room? Your power should change to reflect the setting, and, if possible, you should *practice* in the right setting. Which means that when recording yourself, try to place your phone wherever your target listener is going to be; if you're going to be addressing a large conference room, record from the far end of the room rather than five inches from your face.

Next, listen to *how* you are speaking. As the great poet and author Maya Angelou observed, "Words mean more than what is set down on paper. It takes the human voice to infuse them with deeper meaning." In practical terms, as *every* public speaking expert agrees, this means one thing: if you speak in a robotic, monotonous tone of voice, you *will* put your audience to sleep. There is nothing, *nothing*, more off-putting in a public speaker than a flat or dull tone.

This is where *pitch* and *pause* come into play. What words are you emphasizing and in what way? What tone are you using, and are you varying it from sentence to sentence? Are you pausing at the right spots, for dramatic or even comic effect? A strategic pause can give you a chance to take a breath—and your audience a chance to "digest," as the old saying goes, what you've just told them.

However, be careful of what are known as "vocalized pauses"—those useless filler words between sentences like *umm*, *uhh*, *like*, *y'know*, and the rest. These verbal tics can be highly off-putting for an audience, so the first thing to do if you want to banish filler words from your speech is to be conscious that you are relying on them! (Did I mention that you should record yourself speaking?)

Pay close attention to how you enunciate words, too, and whether or not you are mumbling. This is a big problem for a lot of public speakers. There was a time when I used to swallow my own words live on-air, which I had no idea I was doing until one of my own producers pointed it out to me. It's something I still have to grapple with because, as you may have noticed if you've watched my debates or TV shows, I'm someone who tends to speak pretty damn quickly.

Which brings us to *pace*, my own Achilles' heel. There is a time to "speed up"—to generate excitement among your listeners, says von Dadelszen, and to keep them rapt. And there is time to slow down—to ensure they're following and processing the argument you're making. Every good orator learns how to alternate between the two. Doing so not only helps listeners absorb your points, but it also keeps the act of listening more interesting and engaging.

If you're anything like me, you'll need to practice much more on consciously slowing yourself down, rather than on speeding up. This is common in first-time speakers, and is often hard to notice. You're full of adrenaline and eager to get your points across—so all of a sudden you sound like a sped-up podcast.

By recording yourself speaking you'll be able to hear how *others* hear you—and that's key. Don't be like Hollywood star Adam Driver, aka Kylo Ren, who angrily walked out of a radio interview in 2019 after the hosts played a clip of him singing from one of his movies. Driver, it seems, cannot bear to hear his own voice played back to him. (But there's no need for you to follow in his footsteps and go over to the dark side of the Force!)

The 4 Ps can require a great deal of practice—especially if you're not used to speaking in public. As a father of two kids, I've always found that reading aloud from a children's storybook, and literally performing the different characters' dialogues, can be a superhelpful and natural way of working on your 4 Ps—and *pitch*, in particular. Professional communications coach Helen von Dadelszen agrees: "Reading a child's story, out loud, provides you with a fabulous opportunity to explore the range of your voice and bring more variety into it . . . It provides an opportunity for you to play!" Even if you don't have kids, pick out a book you like and try vocalizing the dialogue—changing up your tone of voice, using different emotions for the different characters. It's an eye-opening experience, showing just how much you can accomplish with your voice.

3. Practice your timing

Whether it's a competitive debate, whether it's a keynote speech, whether it's live television, you're almost always given a time slot, a clock, a scheduled period. And you need to be able to stick to it. Not just because you want to avoid breaking any rules but also because you want to avoid annoying your host or shortchanging your audience.

So this is my final practical piece of advice for honing your delivery: time yourself speaking. Do it again and again until you can deliver your argument, in your sleep, *to time*.

The benefits aren't just about sticking to schedule. Working on your timing beforehand ensures that your speech or presentation is dead-on. It also makes you less likely to ramble, which can be a death knell to a public presentation. I promise: no one wants to hear you meander through a twenty-minute story that you could have told in two. And you're not going to fall into that trap if you've already clocked out each key part of your presentation.

Nailing your timing also makes it easier to *adapt* on the big day, if need be. You may be in a formal debate or a work conference and find out that you need to address new arguments or offer new rebuttals. But now you still have to stay within your existing time constraints. If you're already superfamiliar with your structure and content—if you know your speech inside and out—you can then make changes to one piece or another without wrecking your overall delivery.

To make your timing work best for you, however, I'd even recommend preparing remarks that go *under* your time limit. If you're given ten minutes to speak, try preparing only eight or nine minutes of remarks. This gives you "wiggle room" if you feel the need to include any extra points or arguments on the day-of. If you don't need to, it's not a problem. Everyone will respect your ability to be concise rather than droning on.

There are three ways, in my experience, of making sure your speech or presentation sticks to time.

1. **The bold move:** Write out your speech in full, then time yourself giving it, and then *memorize* the entire thing. Yes, commit all of it to memory! Back in 2005, David Cameron went from outsider in the race for the Conservative Party leadership to front-runner after he famously dazzled the party membership at the annual conference in Blackpool by delivering a speech from memory, without any notes whatsoever. Five years later, he was prime minister. If you have the time and want to wow your audience without any

distractions, memorizing your speech is a surefire way to do so while sticking to your time constraints.

2. **The safer option:** You might say that memorizing your remarks is a high-risk/high-return strategy, just as a young Churchill learned the hard way. My advice, if you decide to go down this road, is to learn from old Churchill and keep a printout of the full speech within arm's reach . . . *just in case*. Write out your speech in full, time yourself giving it, and then deliver it with written remarks on the podium or lectern in front of you. But *do not* read it out to your audience, with your head down, buried in the text. Churchill put so much time into practicing that every sentence and paragraph was deeply familiar and he only needed to glance down at his paper from time to time. This is what I'd recommend, and it's my own preferred method.

3. **The freewheeling route:** Instead of writing out your speech in full, you can also deliver your remarks in note form. Use cue cards with bullet points on them—including only key words and phrases, instead of full sentences or paragraphs. The advantage of this popular technique is that you need not worry about forgetting your speech or having to read your speech word for word. It doesn't let you nail your timing to a T, as writing out the whole speech allows. But it gives you flexibility: if you're running out of time, you can make sure to still get your most important points across.

You can try each method out and pick which works for you. But the key to succeeding with all of these methods is *rehearsal*. Find an audience of friends or colleagues to practice in front of. Be willing to accept feedback, even criticism. Then tweak and retweak your remarks until they're just right—properly timed but also natural to you, in a way that allows you to speak smoothly (bonus points if you can allow room for spontaneity). Practicing in front of friends means you can lean into a conversational style and tone. But remember: your goal is to *be* prepared but not *sound* prepared.

Carmine Gallo, an expert on TED Talks, stresses the importance of rehearsal and feedback, and points to musician Amanda Palmer, who gave "The Art of Asking" TED Talk in 2013:

> Palmer would read the drafts out loud to a group of people. If they seemed bored, she'd go home to rewrite. She practiced in front of anyone who would listen. She told the story to a bartender and a passenger next to her in a plane. She held potluck dinners and invited friends to watch and offer feedback. She delivered it to a class of students. Finally, Palmer performed it twice for the TED team.

Well, not quite "finally." After all that preparation, "The Art of Asking" went off without a hitch and has amassed more than twelve million views.

. . . .

One question I often receive is: How *much* do you need to practice? Some people assume that a short, quick presentation or speech requires only a little practice or preparation time. But nothing could be further from the truth. There is a rather apt quote, which has been ascribed to everyone from Mark Twain to Woodrow Wilson to Winston Churchill, that says: "If you want me to give you a two-hour presentation, I am ready today. If you want only a five-minute speech, it will take me two weeks to prepare."

It takes considerable time, skill, and effort to condense everything you might want to say on a topic into a short yet effective presentation. When I first started out as a pundit on U.S. cable news, I would often spend up to two hours preparing for a three-or four-minute appearance on CNN or MSNBC. It was live TV and I wanted to be prepared.

On one occasion, I was invited by CNN to talk about Trump and anti-Semitism. I knew that I wouldn't have much time, and I had a great deal that I wanted to say on that particular issue. So I researched copiously beforehand and then practiced reeling off a list of examples of Trump's anti-Semitism. Because I am well aware of the time constraints of live television, I timed what I wanted to say to make sure it wasn't more than a minute in length.

When host Jake Tapper turned to me and gave me an opportunity to speak on the subject, I let rip:

> Three times now, he has basically referred to American Jews as secret Israelis with dual loyalties to their prime minister abroad. This is the third time he has done it as president. He's not going to back down. And I just think we need to deal with this very dangerous idea that being pro-Jewish means you have to be pro-Israeli, or being pro-Israeli means you're automatically pro-Jewish or you're immunized from the charge of anti-Semitism. Lots of anti-Semites support Israel and Benjamin Netanyahu. It doesn't mean anything.
>
> And regardless of Donald Trump's views on Israel, he's always been an anti-Semite. This is not a controversial opinion. The facts are there. He was an anti-Semite in the 1980s when Ivana said he kept a book of Hitler speeches next to his bed. He was an anti-Semite in the 1990s when his casino manager said he only wanted short guys in yarmulkes counting his money. He was an anti-Semite in 2013 when he shamed Jon Stewart on Twitter for having a Jewish birth name. And, of course, in 2015 when he said to Republican

Jewish donors, "You won't vote for me because I don't want your money."

And then we see the presidency: neo-Nazis at Charlottesville, "very fine people." It goes on and on and on. I don't know how much more evidence we need that he is an anti-Semite, and it's amazing that not a single Republican today has called him out for it.

Sixty seconds. Dead-on. Live on-air. And soon after, the clip went viral. "A Perfect Distillation of Trump's Anti-Semitism in Just One Minute," as one online headline put it at the time.

"Give me six hours to chop down a tree," Abraham Lincoln is said to have remarked, "and I will spend the first four sharpening the axe." I firmly agree with Honest Abe.

Practice does make perfect. Preparation does deliver success. Spend all the time it takes to sharpen your axe. Hone your delivery— your look, your sound, your timing—until it's as sharp as can be. Because you can never be too prepared. Consider this: days before Lincoln delivered his landmark Gettysburg Address in November 1863, writes Sam Leith in his book *Words Like Loaded Pistols: Rhetoric from Aristotle to Obama*, Lincoln "asked the man who landscaped the cemetery to bring him the plans, so he could familiarize himself with the layout of where he'd be speaking." The sixteenth president never liked leaving anything to chance.

Lincoln, perhaps, was embracing the wisdom attributed to another legendary American political figure: Founding Father Benjamin Franklin. "By failing to prepare," Franklin is said to have remarked, "you are preparing to fail."

Don't prepare to fail. Prepare only to win.

DO YOUR HOMEWORK

Supposing is good, but finding out is better.

—Mark Twain

We called it The Document. The research dossier that my colleagues and I had to prepare each week in the early 2000s while working on ITV's *Jonathan Dimbleby*.

I was a year out of college when I joined the show as a researcher—but nothing I had done during my three years at Oxford University, whether writing essays on Kant or Locke for undergraduate tutorials or giving speeches at the Oxford Union debating society, prepared me for the sheer vastness of The Document.

The award-winning journalist Jonathan Dimbleby, a scion of the Dimbleby broadcasting family, hosted his eponymous political interview show on British television between 1994 and 2006. Every Sunday at lunchtime, he would conduct an hour-long, in-depth interrogation with a top politician, in front of a live studio audience on London's South Bank. And Dimbleby was formidable—one of the most feared and forensic interviewers of that era.

My job was to help him prepare. Every week, in the run-up to the big Sunday interview, three of us—one producer and two researchers—would spend several days digging into the background and record of the confirmed guest: their statements, policies, career highlights and lowlights. We funneled it all into The Document, which we constructed anew each week to build Dimbleby's argument in advance, mapping out the entire hour-long interview ahead of time. We gathered facts, figures, footnotes, charts, graphs, tables, and more. We suggested possible questions for Jonathan to ask; anticipated predicted responses from his guests; and even proposed follow-up questions. We tried to prepare for every eventuality. If the minister said *A*, Jonathan would ask *B*. If the minister then said *X*, Jonathan would be ready with *Y*.

It was all there. In The Document. This was not a couple of sheets of paper, with a handful of bullet points on them. What we produced, week in, week out, was an elaborate, detailed, and wide-ranging *booklet*. (Jonathan once suggested we publish them, after each interview, as resource guides for schools and colleges.)

For Jonathan, as he told me in a recent interview, "The Document was crucial. It provided focus and clarity plus facts." It was a foundation of knowledge that sparked Jonathan's own final research in the run-up to the show, and then kept him steady and in control once the cameras were rolling. Doing homework of the kind we did on his show, Jonathan explained, "is fundamental. Without that, any half-decent interviewee can walk over you to peddle a message without serious challenge."

Looking back more than two decades later, I can honestly say that the four years I spent working, on and off, for ITV's *Jonathan Dimbleby* made me the journalist, and especially the interviewer, I am today. Since leaving ITV, I have had the privilege of working for some of the world's biggest media organizations—the BBC, Sky News, Al Jazeera English, and, currently, NBC News. Yet nothing has had more influence on how I prepare for a public presentation, debate, or interview than my experience working on The Document for the *Dimbleby* show. And what did that experience show me? That, if you want to win an argument, nothing is more important than digging in and doing your homework.

············

You'll be shocked to hear that, as a kid, I hated doing homework. Like most children, I wanted to watch television, ride my bike, play computer games . . . anything *other* than my wretched homework assignment.

As an adult, though, I have become obsessed with doing homework. I always want to be prepared; I always want to have receipts; I always want to know more about a contentious issue than anyone else. And that requires doing the research.

The inconvenient truth is that it doesn't matter how clever, passionate, or eloquent you are—you cannot win an argument without putting in the work.

I have interviewed everyone from John Bolton to John Legend, from the former head of the CIA to the ex–head writer of *Veep*. I have interviewed adults and children; Hollywood superstars and members of the public. And I have never sat down to do a *single* interview without first doing some homework—whether that's to understand my guests, the topic at hand, or the particular story I'm trying to cover.

I would go so far as to argue that *not* doing your homework is a sign of disrespect for your interview guest—or debate opponent. It is a sign of intellectual laziness, and even arrogance.

The problem is that we foolishly assume debating is pure technique. Today, we live in an era of "hot takes"—an age in which everyone seems to have an opinion on everything—and we wrongly assume that debates are all about our *opinions*. And yet, as the philosopher Patrick Stokes has observed, "You are not entitled to your opinion. You are only entitled to what you can argue for."

If you're trying to master a field like medicine or law or accounting, then you know you'll need to read and prepare. You only want a professional opinion from a doctor if it's based on study and expertise. If you want to win a debate on a contentious topic, it's no different. Your opinions and arguments are going to be worthless if they're not based on a foundation of knowledge.

So how can you build your argument the right way? What facts or figures can you bring to bear? Why should your opinion count more than anyone else's? Or as the saying goes, are you willing to do the work required to have an opinion?

In 2012, I was invited to visit Kyiv as part of a democracy-building program organized by the Ukrainian nonprofit Foundation for Effective Governance (FEG). The FEG, in conjunction with Intelligence Squared, was hosting debates in the country's capital on a variety of political and economic issues, to promote free speech and free discussion.

This was two years prior to the Maidan Square protests and the annexation of Crimea by Russia, and a full decade before Vladimir Putin's brutal full-scale invasion of Ukraine. But even back in 2012, the Ukrainian economy was a mess.

The motion for my debate was: "Increasing government spending will prevent the second wave of crisis in Ukraine." I was asked to debate in favor of the motion while, on the other side, would be Viktor Pynzenyk, who served as Ukraine's finance minister between 2007 and 2009.

To be clear: I was being asked to make an argument about the economy of a foreign country about which I knew next to nothing, while visiting that foreign country, against a guy who had literally run the economy of that foreign country.

Crazy, right?

And yet I agreed. Because I was willing to do the work required to have that opinion. (Okay, and because I love a good debate!)

I spent weeks in the run-up to that event reading up on both Keynesian deficit spending and the state of the Ukrainian economy. I devoured every relevant newspaper article and academic study in the English language that I could get my hands on. And then I flew 1,500 miles to Kyiv to hold my own against Viktor Pynzenyk. I may have ended up losing that debate—you'll be stunned to hear that the Ukrainian audience voted in favor of their former finance minister rather than the British-Asian guy who had just landed in their country—but it was a thoroughly exhilarating experience and I wouldn't have dared to do it if I had not done my homework. (As I freely admitted in my opening remarks that night in Kyiv, "I'm not an expert on the Ukrainian economy . . . nor do I pretend or claim to be one. I've only been in your country, in fact, for eighteen hours, on your soil.")

One of the quickest—and perhaps dumbest—ways to badly lose a debate is to turn up unprepared. Personally, I have never understood why people even bother getting into arguments without having done their homework beforehand. It's a fool's errand.

In my view, there are three crucial components to the preparation you'll need to do before any argument, interview, or presentation: brainstorming, researching, and role-playing. Let's take each in turn.

THE BRAINSTORM

We've all experienced that dreaded feeling, haven't we? Staring at a blank computer screen, trying to come up with the right sentence to start off a new essay or presentation. There's so much you could say—so much you *will* say—that you can't settle on where to begin.

Brainstorming, pioneered by advertising executive Alex Osborn in the 1950s, is our way out of this mental block. It's usually conceived of as a group activity, but it can also be done individually—and you might be surprised by how much you enjoy brainstorming solo. It's a process that allows for you to be both creative and reflective, while acquainting yourself with unfamiliar corners of your own mind.

Brainstorming is an ideal first step because it lets you jot down all the jumbled ideas and facts you already know, along with the many questions you have about what you *don't* know. The point is to unlock the ideas already trapped inside your mind, perhaps deep in your subconscious, and to identify the areas that are still murky. Once you do so, you'll know where to focus your research so that you can forge your first-draft thoughts into a formidable argument.

Here are my top three tips on how to pull off a good brainstorm on your own.

1. Quantity not quality

"The best way to have good ideas is to have lots of ideas and throw away the bad ones," said the Nobel Prize–winning chemist Linus Pauling.

When it comes to brainstorming, quantity matters more than quality. Yes, that's right. You read that correctly. The experts say to worry about quantity first, and quality much, *much* later. It's a tried-and-tested principle that goes all the way back to Osborn himself— and is also endorsed by Nobel laureates like Pauling.

When beginning a brainstorming session, throw as many ideas onto the page as possible—whether good or bad, magnificent or mediocre. By prioritizing quantity over quality, you give yourself more choices, more options, more possibilities. Once lots of ideas are on the page, you can decide which ones to keep and develop, and which ones to get rid of. In a brainstorm, as the saying goes, no idea should be considered *too* crazy. Your most absurd ideas might inspire truly clever ones, and in the end, what happens to the bad ideas? You just toss them away.

I often apply this technique to my own question-writing process. I think of every possible question I might want to ask an interviewee on my show, from the ridiculous to the rude, from the irreverent to the irrelevant. Then I narrow it down to the *actual* questions that I need to ask (or, at least, the ones I can get away with asking!).

It's a liberating exercise, and it helps prevent you from getting tunnel-visioned on a single approach from the start. "I sometimes compare my brainstorming on paper to the drilling of oil wells," the entrepreneur Tom Monaghan once remarked, referring to his yellow legal pads and lists of ideas. "My lists are wells, and every once in a while I hit a gusher."

2. Past is prologue

"Every amazing creative thing you've ever seen or idea you've ever heard can be broken down into smaller ideas that existed before," writes author Scott Berkun in his book *The Myths of Innovation*.

Forget about a "eureka" or "aha" moment, or a "bolt from the blue." You don't need to wait, Isaac Newton–style, for an apple to fall on your head, argue tech writers David Kelley and Tom Kelley.

The best ideas are often formed via "small steps," not giant leaps. So says the science. With his team at the University of Pittsburgh, reported *Fast Company*'s Jessica Hullinger, psychologist Christian Schunn analyzed hours of transcripts recounting brainstorming sessions held by a professional engineering team that had been asked to come up with a new handheld printer for children. The subsequent study they published in *Cognitive Science* in 2014 found that new ideas *don't* require big cognitive leaps. Instead, they're often formed by a "chain of little mental advances." We can compare solutions that worked in the past to the present; we can look for previous examples of similar ideas; we can make analogies from one field to the next.

For example, noted Hullinger, the researchers found that the engineers came up with an idea for a roller door as part of their design for a new printer, after one of them reminisced about the flap on old videotapes, which then prompted another team member to suggest the mechanism behind a garage door.

"Your head is filled with solutions you've seen, and analogies are a way of looking through that past history of solutions to say, 'Well, maybe one of those could work here,'" Schunn told business magazine *Fast Company*.

This approach can be liberating for your own brainstorming. Think incrementally. Consider different topics that might hold similarities to your own subject. Don't be afraid to analogize using past experiences, or examples from other fields.

3. Get in your zone

It was the legendary tennis player Arthur Ashe who reportedly was the first to refer to "the zone"—that state of total focus where an athlete is performing to their fullest potential.

The best brainstorms occur when *you* are in *your* zone. When you take a break from the daily grind, give your conscious mind a rest, and let your subconscious take charge.

Switch off from work. Stop checking your email. Let your mind wander. "The greatest geniuses sometimes accomplish more when they work less," Leonardo da Vinci is reported to have declared.

Listen to Leo, a bona fide genius! Listen also to psychologists John Kounios and Mark Beeman, who have conducted neuroimaging research on the brain and have concluded that it is our *idle* or relaxed minds that produce "moments of insight," or what we call "aha" or "eureka" moments. To quote Kounios, when a person is "briefly less aware of his or her environment," that's when the magic happens. It's when we get in our zone.

So how do we make that happen? Every person is different, and you'll need to find the best environment for *you*. Perhaps experiment with different places and processes. Close your eyes. Go for a walk. Take a shower. See what gets your mind wandering.

I'm serious about the shower, by the way. My best ideas and arguments almost always hit me when I'm in the shower. Of course, I then have to frantically note them down somewhere as soon as I get out, and before I even dry off, otherwise I forget them! And, while researching this book, I discovered that I'm not alone: a 2015 survey by acclaimed cognitive psychologist Scott Barry Kaufman found

72 percent of people get "new ideas in the shower"; 14 percent even say they take showers for the "sole purpose" of coming up with new insights. For Kaufman, speaking at an online summit, the study highlights "the importance of relaxation for creative thinking."

RESEARCH, RESEARCH, RESEARCH

Do you know how I prepare for an interview with a big-name guest?

I watch their interviews and speeches, read and study their books, and research their careers. I look for what *they* have said about the topics on which they're experts. And I find out what others have said about *them*, both the good and the bad. Then I piece together all these different bits of information until I find a through line.

For me, it's all about finding the new and undiscovered angle. "Research," according to the Hungarian Nobel Prize–winning biochemist Albert Szent-Györgyi, "is to see what everybody else has seen and think what nobody has thought."

That's what I aim for—even if it's not easy to get there. Doing research can be tricky, time-consuming, and—let's be honest—tedious. Nevertheless, it is absolutely crucial to your success. No argument is complete without it. Remember Aristotle? He famously held that *logos*—the logical, reasoned aspect of an argument—is the heart of persuasion. And there is no *logos* without the underlying research; without the double-checked facts and figures to back it up. That's why research matters so much. As Jonathan Dimbleby said to me, it is "fundamental" to winning any debate.

In December 2015, I persuaded Paul Bremer to do an extended interview with me for Al Jazeera English. Bremer had served as the head of the U.S.-led Coalition Provisional Authority in the wake of the invasion and occupation of Iraq and was the effective "viceroy" in that country between 2003 and 2004. He was also a Yale and Harvard grad who had served in both the Ronald Reagan and George

W. Bush administrations, along with the private sector. Bremer was a smart and savvy opponent, and I wanted to probe him about his time in Iraq—going deeper than the packaged story he'd told in other forums.

How did I prepare for my clash with him? Research, research, research! My team and I pored over not only his 2006 memoir, *My Year in Iraq*, but the memoirs of other former diplomats and reporters who served in Iraq at the same time as Bremer, not to mention documentaries, reports, and studies from PBS, the RAND Corporation, Human Rights Watch, the Special Inspector General for Iraq Reconstruction, and many more. My list of questions and follow-ups for Bremer ran ten pages in length, brimming with quotes, stats, and footnotes. I doubt he had been expecting to be challenged in such detail—or that he had ever been challenged in such a way before! At the end of our rather intense ninety-minute back-and-forth, Bremer took a sip from his glass of water, then leaned forward and stared down at the sheaf of papers on my lap. "Nice research," he said.

Do your homework. Do it well . . . and you might impress *even* your own opponent. As you prepare, here are three things to bear in mind when researching for a debate or presentation of any kind.

1. Google beyond page one

Remember my exchange with Mamoun Fandy at the Intelligence Squared debate on Saudi Arabia? I set a booby trap for him by quoting to him his own words from a three-decade-old op-ed, which left him fumbling to recover.

I had spent hours in advance of that debate googling Fandy's articles. The guy is prolific. He has written four books and literally hundreds of articles in both the English-language and Arabic-language press.

If memory serves me correctly, I only found the 1992 *Christian Science Monitor* op-ed that I used against him on page ten or eleven of the Google search results. Too often, we don't go far enough in our googling. We tend to lazily limit our research to page one of our Google search results, and if nothing interesting pops up, we move on. You have to learn to go beyond that. You have to be willing to do a deep dive into your subject—and into Google itself.

There are so many tricks and techniques to googling that you should familiarize yourself with to make your research process easier. For example: use customized dates to get results, from say 2007 to 2012, which cuts through some of the fluff you get on page one. Track down the source of quotable quotations by putting them inside quote marks (" ") in the Google search bar. Narrow down your inquiry by using the minus (-) sign, advises *Insider*, to "exclude" certain terms, words, or phrases from the search.

In the age of the search engine, there really is no excuse for not being able to find whatever quote, stat, or source you need. As Sam Leith writes in his book *Words Like Loaded Pistols*, "Many of the things that Aristotle talked about when discussing argument—the use of proofs and witnesses, the appeal to commonplaces, and the adducing of evidence—are easier rather than harder in the online age. With the digital equivalent of the Great Library of Alexandria at your fingertips— and the means not only to quote from but to link to it—your resources for serious argument are far greater than they were."

2. Start, don't end, with Wikipedia

Any high school or college student will tell you that teachers and professors don't look kindly on those who cite Wikipedia as a source of information. The argument is that it is nothing short of insane for you to publicly cite only a Wikipedia article, crowdsourced online by anonymous editors and contributors, as a source of information or evidence for your argument.

But here's what the teachers and professors get wrong. Wikipedia *can* play an invaluable role as a research tool, *if* you use it in the right way. To quote Dustin Wax, author of *Don't Be Stupid: A Guide to Learning, Studying, and Succeeding at College,* "Start, don't end, with Wikipedia."

Use it as starting point for your research—to get an "overview" of the topic, and then to dig deeper into that topic by following the provided links to more trusted sources. Think of Wikipedia as a "gateway" to further facts and research, says one administrator.

Take my own Wikipedia entry, which was created in 2010. It has never painted the most accurate or comprehensive picture of my life or career. Nevertheless, there are seventy-two hyperlinked references— at the time of this writing!—at the bottom of the page, leading to a wealth of tweets, interviews, news stories, op-eds, and videos. These are references that you could credibly and legitimately mention and quote from . . . if you were arguing against me.

In short: be skeptical about the main text on Wikipedia, but don't be afraid to use its *citations* as a way to jump-start your research process and seek out primary sources worth relying on.

3. Check your sources

"What's your source for that?" It's a question that will come up in any argument or debate, and you should assume your opponent is going to ask it. So, what's your answer? Do you even have a source?

Too often, these days, we're relying on hearsay or anecdotes to make our point—or in our social media age, some unsourced story or image that was forwarded to us on a WhatsApp group! If you want to make your case or win an argument, especially in front of an audience, please don't cut corners. Find original sources for your claims and familiarize yourself with those sources. Know them inside out.

Make it a habit to search out original sources and cite them in your arguments or presentations. That means: *Don't* just read a book review—buy the book and go through it page by page. *Don't* just watch a clip of an interview on Twitter—go watch the whole thing on YouTube (or on C-SPAN or BBC Parliament). *Don't* just trust a news article that selectively quotes an academic study—go find the actual study and read it, or at least the abstract, for yourself.

When you can go deeper than the headline or the viral clip, you gain a real advantage. Consider this exchange from my interview with controversial businessman Erik Prince in 2019, in which I pressed him on the work done by his company Frontier Services Group (FSG) inside China.

> ME: Why is FSG opening a training center for security guards in, of all places, Xinjiang Province in China, where up to a million Muslim Uighurs are being held in, basically, concentration camps right now?

> ERIK PRINCE: There is a lot of misreporting on that. The company is not opening any training facility up there, that was actually discussed at a board meeting. The reporting got it wrong, the only, there was a, some kind of memorandum assigned for construction services, not training. The company doesn't do any training of any police or security forces inside China at all.

> ME: But why did it say that last year? Why did your company say it was "establishing training facilities"?

> PRINCE: It was, it, it signed an MOU for constructions services.

> ME: They put out a press release, March the second, with your name on it.

PRINCE: For a construction—not my name. It was for construction services.

ME: No, your name's on the press release, your name's on the press release several times and it says—I've got the press release quote here—"Xinjiang China, establishing training facilities and buying security equipment and vehicles."

PRINCE: Uh, again it was for construction services that . . .

ME: It says training facilities.

PRINCE: If, if, if you look at the actual translation from Mandarin to English it was for construction services, okay? The only . . .

ME: Sorry, we didn't translate it; this is your company's English press release, with respect.

How did I pin Prince down in that exchange (and also get a huge laugh from the audience)? By relying on a primary source, and by quoting from the original press release itself—not from a news story.

In fact, up until the day of the interview itself, we didn't even have the original source in our possession. We only had news stories referencing FSG's work in Xinjiang. It was a last-minute coup, and I later asked my producer how she had found such a crucial and revealing document only hours before the interview. "I started looking on the company website, and when I couldn't find anything, I searched the company's name, with 'Xinjiang' and 'pdf,'" she told me. "And it was like the first or second result [at the time]."

Sometimes you have to be a little clever to get Google to bring you what you need.

PLAY THE ROLE

Doing your homework goes beyond just brainstorming and researching. These two steps will constitute the bulk of your preparation. But
there's a third step that, while less widely practiced, is just as important.

1. Find a Partner

Remember The Document? Well, once we finished writing it, we had
to act on it. Literally. Every week, ahead of the big Sunday interview,
Jonathan would arrive at the office on Thursday and Friday, and we
would go through each page of The Document. But the twist was that
one of us would be designated to *play the role* of that Sunday's guest.
A Labour government minister. An opposition Conservative Party
official. A retired general or spy chief. Whoever.

Jonathan would throw questions at us from The Document and
we would have to deliver what we expected Sunday's guest might say
in response. As a former actor in high school, I had a lot of fun doing
it. One of my fondest memories from that period is pretending to
be Tony Blair, on those rare occasions that the then prime minister
agreed to appear on the show. Years later, when I went on to host my
own interview show on Al Jazeera English, I borrowed the *Jonathan
Dimbleby* technique. My team and I role-played every major interview beforehand.

In the summer of 2018, for example, Israel's former deputy
foreign minister Danny Ayalon agreed to appear on my then show
Head to Head. As we approached the date of the interview, one of
the producers on my team morphed into Danny Ayalon—in a truly
astonishing transformation. She had watched and read all of his
interviews, pored over his YouTube videos, and basically *became* him
during our editorial meetings. I threw questions at our own in-house
"Danny," and she responded as Ayalon might.

We had done our homework and obtained our receipts—but we also practiced how to *deploy* those receipts against our interviewee in the form of a role-play. It might sound strange on the surface. But when the time came, I was ready for a smooth-talking Ayalon. When he claimed Iran was in violation of UN Security Council resolutions on nuclear inspections, I knew how I wanted to respond and where to take the conversation next. After a back-and-forth over Israel's secret stockpile of nuclear weapons, which Ayalon pretended to be unaware of, I asked him how he might respond if an Iranian official adopted his line of denialism.

ME: If an Iranian guest came on my show and I asked him about Iran's nuclear weapons and he said: "No, I'm not going to talk about it," would you be okay with that? You'd be outraged.

DANNY AYALON: Of course I would. Because there was, like, sixteen United Nations Security Council resolutions against Iran and . . .

ME: And there is against Israel as well, about your nuclear program?

AYALON: About nuclear issues? No.

ME: Yes, there is. UN resolution 487. Let me read it to you. The UN Security Council in 1981 "calls upon Israel urgently to place its nuclear facilities under the safeguards of the IAEA [International Atomic Energy Agency]." Why haven't you done that?

The exchange went viral, with more than ten million views on TikTok alone. But I couldn't have done it without my research team, especially that producer who had helped me role-play almost the entire exchange beforehand. For weeks and months after that interview, we still jokingly referred to her as Danny. (Okay, fine, maybe only I did.)

Now, you may not have a team of producers to help you prepare for an argument or debate but . . . you can always phone a friend. Get a friend, colleague, or family member, even, to role-play with you before the big speech or pitch meeting. They don't need to be a trained actor to help you become more comfortable with what you want to say. It's all part of public speaking homework.

2. Prepare for the worst

Even if you don't have a partner who doubles as a perfect Danny Ayalon, you can do your own homework to prepare for the worst your opponent can throw at you. And you *should* be ready for the worst.

When any of us prepare an argument, there's a danger of falling into confirmation bias. That's the term coined by the cognitive psychologist Peter Wason in 1960 to describe our human tendency to look only for information that "confirms" what we already believe, while just ignoring any evidence that backs up other or especially opposing viewpoints. In a debate, this often leads us to research our preferred line of argument until we can't imagine losing—even as we fail to anticipate our opponent's *actual* counterattack.

In my opinion, the simplest and surest way to *lose* an argument is to go into it with a set of views or opinions that you have not sufficiently challenged. So how do you avoid this trap?

The only solution is to know *both* sides of the argument—not just the viewpoint you may personally favor. Even at the research stage, you'll want to develop an understanding of your opponent's arguments as you're honing your own. The reason to do that is a simple matter of perspective. As philosopher John Stuart Mill pointed out in *On Liberty*, you *cannot* know your own side of the argument without also knowing the other side—and the other side in its "most plausible and persuasive" form. So your aim should be to reach a point where you know your opponent's arguments better than they do—and where you can also spot the flaws in your own arguments before they do. That means doing your homework on your opponent's arguments, as well as your own.

But how do we truly learn the other side? It's harder than it sounds, because we're fighting against confirmation bias the whole way. We can't be cocky, or lazy, or close-minded.

To get it right requires what is called "steelmanning"—an exercise in constructing the strongest version of your opponent's argument. Steelmanning, as many have pointed out, is the total opposite of the infamous "strawman" argument, which involves dumbing down your opponent's position as a way of undermining them. Instead, if you can steelman your opponent's arguments in advance of that debate—if you can develop an understanding of the smartest and strongest approach to their position—you'll be ready for anything they might throw at you in the debate itself.

So how do you go about the steelmanning process? I'd recommend asking the following questions:

- *What is your opponent's best argument?*
- *What is their best evidence for that argument?*
- *Who is the best advocate for that argument?*
- *What is their best critique of your argument?*

Such questions serve as a one-person role-play exercise. They force you to flip sides and poke holes in your own argument. You should take the time to give serious thought to these questions rather than rushing through them. And I even recommend asking them in two rounds—once *at the start* of your research process, and once *at the end*. The first round will help direct your research, and the second will help polish it off at the end. And you can also keep them in mind throughout, checking with these questions occasionally to gauge whether you still have more work to do.

Steelmanning allows you to be comprehensive, to cover every possible argument and counterargument, both yours *and* theirs. Get it right, and you'll intimidate your opponent from the get-go while dazzling any audience in attendance.

....

In November 2011, the BBC published the shortlist for its annual and prestigious Sports Personality of the Year award—and not a single female athlete made the cut.

It was a hugely controversial decision, and the British press was all over it. "Women Snubbed in the Sports Personality of the Year Shortlist," declared the *Independent*. "Women-Free BBC's Sports Personality Shortlist Sparks Widespread Backlash," was the headline in the *Guardian*. "Sportswomen Criticise BBC Sports Personality Shortlist," reported the BBC's own news website.

The following week, I was invited to appear on the BBC's *Question Time*, hosted by Jonathan Dimbleby's elder brother David. When you appear on *Question Time*, you go in blind: you have no idea what questions will be asked or even what topics will be raised by the audience. You have to be ready for *any* story in the news to be thrown at you by an audience member, with several million people watching you at home.

As with every *Question Time* appearance, I set aside several hours that week to prepare for my appearance. I wasn't sure whether the BBC Sports Personality story would get a mention. It wasn't the top newspaper headline, but it was receiving plenty of attention. So, just in case, I read every piece that I could find about it, in print and online. I googled; I Wikipedia-ed; I made sure I checked all my sources.

As the show came to an end that night, after all the expected questions on the Eurozone crisis, the 2012 London Olympics bid, and the state of the UK economy, a woman in the audience asked:

> Does the lack of recognition in female sporting achievement in the BBC Sports Personality Awards reflect sexist reporting practices in the media?

There it was. The outside-the-box question on the awards controversy. My fellow panelists looked unprepared and made some vague and generic statements about the importance of equality and representation, but this is how I replied to that question:

> When it comes to the gender divide, sport is a male-dominated world, as is politics, as is the media, as is business. What I thought was interesting about the BBC Sports Personality of the Year Award . . . was that it was twenty-seven publications that chose [the shortlist]; all those twenty-seven sports editors were men. And interestingly, two of them were from *Nuts* and *Zoo* magazines; well-known sporting magazines! But it just shows, people who think that representation doesn't matter . . . the sports editor of the *Manchester Evening News* chose Patrick Vieira, who is retired, while Rebecca Adlington, who is a world champion swimmer, lost by one vote getting on that shortlist.

See, unlike the other four guests—two elected politicians, one CEO, and one judge—I avoided mere platitudes and responded directly to the audience member's question with *details*. With facts and figures. It prompted a bewildered David Dimbleby to interrupt me midflow.

"You know so much," he said. "How do you *know* all this?"

How? I did my homework.

Part Four

IN CONCLUSION

THE GRAND FINALE

A speech is like a love affair. Any fool can start it, but to end it requires considerable skill.

—Lord Mancroft, British minister

TUESDAY, MAY 28, 1940

It was a warm day in London, and inside the corridors of government, Winston Churchill was engaged in a heated argument that would determine the course of human history. The war in Europe had been raging for eight months, and the future looked grim. The retreat from Dunkirk had begun. France was on the verge of falling to the Nazis. Great Britain looked like it could be next.

Days prior, amid the carnage, Mussolini's Italy had reached out offering to mediate a deal with Hitler's Germany. The question on the table: Should the British government accept?

For three consecutive days, in front of an audience of government ministers, observe writers Brett and Kate McKay, Churchill had gone back and forth with his foreign secretary, the pragmatic Lord Halifax, who leaned toward accepting the Italian overture and preparing for a negotiated peace with Nazi Germany.

Churchill, who had become prime minister only a few weeks earlier, was dead set against such a move, saying that nations "which

surrendered tamely were finished." Over the course of nine different meetings, he had tried reasoning with the members of his war
cabinet. He had tried *logos*, yet they were still split between him and
Halifax. So it was time for *pathos*—for a last-ditch emotional appeal.

He now stood before his cabinet, ready to deliver one final
speech before the group would decide the matter. As his biographer
Boris Johnson writes, Churchill began his remarks "calmly enough."

> I have thought carefully in these last days whether it was
> part of my duty to consider entering into negotiations with
> That Man [Hitler]. But it [is] idle to think that, if we tried
> to make peace now, we should get better terms than if we
> fought it out. The Germans would demand our fleet—that
> would be called disarmament—our naval bases, and much
> else.

Then he raised the temperature, highlighting the existential
stakes of their decision.

> We should become a slave state, though a British Govern-
> ment which would be Hitler's puppet would be set up . . .
> And where should we be at the end of all that? On the other
> side we have immense reserves and advantages.

There was only one option, in Churchill's mind. And as he
reached his climactic finale, to quote Johnson, it was "almost Shake-
spearean."

> And I am convinced that every one of you would rise up
> and tear me down from my place if I were for one moment
> to contemplate parley or surrender. If this long island story
> of ours is to end at last, let it end only when each one of us
> lies choking in his own blood upon the ground.

Suddenly, the assembled ministers were cheering! Within moments they had left their seats and gathered around Churchill, patting him on the back in total support. Halifax was defeated. The prime minister's grand finale had won the argument—and, say the McKays, "won the day." "Then and there," wrote historian John Lukacs in his landmark work, *Five Days in London: May 1940*, "he saved Britain, and Europe, and Western civilization."

. . . .

Every good speech deserves a grand finale. Once you've done your research and structured your argument; once you've added one part logic, one part emotion, one part humor, and a healthy sprinkling of judo moves; once you've practiced it all until it's perfect—you *still* need to have a rousing finish. You need your audience to remember all the work you put in, and to leave energized.

The ending of a speech or argument is so important that rhetoricians even have a special name for it: *peroration*. Like the word *oration*, peroration is "ultimately derived," says *Merriam-Webster*, from the Latin *orare*, meaning to "plead" or "pray." Your peroration is the grand finale of any argument—your final plea to your audience.

William Safire, who served as speechwriter for President Richard Nixon, cautioned that "a well-prepared, well-delivered speech without a peroration dribbles off and leaves an audience unsatisfied."

"Every oration needs one," said Samuel Rosenman, speechwriter for President Franklin Roosevelt. "A well-written peroration can clinch an argument or inspire confidence or lift morale."

Indeed, many of the greatest speeches in history are remembered *above all* for their stirring perorations, the final lines that we continue to quote to this day. Consider the historic final line of Nelson Mandela's speech at the Rivonia Trial: "It is an ideal for which I am prepared to die." Or the rousing conclusion of Abraham Lincoln's Gettysburg Address: "We here highly resolve that these dead shall not have died in vain—that this nation, under God, shall have a new birth of freedom—and that government of the people, by the people, for the people, shall not perish from the earth." Or even look to William Wallace's decree at the Battle of Stirling Bridge: "Tell our enemies that they may take our lives, but they'll never take our freedom." (Sorry, that last one is technically a *Braveheart* quote, but it's still one hell of a call to arms!)

Your finale is so, *so* crucial—but it isn't easy to get right. So, what should go into that final plea? Over the decades, nay the centuries, much has been said about the art and import of the peroration.

For Aristotle, an ideal peroration is "composed of four things":

1. It *seeks to draw the audience in*, "getting the hearer favorable to oneself, and ill-disposed toward the adversary."
2. It *drives home the stakes of the argument*, by what he calls "amplification and extenuation."
3. It *makes one final appeal to pathos*, "placing the hearer under the influence of the passions."
4. It *summarizes the key points of your argument*, thereby "awakening [the hearer's] recollection."

There is a great degree of consensus among speechwriters and rhetoricians that the peroration, the concluding plea, is the perfect place for pathos. You want to motivate your audience, after all—you want to fire them up and deliver an ovation-worthy closer. But as Aristotle notes in his last point, you also want to make sure they *remember* what it is you talked about.

In my book, the trick to the peroration is to strike a balance between: (1) restating your main argument so that it *sticks*, and (2) grabbing your listeners' emotions and attention, so that they leave on a high! You want to capture both their hearts and their minds, and a great peroration will do both.

But how do you accomplish both those goals? We'll take them each in turn, starting with the question of how to drive your main points home.

USE A PILE DRIVER

There's an old saying that sums up the sheer importance of driving your message home, across the course of your address:

Tell them what you are going to tell them.

Tell them.

Then, tell them what you just told them.

Are you with me? Let speech coach Andrew Dlugan explain:

Tell them what you are going to tell them. That's your introduction.

Tell them. That's the middle of your speech; the body of it.

Then, tell them what you just told them. That is your conclusion.

That conclusion is where you restate, reiterate, *repeat.* And there is nothing wrong with repetition. Don't let anyone tell you otherwise. Repetition can be a vital tool when you're trying to get through to a skeptical crowd. "It is only when you're sick of hearing yourself repeat the same message over and over again that your audience is just beginning to get it" is a line often attributed to Peter Mandelson, the former TV producer and communications guru who went on to become an architect of Tony Blair's triple-election-winning New Labour. In fact, academic study after academic study—whether by experts in marketing, communications, or psychology—shows that a message is much more effective the more it is repeated.

Should I say that again? Actually, let's give Churchill the honors: "If you have an important point to make, don't try to be subtle or clever. Use a pile driver. Hit the point once. Then come back and hit it again. Then hit it a third time—a tremendous whack."

The "third time" is your conclusion, your peroration. A crucial part of your peroration's job is to summarize the main points of your argument—and one of the most effective ways to accomplish that is by harnessing the power of repetition. One tried-and-true structure is to shape your entire speech with a clear plan in mind, with the end coming back to reference the beginning. That's what's called "topping and tailing," or starting and finishing with the same theme, the

same idea, often the same language. The second time around, however, the listener can hear it with newfound understanding.

Why is repetition so important to the conclusion, in particular?
Because this is the "make-or-break" portion of your speech, the section that will decide whether your audience walks away informed,
inspired, and persuaded. It is the part of your address that the crowd
is most likely to *remember*. Speech coach Dom Barnard cites a study
coauthored by the late Yale University psychologist Robert Crowder,
an expert on human memory, that found when people were asked
to recall information they had been given in the form of a series of
names, they had their "best performance at the beginning and end"
of the series. The long middle . . . can be a muddle.

It still amazes me how many speakers put so little effort into how
they finish their remarks. Over the years, I've watched in horror as
opposing debaters or fellow panelists or even interviewees on television offer a cursory and lackluster summary of their key points and
then say, "Thank you." And then . . . stop. Or say, "That's all from me."
And then . . . stop.

No. No. *No.* The peroration is no place for stumbling, mumbling,
or hesitation.

A simple structure, built on the power of repetition, will make
a world of difference. Here is a recipe that I used in my Intelligence
Squared debate on whether the West should cut ties with Saudi Arabia. I won the debate in front of a big crowd in London in 2019, and
I based my concluding sixty-second remarks around a few repeated
themes. First, I recapped my main arguments, both from a human
rights and a national security perspective, pointing out how cutting
political and economic ties with Saudi Arabia was the right thing
to do and would have only "mild consequences" for the West. Next,
I took a page from Aristotle and took a moment to denounce my
adversaries' arguments: *"Don't listen to fearmongering of the opposition."* Then I concluded with callback to my opening remarks about
Jamal Khashoggi and other victims of Saudi abuses.

Vote for justice for Jamal. We are talking about real people here. Jamal Khashoggi, who walked into a Saudi consulate in Istanbul five months ago, was surrounded by a team of Saudi assassins, who put a plastic bag over his head. His last words, reportedly, were: "Do not cover my mouth. I have asthma. Don't. You will strangle me." Vote for Jamal. Vote for all those names you heard tonight. Vote for the motion.

If you look at the shape of my whole argument, I wasn't doing anything complicated. I employed a "top and tail" structure, and I used the power of repetition (along with the rule of three) to ensure that my most important lines resonated.

Of course, you'll notice that I'm not *just* using repetition or neatly summarizing my points. That's just half the battle. The other half is the feeling, the urgency, the anger, and the need to make the audience understand how Jamal felt in that horrifying moment. The other half is the *pathos*.

....

What do you want out of the end of your speech? You need to ask yourself some questions, say the experts. What kind of speech are you giving? What is it that you want to accomplish with your audience? Are you trying to motivate and inspire them? Or persuade and convince them? Maybe a bit of both?

The answers to these questions will help you decide on how to end it. But some things are universal. You want to end with climax, not anticlimax. You want to end with a bang, not a whimper.

And this only happens when your peroration has the passion and the pathos. Once you've driven home your argument, you also need to drive your audience to their feet.

Never forget the words of Sam Seaborn, the fictional deputy White House communications director and presidential speech-writer in *The West Wing*:

The difference between a good speech and a great speech is the energy with which the audience comes to their feet at the end. Is it polite? Is it a chore? Are they standing up because their boss is standing up? No, we want it to come from their socks.

I want to be very, *very* blunt with you here (because others may not!): there is nothing like the adulation of a standing ovation, of an audience rising from their seats to deliver prolonged and thunderous applause because of something you—yes, *you!*—said to them. There is an explosion of endorphins! Forget the false modesty of those who tell you that standing ovations are neither here nor there—the truth is that they are a form of public gratification and validation that you will find in very few other walks of life. They are a sign of *victory*.

So how do you get people to feel the energy "from their socks"? How do you imbue your peroration with the pathos that drives your audience to their feet? Here are three of my favorite techniques to use for the grand finale.

1. End with a quote

Quotes get a bad rap. We've all heard a groaner of a speech that opens with a quote from the dictionary. We've all been treated to inspirational quotes that register as nothing more than dull clichés. You're right to be wary of overused quotes.

But there's a reason they became overused in the first place. Words of wisdom from great leaders, celebrities, or experts can be incredibly memorable. Inspiring. Eloquent. Don't be afraid to use a perfectly apt quotation in your conclusion.

In 2018, I was the keynote speaker at a fundraiser in Toronto for a small Canadian Muslim charity, which was trying to raise money to support its refugee projects. My speech was about the importance of standing in solidarity with refugees and asylum seekers and resisting the urge to treat outsiders as a threat, or as "the other." So I decided to end it with a not-so-famous quote from the famous Muslim leader Imam Ali ibn Abu Talib that reemphasized the purpose of the event as well as the overall theme of my speech.

People are of two types: they are either your brothers in faith, or your equals in humanity.

It hit the perfect note, fit the occasion, and came from an eminent source that the audience would respect. And, more importantly, it was a better line than I was going to come up with in a pinch! So with those wise words, I was done—and the event organizers raised an unexpected $75,000 that night.

The quotes you end with can be inspiring, funny, or even somber, depending on the direction—and subject matter—of your speech. Whatever the case, using a quote to conclude your remarks helps provide a change of pace as you approach your climax. It slows down the end of your address as you bring things to a close. And it allows you, says speech coach Andrew Dlugan, to introduce a "second voice," a fresh voice, to bolster what you have been saying all along. That adds to *your* authority, and ends your speech on a line to remember.

2. End with an anecdote

What's the most powerful way to appeal to your audience's emotions? *Telling stories.*

Stories are how we connect with people, how we tap into the empathy of our listeners, and how we most effectively persuade others to follow along. Ending your speech with a story or a personal anecdote is a clever way of keeping the crowd hooked and attentive right until you've delivered your very last word.

It also allows you, in those very final moments, to transport your audience out of the conference room, or auditorium, or TV studio, and back into the real world. It lets them not only come to terms with what you're saying on a personal level but also to absorb why it ultimately matters.

The most effective instance of this technique that I've ever seen was in November 2008, on the night that Barack Obama won the presidency for the first time. To wrap up his historic speech—to a crowd of more than two hundred thousand people in his home city of Chicago—author Sam Leith reminds us of the story he told.

This election had many firsts and many stories that will be told for generations. But one that's on my mind tonight's about a woman who cast her ballot in Atlanta. She's a lot like the millions of others who stood in line to make their voice heard in this election except for one thing: Ann Nixon Cooper is 106 years old.

She was born just a generation past slavery; a time when there were no cars on the road or planes in the sky; when someone like her couldn't vote for two reasons—because she was a woman and because of the color of her skin.

And tonight, I think about all that she's seen throughout her century in America—the heartache and the hope; the struggle and the progress; the times we were told that we can't, and the people who pressed on with that American creed: Yes we can.

At a time when women's voices were silenced and their hopes dismissed, she lived to see them stand up and speak out and reach for the ballot. Yes we can.

When there was despair in the dust bowl and depression across the land, she saw a nation conquer fear itself with a New Deal, new jobs, a new sense of common purpose. Yes we can.

When the bombs fell on our harbor and tyranny threatened the world, she was there to witness a generation rise to greatness and a democracy was saved. Yes we can.

She was there for the buses in Montgomery, the hoses in Birmingham, a bridge in Selma, and a preacher from Atlanta who told a people that "We Shall Overcome." Yes we can.

A man touched down on the moon, a wall came down in Berlin, a world was connected by our own science and imagination.

And this year, in this election, she touched her finger to a screen, and cast her vote, because after 106 years in America, through the best of times and the darkest of hours, she knows how America can change.

Yes we can.

America, we have come so far. We have seen so much. But there is so much more to do. So tonight, let us ask ourselves—if our children should live to see the next century; if my daughters should be so lucky to live as long as Ann Nixon Cooper, what change will they see? What progress will we have made?

This is our chance to answer that call. This is our moment.

Barack Obama is a masterly orator *because* he is also a masterly storyteller. The way he ended that speech was both inspiring *and* enlightening. On the night of his greatest victory, he wanted to make clear to the world, in the words of his speechwriter Jon Favreau, that change in America might sometimes "come slow, but change is always possible." Finishing his speech with the life story of Ann Nixon Cooper allowed him to do that.

3. End with a call to action

Is there something specific you want your audience to *do* after they've absorbed your argument? Once they've listened to, absorbed, and *agreed* with your words, is the next step to go out and *do* something about it?

If so, end your argument, or conclude your remarks, with a call to action. Something concrete. Something simple. Something singular. Something *memorable*.

You can even combine a call to action *with* an inspiring quote or anecdote. It's something I often like to try, as when I closed out my keynote address in Sydney on the topic of growing anti-Muslim extremism, while on a speaking tour of Australia in 2017.

I'm always reminded of that famous British Army recruitment poster during World War 1, with two kids sitting on their father's lap, and the caption says: "Daddy, what did YOU do during the Great War?"

In decades to come, your kids, your grandkids, might ask you: mum, dad, what did you do during the Great Extremism Frenzy, the Halal Hysteria, of the early twenty-first century, when extremists of all kinds tried to divide and destroy us, tried to undermine our rights and freedoms, in Australia, in the U.S., in the UK, in France, Germany. What did you do when all that was happening, they might ask?

Did you sit on the sidelines, complaining and carping on Facebook, moaning and groaning on Twitter, or did you push back by getting better organized? Did you stay engaged? Did you stay mobilized? Did you build alliances? Did you put your money where your mouth is? Did you invest in the future, invest in hope over fear, love over hate?

What will you tell YOUR kids? Because, ladies and gentlemen, brothers and sisters, now is not the time to give up, now is not the time to roll over, and admit defeat; no, now is the time to stand up and be counted. Now is the time to speak out, loud and proud. Now is the time to be the change that you wish to see in the world. Now is the time to stand up to the bullies and the bigots.

Ladies and gentlemen, if not now, when? If not us, who?

Of course, several of those final lines aren't simply calls to action but also famous quotes. There's a bit of Gandhi and the Jewish sage Hillel the Elder in there. And they *still* have the power to galvanize. Those closing remarks earned me a long and delightful standing ovation from my hosts Down Under.

You shouldn't be afraid to mix and match techniques to bring your audience to their feet. You'll notice that I'm not just using quotes and rhetorical questions to round out my speech but also the rhetorical device known as *anaphora*: I'm repeating the same word or phrase, again and again, at the start of each sentence, to give impact and emphasis. It's especially useful to deploy at the end of a speech or presentation—allowing you to combine pathos *with* the power of repetition.

Try out these three main strategies to create a memorable ending to any speech or argument: (1) employ powerful quotes that echo the theme of your speech; (2) share a humanizing anecdote that reminds people why your argument matters; or (3) deliver a heartfelt call to action that inspires people to *do* something. Choose the option that fits your speech best, or combine them to create your own grand finale.

All three strategies are focused on pathos over logos. All three are about connecting with your audience, one final time, at an emotional level—and leaving them wanting more. As the late American politician and Mormon church leader Carl Buehner remarked: "They may forget what you said—but they will never forget how you made them feel."

....

You'll want to make your peroration memorable and crystal clear, heartfelt and authentic. But bear in mind also that there are some basic contours that any good conclusion needs to follow—and some common pitfalls to try and avoid.

Here are my own brief dos and don'ts, based on my own experiences, as well as the work of top speech coaches.

- *Do* think about *how* you'll want to be speaking when you write out your lines. Add an "exclamation point," suggests motivational speaker Brian Tracy, to your most important closing lines when they warrant it. Those sentences you deliver at the end have to pack a rhetorical punch!
- *Don't* bring in a new argument or point right at the end that you have not mentioned before. That can be both distracting and confusing. The ending is for summarizing. New complications are a no-no.
- *Do* signal to your audience that the speech is coming to a close, that "the end is nigh." It'll force those who have tuned out, gotten bored, or pulled out their phones to snap "back to attention." You can signal this with your own pace and tone—slowing down, taking a pause, raising your voice to a crescendo. Or you can do it with language, using phrases like, "In conclusion . . . ," or "Let me finish by saying this . . . ," or another variant that's authentically *you*.
- *Don't* just come to an abrupt halt. Don't be like the Philadelphia preacher Dr. James Wilson, who would preach for exactly one hour, "no more, no less." When he saw sixty minutes had passed on his watch, he would stop mid-sentence, no matter where he was in his sermon, and say: "Brethren, the hour is up. Let us pray." Don't do that! Make sure your very last sentence is planned out and—at the very least—sounds like a fully formed final thought.
- *Do* try to come up with a "memorable" and ideally pithy phrase of your own at the end. As speech coach Dom Barnard reminds us, the late Steve Jobs of Apple used just four words to end his famous Stanford commencement speech in 2005: "Stay hungry. Stay foolish."
- *Don't* go on too long. If abruptness is bad, tardiness is worse. Set a time to finish, and preplan an ending that allows you to wrap up on time *without the need to rush.*

And if you do go over your time, per one speech coach, do not then end your speech by apologizing (*"Sorry for taking up so much of your time . . ."*). Please do not do that! It's totally unnecessary and takes up time that you could otherwise spend on a meaningful, confident conclusion.

. . . .

A great argument, like a story, has a beginning, a middle, and an end. Churchill, the master orator and debater, called this the "accumulation of the argument." It's an *experience*, for both the audience and the speaker. You start with your plan; they start with pure skepticism. But then you land the initial foray—your most important point—followed by your stacks and stacks of evidence, all of which moves your audience toward, in the words of two commentators on Churchill, "one inescapable conclusion." There's a certain magic to what happens in a great argument—though only Churchill could truly capture it, in his uniquely Churchillian way.

> The climax of oratory is reached by a rapid succession of waves of sound and vivid pictures. The audience is delighted by the changing scenes presented to their imagination. Their ear is tickled by the rhythm of the language. The enthusiasm rises. A series of facts is brought forward all pointing in a common direction. The end appears in view before it is reached. The crowd anticipates the conclusion and the last words fall amid a thunder of assent.

You can practically picture it, can't you?

It's you up onstage now, standing before a crowd, as they hang on your every word. You have no need for your notes, no ounce of nerves left in your body. Every eye is on you as you round the home stretch to deliver your final quote, your last personal anecdote, your sweeping call to action. There's a pin-drop silence for a moment as you call out your last word—then *the thunder of assent*. You don't need to hear *anything* else to know that your grand finale landed. That you have what it takes now, to step up, to deliver a convincing argument.

To win.

NOTES

Introduction

ix **saw an opportunity**: "The Remarkable Salaethus and the Siege of Mytilene," *Hellenic Antidote* blog, January 19, 2021, http://hellenicantidote.blogspot.com/2012/09/the-remarkable-salaethus-and-siege-of.html; "Mytilenean Debate," Wikipedia, last modified April 18, 2022, https://en.wikipedia.org/wiki/Mytilenean_Debate.

ix **"Egged on"**: Ejaz Haider, "The Mytilenian Debate and Us," *Express Tribune*, March 12, 2013, https://tribune.com.pk/story/519704/the-mytilenian-debate-and-us.

x **"penalty of rebellion is death"**: Thucydides, *The History of the Peloponnesian War*, trans. Richard Crawley (London: Global Grey, 2021), 96. Retrieved on May 2, 2022, https://www.globalgreyebooks.com/history-of-the-peloponnesian-war-ebook.html.

x **moderate Athenian political faction**: Donald Kagan, *The Outbreak of the Peloponnesian War* (Ithaca, NY: Cornell University Press, 1969), 155.

xi **"beating them fairly in argument"**: Thucydides, *The History of the Peloponnesian War*, 96.

xi **"And beat Cleon he did"**: Alex Clark, "Why Debating Still Matters," *Guardian*, August 6, 2016, https://www.theguardian.com/education/2016/aug/06/why-debating-still-matters.

xii **"Avoid it as you would avoid rattlesnakes"**: Dale Carnegie, *How to Win Friends & Influence People* (New York: Pocket Books, 1998), 110.

xiii **"Of all the talents"**: Winston Churchill, "The Scaffolding of Rhetoric" (unpublished essay, 1897). Retrieved on May 2, 2022, https://winstonchurchill

.org/images/pdfs/for_educators/THE_SCAFFOLDING_OF_RHETORIC
.pdf.

xiv **"preferring either opinion"**: John Stuart Mill, *On Liberty* (London: Walter Scott, 1901), 67, https://www.gutenberg.org/files/34901/34901-h/34901-h.htm.

Chapter 1: Winning Over an Audience

5 **"No matter how odious and nasty"**: Interview with Jonathan Dimbleby, *Any Questions?*, BBC Radio 4, February 11, 2012, https://www.bbc.co.uk/programmes/b01bmq3c.

6 **"judge and jury"**: Jeff Davenport, "Q&A: Top Delivery Struggles Speakers Face & How to Combat Them Expertly," Duarte, accessed September 20, 2022, https://www.duarte.com/presentation-skills-resources/qa-top-delivery-struggles-speakers-face-how-to-combat-them-expertly/.

7 **"one-size-fits-all"**: Ian Altman, "3 Keys to Deliver an Amazing Presentation Suited to the Room," *Inc.*, August 30, 2018, https://www.inc.com/ian-altman/whether-speaking-in-a-convention-center-or-a-conference-room-you-can-deliver-an-amazing-speech-every-time.html.

10 **attention span of nine seconds**: Kevin McSpadden, "You Now Have a Shorter Attention Span Than a Goldfish," *Time*, May 14, 2015, https://time.com/3858309/attention-spans-goldfish/.

10 **As a group**: "How to Start a Speech with Power and Confidence," *Ginger* blog, December 13, 2019, https://www.gingerleadershipcomms.com/article/how-to-start-a-speech-with-power-and-confidence.

11 **"The First! F-I-R-S-T! First!"**: Dale Carnegie, *How to Develop Self-Confidence and Influence People by Public Speaking* (New York: Pocket Books, 1991), 135.

11 **"Sadly, in the next eighteen minutes"**: Jamie Oliver, "Teach Every Child about Food," filmed 2010, TED video, 21:32, https://www.ted.com/talks/jamie_oliver_teach_every_child_about_food.

11 **"provocative"**: "How to Start a Speech with Power and Confidence," *Ginger* blog.

11 **"a desire to fill knowledge gaps"**: Akash Karia, *How to Deliver a Great TED Talk: Presentation Secrets of the World's Best Speakers* (self-pub., CreateSpace, 2012), 38.

11 **"What do I know that would cause me"**: James Hansen, "Why I Must Speak Out about Climate Change," filmed 2012, TED video, 17:35, https://www.ted.com/talks/james_hansen_why_i_must_speak_out_about_climate_change.

12 **"I was sitting in 1D"**: Ric Elias, "Three Things I Learned While My Plane Crashed," filmed 2011, TED video, 4:46, https://www.ted.com/talks/ric_elias_3_things_i_learned_while_my_plane_crashed.

13   **"saying somebody's name aloud"**: Fia Fasbinder, "Why This Is the Most Widespread Bad Advice in Public Speaking (and You're Probably Following It)," *Inc.*, February 26, 2019, https://www.inc.com/fia-fasbinder/why-most-public-speakers-are-wrong-about-this-one-thing-and-youre-probably-offering-it-as-advice.html.

13   **"seen by you"**: Craig Valentine, "Here is the Secret to Keep Your Audience from Checking Out," Craig Valentine MBA, February 11, 2016, accessed August 10, 2022, https://craigvalentine.com/one-necessary-secret-to-keep-your-audience-from-checking-out/.

15   **"bond with you"**: Bas Van Den Beld, "8 Successful Ways to Connect with Your Audience," Speak with Persuasion, accessed September 8, 2022, https://www.speakwithpersuasion.com/ways-connect-audience/.

15   **ten million views on YouTube**: Oxford Union, "Mehdi Hasan | Islam Is a Peaceful Religion | Oxford Union," YouTube video, 13:48, July 3, 2013, https://www.youtube.com/watch?v=Jy9tNyp03M0.

16   **"Trump makes George Bush look good"**: Interview with Seth Meyers, *Late Night with Seth Meyers*, NBC, December 5, 2018.

17   **Just as often**: Jay Heinrichs, *Thank You for Arguing: What Aristotle, Lincoln, and Homer Simpson Can Teach Us about the Art of Persuasion* (New York: Broadway Books, 2020), 109.

Chapter 2: Feelings, Not (Just) Facts

18   **"the most controversial ever"**: Roger Simon, "Questions That Kill Candidates' Careers," *Politico*, April 20, 2007, https://www.politico.com/story/2007/04/questions-that-kill-candidates-careers-003617.

18   **at 2:00 am**: Simon, "Questions That Kill Candidates' Careers."

18   **"For the next ninety minutes"**: "October 13, 1988, Debate Transcript," Commission on Presidential Debates, accessed May 2, 2022, https://www.debates.org/voter-education/debate-transcripts/october-13–1988-debate-transcript/.

19   **"No, I don't, Bernard"**: "October 13, 1988, Debate Transcript."

20   **How would *he* "feel"**: Paige Parvin, "Professor at the Polls," *Emory Magazine*, https://www.emory.edu/EMORY_MAGAZINE/2007/autumn/westen.html.

21   **"a willingness to declare who he is as a person"**: Richard Cohen, "A Man in Hiding," *Washington Post*, October 16, 1988, https://www.washingtonpost.com/archive/opinions/1988/10/16/a-man-in-hiding/cdc67d76-95f1-454d-86c7-0724c5e52118/.

21   **"killed by a hit-and-run-driver"**: Simon, "Questions That Kill Candidates' Careers."

21   **"to see if there was feeling"**: Tom Shales, "CNN's Blunt Edge," *Washington Post*, October 25, 1988, https://www.washingtonpost.com/archive/lifestyle /1988/10/25/cnns-blunt-edge/7f2c6b1e-488f-4959-9ddc-1d18c48a7656/.

21   **"lost the election"**: Simon, "Questions That Kill Candidates' Careers."

21   **"I didn't think it was that bad"**: Michael Dukakis, interview with Jim Lehrer, *Debating Our Destiny*, PBS, September 9, 2008, https://www.pbs.org /newshour/spc/debatingourdestiny/docrecap.html.

22   **his three proofs or "modes"**: Aristotle, *Rhetoric*, trans. W. Rhys Roberts, bk. 1, chap. 1, sec. 2 (Internet Classics Archive), accessed May 2, 2022, http:// classics.mit.edu//Aristotle/rhetoric.html.

22   **derived from *pathos***: Gini Beqiri, "Ethos, Pathos, Logos: 3 Pillars of Public Speaking and Persuasion," VirtualSpeech, April 11, 2018, https://virtual speech.com/blog/ethos-pathos-logos-public-speaking-persuasion.

23   **"left four children orphaned"**: Jesse O'Neill, "'I Wish I'd Got the Shot': Dad Who Died of COVID along with Wife, Leaving 4 Kids," *New York Post*, October 17, 2021, https://nypost.com/2021/10/17/i-wish-that-id-got -the-shot-dad-of-4-who-died-of-covid/.

23   **pathos beats logos**: Jay Heinrichs, *Thank You for Arguing: What Aristotle, Lincoln, and Homer Simpson Can Teach Us about the Art of Persuasion* (New York: Broadway Books, 2020), 287.

24   **feel, rather than think**: Douglas Van Praet, "The Myth of Marketing," *Fast Company*, March 21, 2013, https://www.fastcompany.com/1682625/the -myth-of-marketing-how-research-reaches-for-the-heart-but-only-connects -with-the-head.

24   **"feeling machines that think"**: Susan Andrews, "Who We Are and Why," *USC News*, November 12, 2010, https://news.usc.edu/28719/Who-We-Are -and-Why/.

25   **a patient referred to as "Elliot"**: Antonio Damasio, *Descartes' Error: Emotion, Reason and the Human Brain* (New York: Penguin, 2005), 34.

25   **"real-life Mr. Spock"**: Christian Jarrett, "The Neuroscience of Decision Making Explained in 30 Seconds," *Wired*, March 10, 2014, https://www .wired.com/2014/03/neuroscience-decision-making-explained-30-seconds/.

25   ***"to know but not to feel"***: Damasio, *Descartes' Error*, 45.

25   **"indispensable for rationality"**: Damasio, *Descartes' Error*, xvii.

26   **"brain-to-brain coupling"**: Uri Hasson, "This Is Your Brain on Communication," filmed 2016, TED video, 14:42, https://www.ted.com/talks/uri _hasson_this_is_your_brain_on_communication.

26   **listened to them**: Carmine Gallo, *Talk Like TED: The 9 Public-Speaking Secrets of the World's Top Minds* (New York: St. Martin's Press, 2014), 49–50.

26   **"When the woman spoke English"**: Joshua Gowin, "Why Sharing Stories Brings People Together," *Psychology Today*, June 6, 2011, https://www

.psychologytoday.com/us/blog/you-illuminated/201106/why-sharing
-stories-brings-people-together.

27 **consist of sharing gossip**: Cody C. Delistraty, "The Psychological Comforts
of Storytelling," *The Atlantic*, November 2, 2014.

27 **In a 2007 study**: Deborah A. Small, George Loewenstein, and Paul Slovic,
"Sympathy and Callousness: The Impact of Deliberative Thought on Dona-
tions to Identifiable and Statistical Victims," *Organizational Behavior and
Human Decision Processes* 102, no. 2 (2007): 143–53.

27 **"checks all of these boxes"**: Deborah Small, personal interview, April 12, 2022.

27 **Hasson observed**: Elena Renken, "How Stories Connect and Persuade Us:
Unleashing the Brain Power Of Narrative," NPR, April 11, 2020, https://www
.npr.org/sections/health-shots/2020/04/11/815573198/how-stories-connect
-and-persuade-us-unleashing-the-brain-power-of-narrative.

28 **"Ladies and gentlemen, good evening"**: Intelligence Squared, "Debate: The
West Should Cut Ties with Saudi Arabia," YouTube video, 1:28:16, March 12,
2019, https://www.youtube.com/watch?v=qi0T0owgW3M.

30 **"water is for fish"**: Jonathan Gottschall, *The Storytelling Animal: How Stories Make Us Human* (New York: Houghton Mifflin Harcourt, 2012), xiv.

30 **"22 times more memorable"**: Women's Leadership Lab Stanford University, "Harnessing the Power of Stories," YouTube video, 8:36, November 18,
2019, https://www.youtube.com/watch?v=oB7FfKPMZvw.

31 **"success of multiculturalism in this country"**: Interview with David
Dimbleby, *Question Time*, BBC1, October 2, 2011.

31 **"the respect-inducing power of personal experiences"**: Emily Kubin et al.,
"Personal Experiences Bridge Moral and Political Divides Better Than
Facts," *Proceedings of the National Academy of Sciences* 118, no. 6 (2021): 1.

32 **"To express emotion"**: Aristotle, *Rhetoric*, bk. 3, chap. 7, sec. 3.

33 **"I support it and he doesn't"**: "October 13, 1988, Debate Transcript."

34 **"embodiment of the passions of the multitude"**: Winston Churchill,
"The Scaffolding of Rhetoric" (unpublished essay, 1897). Retrieved on
May 2, 2022, https://winstonchurchill.org/images/pdfs/for_educators
/THE_SCAFFOLDING_OF_RHETORIC.pdf.

34 **"showing" your emotions**: Andrew Dlugan, "Connect With Your Audience:
Don't Hide Your Emotions When Speaking," Six Minutes, May 22, 2008,
http://sixminutes.dlugan.com/emotions-public-speaking/.

35 **"Do you really think that"**: Oxford Union, "Mehdi Hasan | Islam Is a
Peaceful Religion | Oxford Union," YouTube video, 13:48, July 3, 2013,
https://www.youtube.com/watch?v=Jy9tNyp03M0.

36 **"is an emotional brain"**: Drew Westen, *The Political Brain: The Role of
Emotion in Deciding the Fate of the Nation* (New York: PublicAffairs, 2007), xv.

36 **"marketplace of ideas"**: Westen, *The Political Brain*, 36.

36 **"even if factually inaccurate"**: George Marshall, *Don't Even Think about It: Why Our Brains Are Wired to Ignore Climate Change* (New York: Bloomsbury USA, 2015), 107.

Chapter 3: Show Your Receipts

38 **"I want to see the receipts"**: Seija Rankin, "The Oral History of Memes: Where Did 'Show Me the Receipts' Come From?," E! Online, August 24, 2016, https://www.eonline.com/news/789906/the-oral-history-of-memes-where-did-show-me-the-receipts-come-from.

39 **"alternative facts"**: Kellyanne Conway, interview with Chuck Todd, *Meet the Press*, NBC, January 22, 2017.

39 **"truth isn't truth"**: Rudy Giuliani, interview with Chuck Todd, *Meet the Press*, NBC, August 19, 2018.

39 **"diminishing role of facts"**: Jennifer Kavanagh and Michael D. Rich, *Truth Decay: An Initial Exploration of the Diminishing Role of Facts and Analysis in American Public Life* (Santa Monica, CA: RAND Corporation, 2018), https://www.rand.org/pubs/research_reports/RR2314.html.

39 **word of the year**: Katy Steinmetz, "Oxford's Word of the Year for 2016 Is 'Post-Truth,'" *Time*, November 15, 2016, https://time.com/4572592/oxford-word-of-the-year-2016-post-truth/.

39 **"at lightning speed"**: Michiko Kakutani, "The Death of Truth: How We Gave Up on Facts and Ended Up with Trump," *Guardian*, July 14, 2018, https://www.theguardian.com/books/2018/jul/14/the-death-of-truth-how-we-gave-up-on-facts-and-ended-up-with-trump.

39 **in the journal *Political Behavior***: Thomas Wood and Ethan Porter, "The Elusive Backfire Effect: Mass Attitudes' Steadfast Factual Adherence," *Political Behavior* (2017): 1–68.

40 **"what is factual and what is not"**: Amy Mitchell et al., "Distinguishing between Factual and Opinion Statements in the News," Pew Research Center, June 18, 2018, accessed May 2, 2022, https://www.pewresearch.org/journalism/2018/06/18/distinguishing-between-factual-and-opinion-statements-in-the-news/.

40 **"are stubborn things"**: "Adams' Argument for the Defense: 3–4 December 1770," National Archives, accessed May 2, 2022, https://founders.archives.gov/documents/Adams/05-03-02-0001-0004-0016.

40 **"reducing their potential harm"**: Antonio Damasio, *Descartes' Error: Emotion, Reason and the Human Brain* (New York: Penguin, 2005), 246.

41 **"*shown* the door"**: Paul Jones, "Arm Wrestling—Aristotle Had a Better Way," *Magneto Blog*, accessed May 2, 2022, https://magneto.net.au/blog/get-your-way-aristotle/.

44 **"you said was for fifteen"**: MSNBC on Peacock, "Mehdi Hasan Interviews John Bolton | The Mehdi Hasan Show | Choice on Peacock," YouTube video, 16:42, October 14, 2020, https://www.youtube.com/watch?v=G78OFZ2MDkM.

44 **"So I'd like to talk"**: NBC News, "Elizabeth Warren Attacks 'Arrogant Billionaire' Michael Bloomberg over Treatment of Women | NBC News," YouTube video, 1:25, February 19, 2020, https://www.youtube.com/watch?v=QD4csGWPo6o.

45 **"Died: February 19th, 2020"**: Maayan Jaffe-Hoffman, "Who 'Murdered' Mike Bloomberg?," *Jerusalem Post*, February 20, 2020, https://www.jpost.com/american-politics/on-wikipedia-warren-killed-bloomberg-618250.

45 **"never seemed to recover"**: Ankita Rao, "How Elizabeth Warren Destroyed Mike Bloomberg's Campaign in 60 Seconds," *Guardian*, March 4, 2020, https://www.theguardian.com/us-news/2020/mar/04/mike-bloomberg-out-60-second-attack-elizabeth-warren-destroyed-campaign.

45 **"was totally prepared and practiced"**: Former aide to Elizabeth Warren, personal interview, April 12, 2022.

46 **"You have already conceded"**: Al Jazeera English, "Should the US Get Out of Latin America? | Head to Head," YouTube video, 47:30, December 5, 2014, https://www.youtube.com/watch?v=42PymQ1Cpek.

47 **"okay with an elected government"**: Al Jazeera English, "UpFront—What Is Saudi Arabia's Endgame in Yemen and Syria?," YouTube video, 17:48, March 26, 2016, https://www.youtube.com/watch?v=8z8ME2O5XdY.

49 **"notions of human rights"**: Al Jazeera English, "Slavoj Zizek on a 'Clash of Civilisations' | UpFront," YouTube video, 10:35, December 3, 2016, https://www.youtube.com/watch?v=qkdPZ-UmrSw.

50 **"Those are CBP numbers"**: MSNBC, "Mehdi Hasan Clashes with GOP Rep. Crenshaw on Immigration | MSNBC," YouTube video, 16:36, March 22, 2021, https://www.youtube.com/watch?v=WlUohLyG-wI.

51 **called my interview**: Jon Allsop, "At the Border, Access Is No Substitute for Humanity," *Columbia Journalism Review*, March 24, 2021, https://www.cjr.org/the_media_today/media_border_crisis_immigration.php.

51 **the entertainment news website**: Lindsey Ellefson, "GOP Rep Crenshaw Schooled by MSNBC's Mehdi Hasan on Immigration Numbers (Video)," The Wrap, March 22, 2021, accessed May 2, 2022, https://www.thewrap.com/dan-crenshaw-immigration-mehdi-hasan/.

51 **"How come you didn't mention"**: Al Jazeera English, "Blackwater's Erik Prince: Iraq, Privatising Wars, and Trump | Head to Head," YouTube video, 49:08, March 8, 2019, https://www.youtube.com/watch?v=KOB4V-ukpBI.

52 **"Let's take global poverty"**: Al Jazeera English, "War, Poverty and Inequality: Is There Any Good News? | UpFront," YouTube video, 14:54, March 17, 2018, https://www.youtube.com/watch?v=BkM2wiOwerc.

55   **"always brings receipts"**: Mehdi Hasan, "How to Resist: Live with Ilhan Omar and Michael Moore," *Deconstructed*, podcast audio, October 24, 2019, https://theintercept.com/2019/10/24/how-to-resist-live-with-ilhan -omar-and-michael-moore/.

Chapter 4: Play the Ball . . . and the Man

56   **"schoolyard debate champion"**: Dorie Clark, "Donald Trump Is Your Schoolyard Debate Champion," The Hill, January 31, 2017, https://thehill .com/blogs/pundits-blog/the-administration/317142-donald-trump-is -your-schoolyard-debate-champion/.

56   **"insulted his way to the top"**: Aaron Rupar, "How Donald Trump Insulted His Way to the Top of the GOP," ThinkProgress, May 4, 2016, accessed May 2, 2022, https://archive.thinkprogress.org/how-donald-trump-insulted -his-way-to-the-top-of-the-gop-b5ab95b676ec/.

57   **"gift for invective"**: Sam Leith, *Words Like Loaded Pistols: Rhetoric from Aristotle to Obama* (New York: Basic Books, 2016), 112.

57   **"hairy cheeks and discolored teeth"**: Valentina Arena, "Roman Oratorical Invective," in *A Companion to Roman Rhetoric*, ed. William Dominik and Jon Hall (Chichester: Blackwell, 2010), 152.

57   **"ingrained and accepted"**: Henriette van der Blom, "Character Attack and Invective Speech in the Roman Republic: Cicero as Target," in *Character Assassination throughout the Ages*, ed. Eric Shiraev and Martijn Icks (New York: Palgrave Macmillan, 2014), 37.

57   **"play the ball, not the man"**: Allen Versfeld, "Play the Man, Not the Ball: In Defense of the Ad Hominem Attack," *Now Look Here* blog, July 2, 2017, https://www.nowlookhere.net/2017/07/play-the-man-not-the-ball-in -defense-of-the-ad-hominem-attack/.

58   **"If Adolph Hitler said"**: Michael Austin, "In Defense of Ad Hominem: Why We Really Shouldn't Listen to Dick Cheney on Iraq," Independent Voter News, June 20, 2014, accessed May 2, 2022, https://ivn.us/2014/06/20 /defense-ad-hominem-really-shouldnt-listen-dick-cheney-iraq.

58   **"If ad hominem arguments are illegitimate"**: Tom Whyman, "Only an Idiot Would Dismiss Ad Hominem Arguments," *Outline*, March 10, 2020, accessed May 2, 2022, https://theoutline.com/post/8785/defense-of -ad-hominem.

59   **"most effective means of persuasion he possesses"**: Aristotle, *Rhetoric*, trans. W. Rhys Roberts, bk. 1, chap. 2, sec. 2 (Internet Classics Archive), accessed May 2, 2022, http: //classics.mit.edu//Aristotle/rhetoric.html.

60   **"a necessary and a proper response"**: Austin, "In Defense of Ad Hominem."

61 **"the reputation of the person offering those facts"**: Bruce Thompson, "Ad Hominem—Abusive," Bruce Thompson's Fallacy Page, accessed May 2, 2022, https://www2.palomar.edu/users/bthompson/Abusive.html#:~:text=Con sider%20the%20inductive%20inference%3A%20people,be%20worth%20 listening%20to%20now.

62 **possible bias**: David Hitchcock, "Why There Is No Argumentum Ad Hominem Fallacy," *Rozenberg Quarterly*, 2006, accessed May 2, 2022, https://rozenbergquarterly.com/issa-proceedings-2006-why-there-is-no -argumentum-ad-hominem-fallacy/.

62 **"allegations of conflict of interest"**: Ralph M. Barnes et al., "The Effect of Ad Hominem Attacks on the Evaluation of Claims Promoted by Scientists," *PLOS One* 13, no. 1 (2018): 1–15.

63 **"an illustrious list"**: Arwa Mahdawi, "A Republican Theme on Abortions: 'It's OK for Me, Evil for Thee,'" *Guardian*, August 25, 2018, https://www .theguardian.com/world/2018/aug/25/a-republican-theme-on-abortions -its-ok-for-me-evil-for-thee.

63 **problem with those beliefs**: Whyman, "Only an Idiot Would Dismiss Ad Hominem Arguments."

63 **"explain away"**: Hitchcock, "Why There Is No Argumentum Ad Hominem Fallacy."

63 **"primarily a *rhetorical* phenomenon"**: Alan Brinton, "A Rhetorical View of the *Ad Hominem*," *Australasian Journal of Philosophy* 63, no. 1 (1985): 50–63.

64 **"is not a fallacy"**: Hitchcock, "Why There Is No Argumentum Ad Hominem Fallacy."

65 **"history of anti-semitic statements"**: Allen Versfeld, "Play the Man, Not the Ball: In Defense of the Ad Hominem Attack."

66 **"the racists believe he is a racist"**: CBS Miami, "Gubernatorial Debate: Candidates Asked about Topic of Racism," YouTube video, 2:53, October 24, 2018, https://www.youtube.com/watch?v=u87Fo4lPwyk.

67 **"credentials fallacy"**: "Ad Hominem: When People Use Personal Attacks in Arguments," Effectiviology, accessed September 10, 2022, https:// effectiviology.com/ad-hominem-fallacy/.

67 **"It is not a fallacy"**: Austin, "In Defense of Ad Hominem."

68 **"What I find so amusing"**: Oxford Union, "Mehdi Hasan | Islam Is a Peaceful Religion | Oxford Union," YouTube video, 13:48, July 3, 2013, https://www .youtube.com/watch?v=Jy9tNyp03M0.

69 **"Dr. Gandhi, one of the big criticisms of you"**: MSNBC, "Mehdi Hasan Questions Doctor on Covid Predictions | The Mehdi Hasan Show," YouTube video, 10:33, February 4, 2022, https://www.youtube.com/watch ?v=VaSTb5kNT4s.

70 **"The Man Who Hated Britain"**: Geoffrey Levy, "The Man Who Hated Britain," *Daily Mail*, September 27, 2013, https://www.dailymail.co.uk /news/article-2435751/Red-Eds-pledge-bring-socialism-homage-Marxist -father-Ralph-Miliband-says-GEOFFREY-LEVY.html.

71 **"whiff of anti-Jewish prejudice"**: Jonathan Freedland, "Antisemitism Doesn't Always Come Doing a Hitler Salute," *Guardian*, October 4, 2013, https://www.theguardian.com/commentisfree/2013/oct/04/antisemitism -does-not-always-come-hitler-salute.

71 **"Quentin, let me finish"**: *Question Time*, "BBC Question Time 3 October 2013 (3/10/13) Birmingham FULL EPISODE," YouTube video, 58:45, October 3, 2013, https://www.youtube.com/watch?v=ZBwglrJyYc0.

73 **opportunity to write in the *Mail***: "What a Difference Three Years Makes: How Political Journalist Who Attacked the Daily Mail on Question Time Once Asked If He Could Write for the Paper," *Daily Mail*, October 4, 2013, https://www.dailymail.co.uk/news/article-2444637/Mehdi-Hasan-journalist -attacked-Daily-Mail-Question-Time-asked-write-paper.html.

Chapter 5: Listen, Don't (Just) Speak

76 **"conservative Richmond"**: Jackie Mansky, "The History of the Town Hall Debate," *Smithsonian Magazine*, October 6, 2016, https://www.smithsonian mag.com/history/history-town-hall-debate-180960705/.

77 **notes one commentator**: Santosh Kumar Singh, "'It's the Economy, Stupid' and Marissa Hall's Query That Fell George H. Bush," LinkedIn, August 13, 2020, https://www.linkedin.com/pulse/its-economy-stupid-marissa-halls -query-fell-george-h-bush-santosh.

77 **"Tell me how it's affected you"**: "October 15, 1992, Second Half Debate Transcript," Commission on Presidential Debates, accessed May 2, 2022, https://www.debates.org/voter-education/debate-transcripts/october -15-1992-second-half-debate-transcript/.

78 **After the debate, a CNN/USA Today poll**: "All Politics, CNN Time, The Debates '96: 1992 Presidential Debates," CNN, accessed May 2, 2022, https: //edition.cnn.com/ALLPOLITICS/1996/debates/history/1992/index.shtml.

79 **eighty times**: Julia Naftulin, "Here's How Many Times We Touch Our Phones Every Day," *Insider*, July 13, 2016, https://www.businessinsider.com /dscout-research-people-touch-cell-phones-2617-times-a-day-2016-7.

79 **"unconscious"**: Michael W. Gamble and Teri Kwal Gamble, *Interpersonal Communication: Building Connections Together* (United States: SAGE Publications, 2013), 93.

83 **author Maria Konnikova**: Maria Konnikova, "Lessons from Sherlock Holmes: Cultivate What You Know to Optimize How You Decide," *Sci-*

entific American, August 26, 2011, https://blogs.scientificamerican.com/guest-blog/lessons-from-sherlock-holmes-cultivate-what-you-know-to-optimize-how-you-decide/.

84 **"some people take drugs"**: Drake Baer, "Why Productive People Take Better Notes," *Fast Company*, July 23, 2013, https://www.fastcompany.com/3014646/why-productive-people-take-better-notes.

84 **"the humble pen and paper"**: Kathleen Elkins, "A Habit Bill Gates and Richard Branson Swear by Is One Most People Overlook," CNBC, November 15, 2016, accessed May 2, 2022, https://www.cnbc.com/2016/11/15/a-habit-bill-gates-and-richard-branson-swear-by-is-one-most-people-overlook.html.

84 **"pen is mightier than the keyboard"**: Pam A. Mueller and Daniel M. Oppenheimer, "The Pen Is Mightier Than the Keyboard: Advantages of Longhand over Laptop Note Taking," *Psychological Science* 25, no. 6 (2014): 1159–68.

85 **"Just on a factual point"**: Oxford Union, "Mehdi Hasan | Islam Is a Peaceful Religion | Oxford Union," YouTube video, 13:48, July 3, 2013, https://www.youtube.com/watch?v=Jy9tNyp03M0.

86 **"full attention"**: Ximena Vengoechea, "Why Empathetic Listening Is Crucial for Your Career—and How to Do It Well," The Muse, accessed May 2, 2022, https://www.themuse.com/advice/what-is-empathetic-listening-definition-examples.

86 **"and with your heart"**: Stephen R. Covey, *The 7 Habits of Highly Effective People* (New York: Simon & Schuster, 2013), 252.

86 **"the damn thing was over"**: George H. W. Bush, interview with Jim Lehrer, *Debating Our Destiny*, PBS, April 10, 1999, https://www.pbs.org/newshour/spc/debatingourdestiny/interviews/bush.html.

86 **"out of touch"**: Alex Markels, "George H. W. Bush Checks His Watch During Debate with Bill Clinton and Ross Perot," *U.S. News and World Report*, January 17, 2008, https://www.usnews.com/news/articles/2008/01/17/a-damaging-impatience.

87 **"That was Bill Clinton"**: *Face the Nation*, "Dickerson's Debate History: George Bush Caught in the Cutaway in 1992," YouTube video, 3:17, October 19, 2016, accessed May 2, 2022, https://www.youtube.com/watch?v=T293aYx3uw0.

87 **"fully present"**: Melody Wilding, "7 Habits of Highly Empathetic People," *Inc.*, January 7, 2019, https://www.inc.com/melody-wilding/7-habits-of-highly-empathetic-people.html.

88 **"gathered in a circle"**: Richard Stengel, "Mandela: His 8 Lessons of Leadership," *Time*, July 9, 2008, http://content.time.com/time/subscriber/article/0,33009,1821659-2,00.html.

88 **"try to find consensus"**: Richard Stengel, personal interview, November 23, 2021.

89   **"Quiet your inner monologue"**: Ximena Vengoechea, "Why Empathetic Listening Is Crucial for Your Career."

89   **"patient perceptions of clinician empathy"**: Enid Montague et al., "Nonverbal Interpersonal Interactions in Clinical Encounters and Patient Perceptions of Empathy," *Journal of Participatory Medicine* 5 (2013): 1–17.

89   **"speaker with averted gaze"**: Helene Kreysa, Luise Kessler, and Stefan R. Schweinberger, "Direct Speaker Gaze Promotes Trust in Truth-Ambiguous Statements," *PLOS One* 11, no. 9 (2016).

90   **"yes" or "no"**: Vengoechea, "Why Empathetic Listening Is Crucial for Your Career—and How to Do It Well."

Chapter 6: Make Them Laugh

93   **"On the specific question of free speech"**: smtm: Entertainment, "Question Time in Lincoln—15/01/2014," YouTube video, 59:01, January 22, 2015, https://www.youtube.com/watch?v=5BP8_UyQWc4.

94   **"universal language"**: Gareth Davies, "Laughter Is a Universal Language," *Daily Telegraph*, January 26, 2010, https://www.telegraph.co.uk/news/7071629/Laughter-is-a-universal-language.html.

94   **shared by all human beings**: Disa A. Sauter et al., "Cross-Cultural Recognition of Basic Emotions through Nonverbal Emotional Vocalizations," *Proceedings of the National Academy of Sciences* 107, no. 6 (2010): 2408–12.

95   *benefits* **of laughter**: John Zimmer, "Using Humour in a Presentation—It's No Laughing Matter," Presentation-Guru, January 2, 2018, https://www.presentation-guru.com/using-humour-in-a-presentation-its-no-laughing-matter/.

95   **"more memorable after the fact"**: Matt Abrahams, "Make 'Em Laugh: How to Use Humor as a Secret Weapon in Your Communication," *Think Fast, Talk Smart*, podcast audio, June 22, 2020, https://art19.com/shows/think-fast-talk-smart?q=laugh.

95   **Researchers at the University of North Carolina**: Laura E. Kurtz and Sara B. Algoe, "When Sharing a Laugh Means Sharing More: Testing the Role of Shared Laughter on Short-Term Interpersonal Consequences," *Journal of Nonverbal Behavior* 41 (2017): 45–65.

95   **"For people who are laughing together"**: Jill Suttie, "How Laughter Brings Us Together," *Greater Good Magazine*, July 17, 2017, accessed May 2, 2022, https://greatergood.berkeley.edu/article/item/how_laughter_brings_us_together.

95   **"once they're smoked"**: CNN, "CNN: SOTU Address, President Obama Cracks Smoked Salmon Joke," YouTube video, 44 seconds, January 25, 2011, https://www.youtube.com/watch?v=BFcWz9eyovA.

95 **NPR asked its listeners**: "The State of the Union, in Your Words," NPR, January 25, 2011, https://www.npr.org/2011/01/28/133211131/the-state-of -the-union-in-your-words.

96 **"laughter with seriousness"**: Steve Sherwood, "Intersections of Wit and Rhetoric: Humor as a Rhetorical Enterprise," *PROTEUS: A Journal of Ideas, Humor and Culture* 29, no. 1 (2013), 45–52.

96 **"Ridicule was a standard weapon"**: Mary Beard, *Confronting the Classics: Traditions, Adventures, and Innovations* (New York: W. W. Norton, 2013), 57.

96 **"by making our enemy small"**: Jack Martinez, "Humor Is the Best Weapon in Presidential Debates," *Newsweek*, October 13, 2015, https://www .newsweek.com/best-presidential-debate-funny-lines-humor-382831.

96 **"Memmius thinks"**: Marcus Tullius Cicero, *How to Tell a Joke: An Ancient Guide to the Art of Humor*, trans. Michael Fontaine (Princeton, NJ: Princeton University Press, 2021), 99.

97 **"winning and winning"**: Linda B. Glaser, "Translation Updates Cicero's Treatise on Jokes as 'Weapons,'" *Cornell Chronicle*, March 16, 2021, accessed May 2, 2022, https://as.cornell.edu/news/translation-updates -ciceros-treatise-jokes-weapons.

97 **"If I can get you to laugh"**: Zimmer, "Using Humour in a Presentation."

97 **Esther Snippe**: Esther Snippe, "5 Tips on Using Humor to Engage Your Audience," SpeakerHub, April 11, 2017, https://speakerhub.com/skillcamp /5-tips-using-humor-engage-your-audience.

97 **"bonds"**: Zimmer, "Using Humour in a Presentation."

97 **TJ Walker**: TJ Walker, Howcast, "How to Use Humor in a Speech," YouTube video, 1:56, July 20, 2013, https://www.youtube.com/watch?v=WvT9WjSlk8E.

98 **defuse the tension**: Matt Abrahams, "Make 'Em Laugh: How to Use Humor as a Secret Weapon in Your Communication."

99 **"no reason only poor people"**: Bill Gates, "Mosquitos, Malaria and Education," filmed 2009, TED video, 20:04, https://www.ted.com/talks/bill _gates_mosquitos_malaria_and_education/transcript?language=en.

100 **"The BNP might have something to say"**: Oxford Union, "Mehdi Hasan | Islam Is a Peaceful Religion | Oxford Union," YouTube video, 13:48, July 3, 2013, https://www.youtube.com/watch?v=Jy9tNyp03M0.

100 **went on to join the UK Independence Party**: David Lawrence, "Who Is Anne Marie Waters?," Hope Not Hate, April 30, 2021, accessed May 2, 2022, https://hopenothate.org.uk/2021/04/30/who-is-anne-marie-waters/.

101 **"worth the entry ticket in and of itself"**: Intelligence Squared, "Debate: Anti-Zionism Is Anti-Semitism," YouTube video, 1:20:07, July 26, 2019, https://www.youtube.com/watch?v=K1VTt_THL4A&ab_channel =IntelligenceSquared.

101 **"so close to twit"**: Glaser, "Cicero's Treatise."

102 **relatable**: Hrideep Barot, "A Guide to Using Humor in Your Speech," Frantically Speaking, accessed September 9, 2022, https://franticallyspeaking.com/a-guide-to-using-humor-in-your-speech/.

102 **"You already are the oldest"**: "October 21, 1984, Debate Transcript," Commission on Presidential Debates, accessed May 2, 2022, https://www.debates.org/voter-education/debate-transcripts/october-21-1984-debate-transcript/.

103 **"got the audience with that"**: Andreas Serafim, "No Laughing Matter: Rhetorical Humour in Ancient and Contemporary Public Speaking" (paper, Classical Association Annual Conference 2015, University of Bristol, April 12, 2015), https://www.academia.edu/10616074/No_Laughing_Matter_Rhetorical_Humour_in_Ancient_and_Contemporary_Public_Speaking.

103 **"on your feet"**: Walker, "How to Use Humor in a Speech."

104 **"I should be afraid of you"**: Al Jazeera English, "Top US General Defends Donald Trump—UpFront," YouTube video, 10:39, May 19, 2016, accessed May 2, 2022, https://www.youtube.com/watch?v=JZ88WRfR66w.

105 **"it was like Special Olympics"**: Steve Padilla, "Opinion: Obama Apologizes to Tim Shriver for Special Olympics Remark," *Los Angeles Times* blog, March 20, 2009, accessed May 2, 2022, https://latimesblogs.latimes.com/washington/2009/03/as-our-friend-m.html.

106 **"Don't use humor"**: Zimmer, "Using Humour in a Presentation."

106 **read in monotone**: Barot, "A Guide to Using Humor in Your Speech."

107 **"a lesson I never forgot"**: Sam Horn, *Got Your Attention? How to Create Intrigue and Connect with Anyone* (Oakland, CA: Berrett-Koehler, 2015), 72.

Chapter 7: The Rule of Three

111 **and future**: Chris Heivly, "How The 'Rule of Three' Can Simplify Your Daily Life," *Inc.*, March 23, 2017, https://www.inc.com/chris-heivly/how-the-rule-of-three-can-simplify-your-daily-life.html.

112 **"we are calling it iPhone"**: Rob Price and Mary Meisenzahl, "The First iPhone Was Announced 13 Years Ago Today—Here's How Steve Jobs Introduced It," *Insider*, January 9, 2020, accessed May 2, 2022, https://www.businessinsider.com/watch-steve-jobs-first-iphone-10-years-ago-legendary-keynote-macworld-sale-2017-6.

112 **saw magic in the number three**: Carmine Gallo, "Apple Is Obsessed With the Magical Number 3. It Will Transform Your Presentations, Too," *Inc.*, September 19, 2018, https://www.inc.com/carmine-gallo/apple-is-obsessed-with-magical-number-3-it-will-transform-your-presentations-too.html.

112 **"Just three stories"**: Stanford, "Steve Jobs' 2005 Stanford Commencement Address," YouTube video, 15:04, March 7, 2008, accessed May 2, 2022, https://www.youtube.com/watch?v=UF8uR6Z6KLc.

112 **speech coach Dave Linehan**: Dave Linehan, "Rule of Three in Speech Writing," Dave Linehan blog, accessed August 2, 2022, https://davelinehan.com/rule-of-three-speechwriting/.

113 **stabbed it with her hairpin**: Barry Strauss, *The Death of Caesar: The Story of History's Most Famous Assassination* (New York: Simon & Schuster, 2015), 214.

113 **"building to a climax"**: Cicero, *Verrines II.1*, trans. and ed. T. N. Mitchell (Oxford: Oxbow Books, 1986), 161.

113 **American presidents**: John Zimmer, "Rhetorical Devices: Tricolon," *Manner of Speaking* (blog), March 16, 2015, accessed May 2, 2022, https://mannerofspeaking.org/2015/03/16/rhetorical-devices-tricolon/.

115 **Writing for Forbes**: Nick Morgan, "Martin Luther King's Rhetorical Genius," *Forbes*, February 12, 2015, https://www.forbes.com/sites/nickmorgan/2015/02/12/martin-luther-kings-rhetorical-genius.

116 **"chunks of information"**: "Theory Name: Information Processing Theory," SUNY Cortland website, accessed September 9, 2022, https://web.cortland.edu/frieda/id/IDtheories/24.html.

116 **"The Magical Number Seven"**: George A. Miller, "The Magical Number Seven Plus or Minus Two: Some Limits on Our Capacity for Processing Information," *Psychological Review* 63, no. 2 (1956): 81–97, https://doi.org/10.1037/h0043158.

116 **"short-term memory"**: Kendra Cherry, "What Is Short-Term Memory?," Verywell Mind, February 17, 2022, https://www.verywellmind.com/what-is-short-term-memory-2795348.

116 **"but not beyond"**: Nelson Cowan, personal interview, August 27, 2021.

116 **"mathematical simulations suggest"**: Nelson Cowan, "The Magical Mystery Four: How Is Working Memory Capacity Limited, and Why?," *Current Directions in Psychological Science* 19, no. 1 (2010): 51–57.

117 **see a pattern**: "How to Use the Rule of Three in Writing," Masterclass, August 20, 2021, accessed August 10, 2022, https://www.masterclass.com/articles/how-to-use-the-rule-of-three-in-writing.

117 **In his book on speeches**: Max Atkinson, *Our Masters' Voices: The Language and Body Language of Politics* (London: Routledge, 1984), 47.

118 **"segregation forever"**: "'Segregation Forever': A Fiery Pledge Forgiven, But Not Forgotten," NPR, January 10, 2013, accessed May 2, 2022, https://www.npr.org/2013/01/14/169080969/segregation-forever-a-fiery-pledge-forgiven-but-not-forgotten.

118 **"Ask me the three most important things"**: Peter Bull, "Claps and

Claptrap: The Analysis of Speaker-Audience Interaction in Political Speeches," *Journal of Social and Political Psychology* 4, no. 1 (2016): 473–92.

119 **"a beginning, a middle, and an end"**: Nelson Cowan, personal interview.

119 **"a whole [story] is"**: Aristotle, *Poetics*, trans. S. H. Butcher, sec. 1, pt. 7 (Internet Classics Archive), accessed May 2, 2022, http://classics.mit.edu /Aristotle/poetics.1.1.html.

119 **"completeness, wholeness, roundness"**: Roy Peter Clark, *Writing Tools: 50 Essential Strategies for Every Writer* (New York: Little, Brown, 2006), 102.

119 **say the experts**: Gini Beqiri, "How to Use the 'Rule of Three' to Create Engaging Speeches," VirtualSpeech, May 17, 2021, https://virtualspeech .com/blog/rule-of-three-speech.

120 **Andrew Dlugan, the founder and editor**: Andrew Dlugan, "Why Success-ful Speech Outlines Follow the Rule of Three," Six Minutes, June 3, 2009, accessed May 2, 2022, http://sixminutes.dlugan.com/speech-outline-rule -of-three/.

Chapter 8: Judo Moves

122 **pulled him out**: "Kanō Jigorō," Wikipedia, last modified September 8, 2022, https://en.wikipedia.org/wiki/Kanō_Jigorō.

122 **twelve tatami mats**: Brian N. Watson, *The Father of Judo: A Biography of Jigoro Kano* (New York: Kodansha America, 2000), 21–26, 39.

123 **the verb *kuzusu***: "Kuzushi," Wikipedia, last modified June 17, 2021, https:// en.wikipedia.org/wiki/Kuzushi.

123 **"The philosophy of judo"**: THNKR, "The Art of Debate: Never Lose an Argument Again," YouTube video, 5:09, October 18, 2012, https://www .youtube.com/watch?v=LesGw274Kjo&t=185s.

123 **"maximum efficiency, minimum effort"**: Rosemary Feitelberg, "UFC Champion Ronda Rousey Breaks Out," *Women's Wear Daily*, October 30, 2014, accessed May 2, 2022, https://wwd.com/eye/people/rousey-breaks -out-of-the-octagon-8014665/?navSection=issues.

124 **conceding one or more**: Jay Heinrichs, *Thank You for Arguing: What Aris-totle, Lincoln, and Homer Simpson Can Teach Us about the Art of Persuasion* (New York: Broadway Books, 2020), 20–21.

124 **"want to attack that"**: THNKR, "The Art of Debate."

125 **"honest and scrupulous"**: Sam Leith, *Words Like Loaded Pistols: Rhetoric from Aristotle to Obama* (New York: Basic Books, 2016), 68.

125 **"in order to make a stronger one"**: *Collins English Dictionary*, s.v. "syn-choresis," accessed May 2, 2022, https://www.collinsdictionary.com/us /dictionary/english/synchoresis.

125 **"strength and firmness"**: "Synchoresis," Ifioque, accessed August 10, 2022, https://ifioque.com/figures-of-speech/trope/synchoresis.

126 **"which is absurd"**: Intelligence Squared, "Debate: Anti-Zionism Is Anti-Semitism," YouTube video, 1:20:07, July 26, 2019, https://www.youtube.com/watch?v=K1VTt_THL4A&ab_channel=IntelligenceSquared.

127 **"anticipation"**: "Procatalepsis," accessed September 8, 2022, https://ifioque.com/figures-of-speech/trope/procatalepsis.

127 **"throw the orator on the defensive"**: George A. Kennedy, *New Testament Interpretation through Rhetorical Criticism* (Chapel Hill: University of North Carolina Press, 1984), 43.

128 **"be distracted by the opposition"**: Intelligence Squared, "Debate: The West Should Cut Ties with Saudi Arabia," YouTube video, 1:28:16, March 12, 2019, https://www.youtube.com/watch?v=qi0T0owgW3M.

128 **"filters"**: David Hoffeld, "This Is the Scientific Way to Win Any Argument (And Not Make Enemies)," *Fast Company*, January 19, 2018, https://www.fastcompany.com/40517659/this-is-the-scientific-way-to-win-any-argument-and-not-make-enemies.

128 **It all depends**: Jay Heinrichs, *Thank You for Arguing*, 119–22.

129 **"redefine"**: Jay Heinrichs, *Thank You for Arguing*, 125; Hoffeld, "This Is The Scientific Way To Win Any Argument (And Not Make Enemies)."

129 **"that's what we want you to vote for"**: Intelligence Squared, "Debate: The West Should Cut Ties with Saudi Arabia."

130 **"religious establishment in China"**: Al Jazeera English, "What Is the Human Cost to China's Economic Miracle? | Head to Head," YouTube video, 49:12, March 15, 2019, https://www.youtube.com/watch?v=yZs4PqKlph0.

131 **"And today, he tweeted"**: "Trump on Coronavirus: 'We Closed It Down, We Stopped It'; Mulvaney Out as Trump's Acting Chief of Staff; Former Senator Al Franken to 2020 Democrats: Focus on Trump. Aired 9–10p ET," CNN, March 6, 2020, accessed May 2, 2022, http://edition.cnn.com/TRANSCRIPTS/2003/06/CPT.01.html.

132 **"Resisting a more powerful opponent"**: Kanō Jigorō, *Mind over Muscle: Writings from the Founder of Judo*, trans. Nancy H. Ross (Kodansha International, 2005), 39–40.

Chapter 9: The Art of the Zinger

133 **"junior senator from Indiana"**: Jack Nelson and Richard E. Meyer, "Bush Selects Quayle as His Running Mate: Calls Indiana Senator, 41, Future Leader," *Los Angeles Times*, August 17, 1988, https://www.latimes.com/archives/la-xpm-1988-08-17-mn-446-story.html.

133 **"with scant national reputation"**: R. W. Apple Jr., "Bush Chooses Senator Quayle of Indiana, a 41-Year-Old Conservative, for No. 2 Spot," *New York Times*, August 17, 1988, https://archive.nytimes.com/www.nytimes.com /library/politics/camp/880817convention-gop-ra.html.

133 **fourteen years**: "Senator, You're No Jack Kennedy," Wikipedia, last modified September 21, 2022, https://en.wikipedia.org/wiki/Senator,_you're _no_Jack_Kennedy.

134 **"not respond well to the lighting"**: Noah Bierman, "'Senator, You're No Jack Kennedy' Almost Didn't Happen. How It Became the Biggest VP Debate Moment in History," *Los Angeles Times*, October 4, 2016, https: //www.latimes.com/politics/la-na-pol-debate-quayle-bentsen-20161004 -snap-story.html.

134 **"you are no Jack Kennedy"**: "October 5, 1988, Debate Transcript," Commission on Presidential Debates, accessed May 2, 2022, https://www .debates.org/voter-education/debate-transcripts/october-5-1988-debate -transcripts/.

135 **"teeth knocked down his throat"**: Mary McGrory, "Bentsen Bags a Quayle," *Washington Post*, October 9, 1988, https://www.washingtonpost .com/archive/opinions/1988/10/09/bentsen-bags-a-quayle/d6292884 -d3a9-42cf-8b0c-719fe5568666/.

135 **"biggest VP debate moment"**: Bierman, "'Senator, You're No Jack Kennedy.'"

135 **parodied and echoed**: Wikipedia, "Senator, You're No Jack Kennedy."

135 **"good line"**: Dan Quayle, interview with Jim Lehrer, *Debating Our Destiny*, PBS, December 2, 1999, https://www.pbs.org/newshour/spc /debatingourdestiny/interviews/quayle.html.

135 *listener* **off guard**: Chuck McCutcheon, "Speaking Politics Term of the Week: Zinger," *Christian Science Monitor*, September 16, 2016, https://www .csmonitor.com/USA/Politics/Politics-Voices/2016/0926/Speaking -Politics-term-of-the-week-zinger.

135 **"insult, quip, burn"**: Pauline Bickford-Duane, *The Little Book of Zingers: History's Finest One-Liners, Comebacks, Jests, and Mic-Droppers* (Kennebunkport, ME: Whalen Book Works, 2020), 4.

136 **"from the Latin word *retortus*"**: Mardy Grothe, *Viva la Repartee: Clever Comebacks & Witty Retorts from History's Great Wits & Wordsmiths* (New York: HarperCollins, 2005), 2.

136 **"superiority over a rival"**: Chris Lamb, "Introduction," in *The Art of the Political Putdown: The Greatest Comebacks, Ripostes, and Retorts in History*, ed. Chris Lamb and Will Moredock (San Francisco: Chronicle Books, 2020), 10.

136 **"kind of the cute line"**: George W. Bush, interview with Jim Lehrer,

"'Debating Our Destiny' Takes Unique Look at Debates," PBS, September 8, 2008, https://www.pbs.org/newshour/show/debating-our-destiny-takes -unique-look-at-debates.

136 **"old as humankind"**: Bickford-Duane, *Little Book of Zingers*, 4.

137 **says one writer**: Leah Goldrick, "Was This Philosopher History's Most Successful Troll?," Brain Fodder, accessed September 10, 2022, https:// brainfodder.org/diogenese-of-sinope/.

137 **On one occasion**: Bickford-Duane, *Little Book of Zingers*, 11; Robert E. Buxbaum, "Diogenes the Cynic," *REB Research* Blog, accessed May 2, 2022, http://www.rebresearch.com/blog/diogenes-the-cynic/.137; Joshua J. Mark, "The Life of Diogenes of Sinope in Diogenes Laertius," World History Encyclopedia, August 6, 2014, https://www.worldhistory.org/article /740/the-life-of-diogenes-of-sinope-in-diogenes-laertiu/.

137 **"spine tingling arrangement of words"**: Bickford-Duane, *Little Book of Zingers*, 4.

138 **"a comic's timing"**: Lamb, *Art of the Political Putdown*, 10.

138 **"compare himself to Kennedy"**: Bierman, "'Senator, You're No Jack Kennedy.'"

139 **"prepared days beforehand"**: Lamb, *Art of the Political Putdown*, 10.

139 **"the example of the bees"**: "Seneca on Gathering Ideas and Combinatorial Creativity," *Farnam Street* blog, accessed September 8, 2022, https://fs .blog/seneca-on-combinatorial-creativity/.

139 **"In the name of God, go"**: Martyn Bennett, "'In the Name of God, Go': The History of a Speech That Has Brought Down Parliament and a Prime Minister," The Conversation, January 20, 2022, accessed May 2, 2022, https:// theconversation.com/in-the-name-of-god-go-the-history-of-a-speech -that-has-brought-down-parliament-and-a-prime-minister-175368; "Norway Debate," Wikipedia, last modified August 2, 2022, https://en .wikipedia.org/wiki/Norway_Debate.

142 **"short and sweet"**: Kendall Payne and Hannah Madden, "How to Create One Liners," wikiHow, February 8, 2022, accessed August 10, 2022, https://www.wikihow.com/Create-One-Liners.

142 **dry wit**: "Laconic phrase," Wikipedia, last modified October 20, 2022, https://en.wikipedia.org/wiki/Laconic_phrase.

142 **"friend or foe"**: Bickford-Duane, *Little Book of Zingers*, 12.

143 **"my name is Mehdi, not Ahmed"**: smtm: Entertainment, "Question Time in Lincoln—15/01/2014," YouTube video, 59:01, January 22, 2015, https:// www.youtube.com/watch?v=5BP8_UyQWc4.

144 **"the memorized twenty-five-second speech"**: CBSN, "Chris Christie Takes Down Marco Rubio," YouTube video, 3:15, February 7, 2016, accessed May 11, 2022, https://www.youtube.com/watch?v=CkdpzRDxTXU.

145 **"Most of those precanned lines"**: Katie Glueck, "How to Prepare a Debate Zinger That Doesn't Sound Prepared," *New York Times*, October 15, 2019, https://www.nytimes.com/2019/10/15/us/politics/democratic-debate -highlights.html.

146 **it was Quayle**: Bierman, "'Senator, You're No Jack Kennedy' Almost Didn't Happen."

Chapter 10: Setting Booby Traps

148 **"a trap for the unwary"**: *Merriam-Webster*, s.v. "booby trap," accessed May 11, 2022, https://www.merriam-webster.com/dictionary/booby%20trap.

148 **"stupid, daft, naive"**: "Booby trap," Wikipedia, last modified June 26, 2022, https://en.wikipedia.org/wiki/Booby_trap#Etymology.

149 **"You keep going on"**: Al Jazeera English, "Who Is to Blame for the Rise of ISIL? | Head to Head," YouTube Video, 47:31, August 13, 2015, https://www.youtube.com/watch?v=-EghwCDNyiY.

151 **"Let me make one very quick point"**: Intelligence Squared, "Debate: The West Should Cut Ties with Saudi Arabia," YouTube video, 1:28:16, March 12, 2019, https://www.youtube.com/watch?v=qi0T0owgW3M.

153 **"You repeatedly refer in the book"**: Al Jazeera English, "Immigration: How Much Is Too Much? | Head to Head," YouTube video, 47:28, August 7, 2015, https://www.youtube.com/watch?v=dA1-JtBACeg.

156 **"Let me ask a question"**: Ayush Tiwari, "Christopher Hitchens to Charlton Heston: 'Keep Your Hairpiece On' (1991)," YouTube video, 3:06, May 7, 2015, https://www.youtube.com/watch?v=nZUMGid0IvI&t=26s.

158 **"the wrong question"**: Al Jazeera English, "Is Democracy Wrong for China? | Head to Head," YouTube video, 47:30, December 19, 2014, https://www.youtube.com/watch?v=F821Fe2_wBk.

Chapter 11: Beware of the Gish Galloper

160 **"Mr. President, two minutes"**: Fox Business, "First Trump-Biden Presidential Debate Moderated by Fox News' Chris Wallace | FULL," YouTube video, 1:36:53, September 29, 2020, https://www.youtube.com/watch?v=2TTtlFpM5Ss.

163 **"spewing so much bullshit"**: *Urban Dictionary*, s.v. "Gish Gallop," accessed May 11, 2022, https://www.urbandictionary.com/define.php ?term=Gish%20Gallop.

163 **"champion of the Gish Gallop"**: William Rivers Pitt, "Trump and the Gish Gallop: A Million Lies and One Truth," Truthout, January 30, 2017, accessed May 11, 2022, https://truthout.org/articles/trump-and-the-gish -gallop-a-million-lies-and-one-truth/.

164 **"flood the zone with shit"**: Sean Illing, "'Flood the Zone with Shit'": How Misinformation Overwhelmed Our Democracy," Vox.com, February 6, 2020, https://www.vox.com/policy-and-politics/2020/1/16/20991816/impeachment-trial-trump-bannon-misinformation.

164 **"false claim"**: Carl Alviani, "There's a Name for Trump's Technique to Overwhelm the Public with a Stream of Tiny Lies," *Quartz*, February 8, 2017, https://qz.com/905252/donald-trumps-lies-are-all-part-of-a-debate-tactic-called-the-gish-gallop/.

164 **proof by verbosity**: "Gish Gallop," RationalWiki, last modified July 1, 2022, https://rationalwiki.org/wiki/Gish_Gallop.

164 **"illusion of authority"**: "Gish Gallop," RationalWiki.

165 **"full of irrelevant information"**: Melissa Ludwig, "Texas Judge Tosses Creationists' Plan for Science Degrees," *San Antonio Express-News*, August 19, 2011, accessed May 11, 2022, https://www.chron.com/news/houston-texas/article/Texas-judge-tosses-creationists-plan-for-science-1601606.php.

165 **"the audiences liked him"**: "Remembering Dr. Duane T. Gish, Creation's 'Bulldog,'" Institute for Creation Research, March 6, 2013, accessed May 11, 2022, https://www.icr.org/article/remembering-dr-duane-t-gish-creations/.

165 **"extraordinary charisma"**: Richard Trott, "Debating the ICR's Duane Gish," Talk.origins, July 7, 1994, accessed May 11, 2022, http://www.talkorigins.org/faqs/debating/gish.html.

165 **"Gish would insist"**: John Grant, *Debunk It! Fake News Edition: How to Stay Sane in a World of Misinformation* (Minneapolis: Zest Books, 2019), 55.

166 **more than three hundred debates**: "Remembering Dr. Duane T. Gish, Creation's 'Bulldog.'"

166 **"spewing out nonsense with every paragraph"**: Eugenie Scott, "Debates and the Globetrotters," Talk.origins, July 7, 1994, accessed May 11, 2022, http://www.talkorigins.org/faqs/debating/globetrotters.html.

166 **"publicly corrected Gish"**: Joyce Arthur, "Creationism: Bad Science or Immoral Pseudoscience?," *Skeptic*, 1996, accessed May 11, 2022, https://www.fullmoon.nu/sources.bak/CHAPTER%2010/PART%202/gish%20exposed.html.

167 **"spreading"**: Daniel Kruger, "How to Win a High-School Debate: Talk Like a Cattle Auctioneer," *Wall Street Journal*, February 7, 2018, https://www.wsj.com/articles/ifyoucanunderstandthisyoumightbeahighschooldebater-1518021742.

168 **"fire hose of lying"**: "'A Fire Hose of Lying': Dale Fact-Checks Trump Town Hall," *Don Lemon Tonight*, CNN, September 16, 2020, https://www.cnn.com/videos/politics/2020/09/16/daniel-dale-fact-check-trump-abc-town-hall-ctn-sot-bts-vpx.cnn.

168 **"whips up fears of Islam"**: Oxford Union, "Anne-Marie Waters | Islam Is Not a Peaceful Religion | Oxford Union," YouTube video, 8:17, July 3, 2013, https://www.youtube.com/watch?v=VQjZHFnmADQ.

170 **"refutes the overall stance"**: "Gish Gallop: When People Try to Win Debates by Using Overwhelming Nonsense," Effectiviology, accessed May 11, 2022, https://effectiviology.com/gish-gallop/.

170 **"This is about disorientation"**: Brian Stelter, "This Infamous Steve Bannon Quote Is Key to Understanding America's Crazy Politics," CNN, November 16, 2021, https://www.cnn.com/2021/11/16/media/steve-bannon-reliable -sources/index.html.

171 **"hammer away"**: JK Ames's answer to "How do you respond to a Gish Gallop? Can one defend, attack or escape?," Quora, June 6, 2022, https:// www.quora.com/How-do-you-respond-to-a-Gish-Gallop-Can-one-defend -attack-or-escape.

171 **"The figure I look at"**: "Interview: Jonathan Swan of Axios Interviews Donald Trump—August 3, 2020," Factba.se, accessed May 11, 2022, https:// factba.se/transcript/donald-trump-interview-axios-jonathan-swan-hbo -august-3-2020.

175 **"the hardest possible interview"**: Jonathan Swan, personal interview, February 17, 2022.

175 **"call out"**: "Gish Gallop," Effectiviology.

176 **"squirt gun of truth"**: Christopher Paul and Miriam Matthews, "The Russian 'Firehose of Falsehood' Propaganda Model," RAND Perspectives, 2016, accessed May 11, 2022, https://www.rand.org/pubs/perspectives/PE198.html.

177 **made 30,573 false claims**: Glenn Kessler, Salvador Rizzo, and Meg Kelly, "Trump's False or Misleading Claims Total 30,573 over 4 Years," *Washington Post*, January 24, 2021, accessed May 11, 2022, https://www .washingtonpost.com/politics/2021/01/24/trumps-false-or-misleading -claims-total-30573-over-four-years/.

177 **"[Trump] said during the campaign"**: Mehdi Hasan, Twitter post, November 14, 2018, 8:58 AM, https://twitter.com/mehdirhasan/status /1062706401804455937.

Chapter 12: Confidence Is Everything

183 **"feel betrayed"**: 2yyiam, "Mehdi Hasan—Question Time Part 1 of 6," YouTube video, 9:59, May 18, 2010, https://www.youtube.com/watch?v =htCdyajC-Os&t=127s.

184 **"surge of subscriptions"**: Jon Allsop, "The Debater: Mehdi Hasan's Challenging Transatlantic Rise," *Columbia Journalism Review*, 2021, accessed

May 11, 2022, https://www.cjr.org/special_report/mehdi_hasan_america .php.

185 **author Carmine Gallo**: Carmine Gallo, *Talk Like TED: The 9 Public Speaking Secrets of the World's Top Minds* (New York: St. Martin's Press, 2014), 91.

185 **"a belief in oneself"**: "Confidence," *Psychology Today*, accessed May 11, 2022, https://www.psychologytoday.com/us/basics/confidence.

185 **notes Wikipedia**: "Confidence," last modified July 8, 2022, https://en .wikipedia.org/wiki/Confidence.

185 **"confidence breeds confidence"**: Richard Branson, "Confidence Breeds Confidence and Negativity Breeds Negativity," Facebook post, January 28, 2015, https://m.facebook.com/RichardBranson/photos/a.10150152138395872 /10152576593725872/?type=3&p=30.

185 **"as competence"**: Katty Kay and Claire Shipman, "The Confidence Gap," *Atlantic*, May 2014, https://www.theatlantic.com/magazine/archive/2014/05 /the-confidence-gap/359815/.

185 **"forgive a poor track record"**: Peter Aldhous, "Humans Prefer Cockiness to Expertise," *New Scientist*, June 3, 2009, https://www.newscientist.com /article/mg20227115-500-humans-prefer-cockiness-to-expertise/?ignored =irrelevant.

186 **"Find a quiet place"**: "Use Creative Visualization to Succeed During a Speech," Presentation Training Institute, July 24, 2018, accessed August 10, 2022, https://www.presentationtraininginstitute.com/use-creative-visualization -to-succeed-during-a-speech/.

187 **"trick" your mind**: "How Visualizing Something into Existence Works," Gravity Learning, accessed September 9, 2022, https://gravitylearning. com/how-visualizing-something-into-existence-works/; "18 Tips for Being Confident from Within," Tony Robbins, accessed September 9, 2022, https:// www.tonyrobbins.com/building-confidence/how-to-be-confident/.

188 **"lift your right hand"**: Srinivasan Pillay, "The Science of Visualization: Maximizing Your Brain's Potential during the Recession," HuffPost, April 3, 2009, accessed May 11, 2022, https://www.huffpost.com/entry/the -science-of-visualizat_b_171340.

188 **better than trainees who didn't**: Sheryl Ubelacker, "Surgeons Study Benefits of Visualizing Procedures," *Globe and Mail*, January 28, 2015, https: //www.theglobeandmail.com/life/health-and-fitness/health/surgeons -study-benefits-of-visualizing-procedures/article22681531/.

188 **"visualizations under hypnosis"**: Donald R. Liggett and Sadao Hamada, "Enhancing the Visualization of Gymnasts," *American Journal of Clinical Hypnosis* 35, no. 3 (1993): 190–97.

188 **"need to finish the race"**: Michael Phelps with Brian Cazeneuve, *Beneath the Surface: My Story* (Champaign, IL: Sports Publishing, 2016), 3.

188 **"He knew exactly was going to happen"**: Mastery Blueprint, "Scientific Benefits of Visualization for Athletes," YouTube video, 5:49, February 4, 2019, https://www.youtube.com/watch?v=VHISQ6xIGZE.

189 **"You gain strength"**: Eleanor Roosevelt, *You Learn by Living* (Louisville, KY: Westminster John Knox Press, 1983), 29.

189 **"taking risks"**: John Baldoni, "Want to Build Your Confidence? Take a Risk!," *Forbes*, April 27, 2018, https://www.forbes.com/sites/johnbaldoni /2018/04/27/want-to-build-your-confidence-take-a-risk.

189 **"Confidence comes with familiarity"**: Megan Bruneau, "'Confidence Starts Within' and 3 Other Myths That Are Making You More Insecure," *Forbes*, October 23, 2016, https://www.forbes.com/sites/meganbruneau/2016 /10/23/confidence-comes-from-within-and-3-other-myths-that-are-making -you-more-insecure/?sh=547c120923db.

190 **"Seize every opportunity"**: Simon Trevarthen, "Speak Like a Master: 7 Ways to Be an Extraordinary Speaker," *Vunela*, April 11, 2017, https://magazine .vunela.com/all-great-leaders-are-inspiring-speakers-5f3168dec2c2.

190 **"*high* levels of stress"**: Sian Beilock, *Choke: What the Secrets of the Brain Reveal about Getting It Right When You Have To* (New York: Free Press, 2011), 34.

190 **comfort zones**: John Baldoni, "Want To Build Your Confidence? Take A Risk!"

191 **"kind of virtuous circle"**: Erin Delmore, "6 Ways to Help Our Daughters Live 'The Confidence Code,'" MSNBC, February 23, 2021, https://www .msnbc.com/know-your-value/6-ways-help-our-daughters-live-confidence -code-n1258685.

191 **"Taking more shots"**: Barbara Markway, "Why Self-Confidence Is More Important Than You Think," *Psychology Today*, September 20, 2018, https://www.psychologytoday.com/us/blog/shyness-is-nice/201809 /why-self-confidence-is-more-important-you-think.

191 **"Bam, there's a jewel"**: BBC Radio 1, "Zane Lowe Meets Kanye West 2015—Contains Strong Language," YouTube video, 43:15, February 26, 2015, https://www.youtube.com/watch?v=4Rn0hDB6Z8k.

192 **"rooting for you"**: Lybi Ma, "Fighting Stage Fright," *Psychology Today*, December 6, 2005, https://www.psychologytoday.com/us/articles/200512 /fighting-stage-fright.

193 **"the voice in our head"**: Stephanie Catahan, "13 Ways to Actually Build Confidence in Yourself, from Experts," Mindbodygreen, November 3, 2021, accessed May 11, 2022, https://www.mindbodygreen.com/articles /how-to-build-confidence/.

194 **"Don't fake it"**: Amy Cuddy, "Your Body Language May Shape Who You

Are," filmed 2012, TED video, 20:46, https://www.ted.com/talks/amy
_cuddy_your_body_language_may_shape_who_you_are.

194 **"waste of tears"**: *E! News*, "Rihanna's Tips for Confidence #shorts," YouTube
video, 17 seconds, August 27, 2021, https://www.youtube.com/watch?v
=d3kp3eMcBco.

194 **"you already had it"**: Norman Vincent Peale, *Enthusiasm Makes the Difference* (New York: Fireside, 2003), 13.

195 **"become more confident"**: Peter Mabbutt and Mike Bryant, *Hypnotherapy
For Dummies* (Germany: Wiley, 2011).

195 **famous 7–38–55 rule**: "How to Use the 7-38-55 Rule to Negotiate Effectively," Masterclass, November 8, 2020, accessed September 20, 2022, https:
//www.masterclass.com/articles/how-to-use-the-7-38-55-rule-to-negotiate
-effectively.

195 **cites research**: Carmine Gallo, "How to Look and Sound Confident During
a Presentation," *Harvard Business Review*, October 23, 2019, https://hbr
.org/2019/10/how-to-look-and-sound-confident-during-a-presentation.

196 **inspired in part**: Katherine Noel, "8 Body Language Tricks to Instantly
Appear More Confident," *Insider*, March 31, 2016, accessed August 10,
2022, https://www.businessinsider.com/body-language-tricks-appear-more
-confident-2016-3.

196 **speech coach Carmine Gallo**: Carmine Gallo, *Talk Like TED: The 9 Public-
Speaking Secrets of the World's Top Minds* (New York: St. Martin's Press,
2014).

196 **"Our nonverbals"**: Cuddy, "Your Body Language May Shape Who You
Are."

196 **Follow-up studies**: Kim Elsesser, "Power Posing Is Back: Amy Cuddy
Successfully Refutes Criticism," *Forbes*, April 3, 2018, https://www.forbes
.com/sites/kimelsesser/2018/04/03/power-posing-is-back-amy-cuddy
-successfully-refutes-criticism/?sh=6b1621bd3b8e.

197 **"The human voice"**: Julian Treasure, "How to Speak So That People Want
to Listen," filmed 2013, TED video, 9:45, https://www.ted.com/talks/julian
_treasure_how_to_speak_so_that_people_want_to_listen.

198 **"hear you clearly"**: Justin Aquino, "How to Project Your Voice: 8 Strategies to Get Louder," Cool Communicator, accessed May 11, 2022, https://
coolcommunicator.com/how-to-project-your-voice/.

198 **Multiple studies**: Gallo, "How to Look and Sound Confident During a
Presentation."

198 **"scanned for information"**: Sarah Jessen and Tobias Grossmann, "Unconscious Discrimination of Social Cues from Eye Whites in Infants," *Proceedings of the National Academy of Sciences* 111, no. 45 (2014): 16208–13.

198 **"establishes dominance"**: Ruth Umoh, "How Making Eye Contact Can Help You Appear More Confident at Work," CNBC, August 17, 2017, https://www.cnbc.com/2017/08/17/how-making-eye-contact-can-help -you-appear-more-confident-at-work.html.

199 **60 to 70 percent of the time**: Sue Shellenbarger, "Just Look Me in the Eye Already," *Wall Street Journal*, May 28, 2013, https://www.wsj.com /articles/SB10001424127887324809804578511290822228174.

199 **"interest and confidence"**: Jodi Schulz, "Eye Contact: Don't Make These Mistakes," Michigan State University Extension, December 31, 2012, accessed May 11, 2022, https://www.canr.msu.edu/news/eye_contact_dont_make _these_mistakes.

199 **"Personally I am always very nervous"**: Sam Leith, *Words Like Loaded Pistols: Rhetoric from Aristotle to Obama* (New York: Basic Books, 2016), 109–10.

200 **on any other muscle**: Anna Leach, "Not Feeling Confident? Here Are Six Ways to Fake It," *Guardian*, May 18, 2016, https://www.theguardian .com/education/2016/may/18/not-feeling-confident-here-are-six-ways-to -fake-it.

200 **"You have to earn it"**: Mindy Kaling, *Why Not Me?* (New York: Three Rivers Press, 2016), 220.

Chapter 13: Keep Calm and Carry On

201 **"conditions for Muslims in Europe"**: Douglas Murray, "What Are We to Do About Islam? A Speech to the Pim Fortuyn Memorial Conference on Europe and Islam," transcript of speech delivered in the Hague in February 2006, accessed July 1, 2022, https://web.archive.org/web/20080201133647/ http://www.socialaffairsunit.org.uk/blog/archives/000809.php.

201 **"less Islam"**: Douglas Murray, "Never Mind Singing John Lennon Songs . . . If We Want Peace Then We Need One Thing—Less Islam," *The Sun*, June 4, 2017, https://www.thesun.co.uk/news/3722649/never-mind-singing-john-lennon-songs-if-we-want-peace-then-we-need-one-thing-less-islam/.

201 **"London has become a foreign country"**: Douglas Murray, "Census That Revealed a Troubling Future," Standpoint, March 2013, accessed July 1, 2022, https://web.archive.org/web/20190703105135/https://standpointmag .co.uk/issues/march-2013/features-march-13-census-that-revealed-a -troubling-future-douglas-murray-immigration-multiculturalism-race -ethnicity/.

202 **the event on YouTube**: The Orwell Foundation, "Oxford University Part 2—What Can't You Speak about in the 21st Century?," YouTube video, 9:21, February 25, 2010, https://www.youtube.com/watch?v=vD-jB8f4SNQ.

202 **actual facts and data:** The Orwell Foundation, "Oxford University Part 3—What Can't You Speak about in the 21st Century?," YouTube video, 7:30, February 25, 2010, https://www.youtube.com/watch?v=33KM-dUS0IU.

204 **"spots of blood":** Kamal Ahmed, "War of the Words," *Observer*, June 29, 2003, https://www.theguardian.com/media/2003/jun/29/iraqandthemedia .politicsandiraq.

204 **"When the breath wanders":** Anna V. Shapiro, *Parents and Children: Relationships Born from Love; Inspired by the Wisdom of Yoga* (Lulu Publishing Services, 2017), 157.

204 **"locus coeruleus":** Kevin Yackle et al., "Breathing Control Center Neurons That Promote Arousal in Mice," *Science* 355, no. 6332 (2017): 1411–15.

204 **"liaison to the rest of the brain":** Alice Park, "This Is the Fastest Way to Calm Down," *Time*, March 30, 2017, https://time.com/4718723/deep -breathing-meditation-calm-anxiety/.

205 **"to your body":** Jonathan S. Abramowitz, *The Stress Less Workbook* (New York: The Guilford Press, 2012), 177.

206 **"shock absorber of life":** Peggy Noonan, *What I Saw at the Revolution: A Political Life in the Reagan Era* (New York: Random House, 2010), 179.

206 **Laughter has been shown:** Katey Davidson, "Why Do We Need Endorphins?," Healthline.com, November 30, 2021, accessed August 10, 2022, https://www.healthline.com/health/endorphins.

206 **"or no tape":** Nancy A. Yovetich, Alexander A. Dale, and Mary A. Hudak, "Benefits of Humor in Reduction of Threat-Induced Anxiety," *Psychological Reports* 66, no. 1 (1990): 51–58.

206 **As the famous psychologist:** Rod A. Martin and Thomas E. Ford, *The Psychology of Humor: An Integrative Approach* (San Diego: Academic Press, 2018), 299.

207 **"frightening situations we are facing":** Andie Kramer, "Using Humor to Manage Stress and Stay Positive," *Forbes*, May 15, 2020, https://www.forbes .com/sites/andiekramer/2020/05/15/using-humor-to-manage-stress-and -stay-positive/.

207 **"Gentlemen, why don't you laugh":** Merrill D. Peterson, *Lincoln in American Memory* (New York: Oxford University Press, 1995), 97.

207 **"the scar on his forehead":** J. K. Rowling, *Harry Potter and the Order of the Phoenix* (New York: Scholastic Press, 2003), 178.

208 **"effortless form of self-control":** Jason S. Moser et al., "Third-Person Self-Talk Facilitates Emotion Regulation without Engaging Cognitive Control: Converging Evidence from ERP and fMRI," *Scientific Reports* 7 (2017): 4519.

209 **"control what goes on inside":** Linda Esposito, "22 Calming Quotes for People with Anxiety," *Psychology Today*, September 17, 2014, https://www

.psychologytoday.com/us/blog/anxiety-zen/201409/22-calming-quotes-people-anxiety.

210 **which he denied**: Al Jazeera English, "UpFront—Klitschko on Ukraine, Russia and a New Cold War Threat," YouTube video, 11:37, February 27, 2016, https://www.youtube.com/watch?v=ezW2D9ZE-ug.

211 **"get more toast"**: humor101channel, "Mustard Spreading the Birdcage," YouTube video, 1:59, June 9, 2011, https://www.youtube.com/watch?v=p85FTLv5_-M.

Chapter 14: Practice Makes Perfect

212 **Reps, reps, reps**: Carmine Gallo, "The Best TED Speakers Practice This 1 Habit Before Taking the Stage," *Inc.*, March 7, 2017, https://www.inc.com/carmine-gallo/the-best-ted-speakers-practice-this-1-habit-before-taking-the-stage.html.

212 **during World War II**: "Demosthenes," Wikipedia, last modified June 28, 2022, https://en.wikipedia.org/wiki/Demosthenes.

212 **"fountain of genius"**: Simon Maier and Jeremy Kourdi, *The 100: Insights and Lessons from 100 of the Greatest Speakers and Speeches Ever Delivered*, rev. ed. (London: Marshall Cavendish, 2011), 88.

212 **"perfect orator"**: Carl P. E. Springer, *Cicero in Heaven: The Roman Rhetor and Luther's Reformation* (Leiden: Brill, 2018), 62.

213 **"at a single breath"**: Plutarch, *Parallel Lives*, trans. Bernadotte Perrin, Lacus-Curtius.

213 **took up arms**: Steven John, "The Top 10 Famous Speeches That Stand the Test of Time," *The Manual*, January 8, 2022, accessed, 30 August 2022, https://www.themanual.com/culture/famous-speeches-from-history/.

214 **"90 percent of how well"**: Aisha Langford, "Ready, Set, Speak," Inside Higher Ed, July 10, 2015, https://www.insidehighered.com/advice/2015/07/10/how-improve-your-public-speaking-skills-essay.

215 **"Mr. Churchill and oratory"**: Boris Johnson, *The Churchill Factor: How One Man Made History* (New York: Riverhead Books, 2014), 87.

215 **"heckle" him**: Brett McKay and Kate McKay, "The Winston Churchill Guide to Public Speaking," *Art of Manliness* blog, last modified October 29, 2021, https://www.artofmanliness.com/character/behavior/guide-to-public-speaking/.

215 **head in his hands**: Johnson, *Churchill Factor*, 84; McKay and McKay, "The Winston Churchill Guide to Public Speaking."

216 **"as well as for brilliant oratory"**: "The Nobel Prize in Literature 1953," The Nobel Prize, accessed May 11, 2022, https://www.nobelprize.org/prizes/literature/1953/summary/.

216 **"she-bear licks her cubs"**: Johnson, *Churchill Factor*, 85.

216 **"before they get up"**: Brett McKay and Kate McKay, "The Winston Churchill Guide to Public Speaking."

216 **"declamations of text"**: Johnson, *Churchill Factor*, 89.

216 **none the wiser**: William Manchester, *The Last Lion: Winston Spencer Churchill*, vol. 2: *Alone, 1932–1940* (New York: Bantam Books, 2013), 104; McKay and McKay, "Winston Churchill Guide to Public Speaking."

216 **"Spanish ships I cannot see"**: Thomas Montalbo, "Seven Lessons in Speechmaking from One of the Greatest Orators of All Time," *Finest Hour* 69, June 17, 2016, accessed May 11, 2022, https://winstonchurchill .org/publications/finest-hour/finest-hour-069/churchill-a-study-in -oratory/.

216 **"is no hindrance"**: William Manchester, *The Last Lion: Winston Spencer Churchill*, vol. 1: *Visions of Glory, 1874–1932* (New York: Bantam Books, 2013), 267.

217 **"I wasn't talking to you"**: Manchester, *Visions of Glory*, 32.

217 **"get his point across"**: Cynthia Haven, "Stanford Archive Shows Origins of Martin Luther King's 1963 'I Have a Dream' Speech," *Stanford Report*, August 25, 2011, accessed May 11, 2022, https://news.stanford.edu/news /2011/august/i-have-a-dream-082511.html.

217 **"It's well known that King"**: Scott Eblin, "Six Leadership Communication Lessons from Martin Luther King, Jr.," *Government Executive*, January 16, 2012, accessed May 11, 2022, https://www.govexec.com/management/2012 /01/six-leadership-communication-lessons-from-martin-luther-king-jr /40840/.

218 **writing and rewriting it**: Gary Younge, "Martin Luther King: The Story Behind His 'I Have a Dream' Speech," *Guardian*, August 9, 2013, https://www .theguardian.com/world/2013/aug/09/martin-luther-king-dream-speech -history.

218 **"equivalent of having a Ferrari"**: Carmine Gallo, *Talk Like TED: The 9 Public-Speaking Secrets of the World's Top Minds* (New York: St. Martin's Press, 2014), 76.

219 **to borrow a line**: Marie Tjernlund, "Are Your Non-Verbals Helping or Hurting Your Presentation?," *NobleEdge* blog, July 12, 2022, https://www .nobleedgeconsulting.com/post/are-your-non-verbals-helping-or-hurting -your-presentation.

219 **without volume**: Jen Glantz, "5 Activities You Can Do at Home to Help You Become a Stronger Public Speaker," *Insider*, March 18, 2020, https://www .businessinsider.com/5-activities-at-home-to-become-a-stronger-public -speaker-2020-3.

219 **"useless movements and gestures"**: Gallo, *Talk Like TED*, 102.

220 **"clasping"**: Sam Leith, *Words Like Loaded Pistols: Rhetoric from Aristotle to Obama* (New York: Basic Books, 2016), 184.

220 **"the tone in my voice"**: Likipedia, "Seinfeld—Tone of Voice," YouTube video, 5:29, July 26, 2017, accessed May 11, 2022, https://www.youtube.com/watch?v=T6yFDm9xT2E.

221 **"loudly or quietly"**: Helen von Dadelszen, "Add Colour to Your Voice to Engage Your Audience," LinkedIn, January 24, 2022, https://www.linkedin.com/pulse/add-colour-your-voice-engage-audience-helen-von-dadelszen.

221 **"Words mean more"**: Maya Angelou, Twitter post, April 29, 2019, 10:44 PM, https://twitter.com/drmayaangelou/status/1123055575632420865.

223 **dark side of the Force**: Maxwell Tani, "Adam Driver Walks Out of NPR 'Fresh Air' Interview over 'Marriage Story' Clip," *Daily Beast*, December 17, 2019, accessed May 11, 2022, https://www.thedailybeast.com/adam-driver-walks-out-of-npr-fresh-air-interview-over-marriage-story-clip.

223 **"opportunity for you to play!"**: Helen von Dadelszen, "The Hidden Benefits of the Bedtime Story," Present Potential Academy blog, April 29, 2011, accessed May 11, 2022, https://presentpotential.ch/2018/10/25/the-hidden-benefits-of-the-bedtime-story/.

224 **"wiggle room"**: "7 Deadly Fears of Public Speaking," *The Big Fish* blog, December 9, 2013, https://bigfishpresentations.com/2013/12/09/7-deadly-fears-of-public-speaking/.

226 **rehearsal and feedback**: Carmine Gallo, *Talk Like TED: The 9 Public-Speaking Secrets of the World's Top Minds* (New York: St. Martin's Press, 2014), 78.

226 **"twice for the TED team"**: Carmine Gallo, "The Best TED Speakers Practice This 1 Habit Before Taking the Stage."

227 **"Three times now"**: Mehdi Hasan, Twitter post, August 22, 2019, 10:30 AM, https://twitter.com/mehdirhasan/status/1164545476747780096.

228 **"A Perfect Distillation"**: Katherine Krueger, "A Perfect Distillation of Trump's Anti-Semitism in Just One Minute," Splinter, August 22, 2019, accessed May 11, 2022, https://splinternews.com/a-perfect-distillation-of-trumps-anti-semitism-in-just-1837479676.

228 **"where he'd be speaking"**: Sam Leith, *Words Like Loaded Pistols: Rhetoric from Aristotle to Obama* (New York: Basic Books, 2016), 143.

Chapter 15: Do Your Homework

230 **"clarity plus facts"**: Jonathan Dimbleby, personal interview, March 28, 2022.

231 **"what you can argue for"**: Patrick Stokes, "No, You're Not Entitled to Your Opinion," The Conversation, October 4, 2012, https://theconversation.com/no-youre-not-entitled-to-your-opinion-9978.

232 **do the work**: "The Work Required to Have an Opinion," *Farnam Street* blog, accessed September 20, 2022, https://fs.blog/the-work-required-to-have-an-opinion/.

233 **"on your soil"**: Foundation for Effective Governance, "Mehdi Hasan: Ukraine Shoud Attack Unemployment," YouTube video, 2:52, accessed May 11, 2022, https://www.youtube.com/watch?v=73-xOpqzD9c.

233 **Alex Osborn in the 1950s**: "Brainstorming: New Ways to Find New Ideas," *Time*, February 18, 1957, accessed May 11, 2022, https://content.time.com/time/subscriber/printout/0,8816,809155,00.html.

234 **"The best way to have good ideas"**: "Clarifying Three Widespread Quotes," *The Pauling Blog*, October 28, 2008, accessed May 11, 2022, https://paulingblog.wordpress.com/2008/10/28/clarifying-three-widespread-quotes/.

235 **"I hit a gusher"**: Jean Gruss, "Burger Hustle," *Business Observer*, November 12, 2012, https://www.businessobserverfl.com/article/burger-hustle.

235 **"Every amazing creative thing"**: Scott Berkun, *The Myths of Innovation* (Sebastopol, CA: O'Reilly Media, 2010), 168.

235 **fall on your head**: David Kelley and Tom Kelley, *Creative Confidence: Unleashing the Creative Potential Within Us All* (New York: Crown Business, 2013), 22.

235 **"little mental advances"**: University of Pittsburgh, "Psychology Researchers Explore How Engineers Create: It's Not So Much 'Eureka' Moments As It's the Sweat of One's Brow," *ScienceDaily*, June 17, 2014, accessed August 2, 2022, https://www.sciencedaily.com/releases/2014/06/140617144814.htm.

235 **"Your head is filled"**: Jessica Hullinger, "The Science of Brainstorming," *Fast Company*, June 30, 2014, https://www.fastcompany.com/3032418/the-science-of-brainstorming.

236 **legendary tennis player Arthur Ashe**: "In the Zone," Quote Investigator, September 16, 2016, accessed May 11, 2022, https://quoteinvestigator.com/2016/09/16/zone/.

236 **when the magic happens**: Lauren Ingeno, "In Fact, Mark Zuckerberg, 'Eureka Moments' Do Exist," *Drexel News Blog*, June 5, 2017, accessed May 11, 2022, https://drexel.edu/coas/news-events/news/2017/June/In-Fact-Mark-Zuckerberg-Eureka-Moments-Do-Exist/.

236 **a 2015 survey**: "Hansgrohe Study: The Brightest Ideas Begin in the Shower," *Plumbing & Mechanical*, January 26, 2015, accessed May 11, 2022, https://www.pmmag.com/articles/96968-hansgrohe-study-the-brightest-ideas-begin-in-the-shower.

237 **"importance of relaxation for creative thinking"**: Jacquelyn Smith, "72% of People Get Their Best Ideas in the Shower—Here's Why," *Business Insider*,

January 14, 2016, https://www.businessinsider.com/why-people-get-their -best-ideas-in-the-shower-2016-1.

237 **In December 2015**: Al Jazeera English, "Did the US Occupation Create ISIL? | Head to Head," YouTube video, 47:39, December 4, 2015, accessed May 16, 2022, https://www.youtube.com/watch?v=L7xfS3LXSOk.

238 *Christian Science Monitor* **op-ed**: Mamoun Fandy, "Egypt, Mubarak Bow to Saudi-Style Islam," *Christian Science Monitor*, August 20, 1992, https:// www.csmonitor.com/1992/0820/20191.html.

239 **"exclude" certain**: Lisa Eadicicco, "5 Google Tricks for Getting the Best Search Results," *Insider*, November 19, 2019, https://www.businessinsider .com/google-tricks-for-best-search-results-2019-11.

239 **"digital equivalent of the Great Library of Alexandria"**: Sam Leith, *Words Like Loaded Pistols: Rhetoric from Aristotle to Obama* (New York: Basic Books, 2016), xix.

240 **"Start, don't end, with Wikipedia"**: Dustin Wax, "Advice for Students: 10 Steps Toward Better Research," Lifehack, accessed May 16, 2022, https:// www.lifehack.org/articles/communication/advice-for-students-10-steps -toward-better-research.html.

240 **"gateway"**: Ikhwan Hastanto, "We Asked a Wikipedia Contributor Why Everyone Thinks They're Unreliable," *Vice*, September 3, 2019 https://www .vice.com/en/article/8xwgev/we-asked-a-wikipedia-contributor-why -everyone-thinks-theyre-unreliable.

241 **"Why is FSG opening a training center"**: Al Jazeera English, "Blackwater's Erik Prince: Iraq, Privatising Wars, and Trump | Head to Head," YouTube video, 49:08, March 8, 2019, https://www.youtube.com/watch?v=KOB4V -ukpBI.

244 **"If an Iranian guest"**: Al Jazeera English, "Gaza Killings: Who Is to Blame? | Head to Head," YouTube video, 49:27, July 20, 2018, https://www.youtube .com/watch?v=pfw2AVqcne0.

246 **as many have pointed out**: Chris Meyer, "Steelmanning: How to Discover the Truth by Helping Your Opponent," The Mind Collection, accessed September 20, 2022, https://themindcollection.com/steelmanning-how-to -discover-the-truth-by-helping-your-opponent/.

248 **"lost by one vote getting on that shortlist"**: 2yyiam, "Mehdi Hasan on Question Time 08.12.11," YouTube video, 59:12, December 12, 2011, accessed May 16, 2022, https://www.youtube.com/watch?v=N3Mka0EOVGw.

Chapter 16: The Grand Finale

251 **"in front of an audience"**: Brett McKay and Kate McKay, "The Winston Churchill Guide to Public Speaking," *Art of Manliness* blog, last modified

October 29, 2021, https://www.artofmanliness.com/character/behavior/guide-to-public-speaking/.

252 **"lies choking in his own blood upon the ground"**: Boris Johnson, *The Churchill Factor: How One Man Made History* (New York: Riverhead Books, 2014), 18–19.

253 **"and Western civilization"**: John Lukacs, *Five Days in London, May 1940* (New Haven, CT: Yale University Press, 2001), 2.

253 **"ultimately derived"**: *Merriam-Webster*, s.v. "peroration," accessed September 10, 2022, https://www.merriam-webster.com/dictionary/peroration.

253 **"leaves an audience unsatisfied"**: William Safire, *Safire's Political Dictionary* (New York: Oxford University Press, 2008), 538.

253 **"Every oration needs one"**: Safire, *Safire's Political Dictionary*, 538.

254 **"composed of four things"**: Richard Nordquist, "Peroration: The Closing Argument," ThoughtCo., May 24, 2019, accessed May 16, 2022, https://www.thoughtco.com/peroration-argument-1691612.

255 **let speech coach**: Andrew Dlugan, "Why Successful Speech Outlines Follow the Rule of Three," Six Minutes, June 3, 2009, accessed May 2, 2022, http://sixminutes.dlugan.com/speech-outline-rule-of-three/.

255 **triple-election-winning New Labour**: Robert Taylor, "Does Endless Message Repetition Really Work?," *Andy Black Associates Blog*, May 10, 2017, accessed May 16, 2022, https://www.andyblackassociates.co.uk/does-endless-message-repetition-really-work/.

255 **"a tremendous whack"**: Rose King, "A Tremendous Whack: Hitting the Key Message of Your Next Talk," Rose King blog, October 16, 2019, accessed May 17, 2022, https://www.rosespeechwriter.com/blog/spotlighteffect/2019/10/16/a-tremendous-whack-hitting-the-key-message-of-your-next-talk.

256 **cites a study**: Dom Barnard, "Different Ways to End a Presentation or Speech," VirtualSpeech, November 6, 2017, https://virtualspeech.com/blog/different-ways-to-end-presentation-speech.

256 **The late Yale University psychologist**: Henry L. Roediger III and Robert G. Crowder, "A Serial Position Effect in Recall of United States Presidents," *Bulletin of the Psychonomic Society* 8, no. 4 (1976): 275–78.

257 **"Vote for the motion"**: Intelligence Squared, "Debate: The West Should Cut Ties with Saudi Arabia," YouTube video, 1:28:16, March 12, 2019, https://www.youtube.com/watch?v=qi0T0owgW3M.

257 **say the experts**: Brian Tracy, "9 Tips to End a Speech with a Bang," *Brian Tracy* blog, accessed August 27, 2022, https://www.briantracy.com/blog/public-speaking/how-to-end-a-speech-the-right-way/; Susan Dugdale, "3 Ways to Close a Speech Effectively," write-out-loud, September 5, 2022, https://www.write-out-loud.com/how-to-end-a-speech.html.

258 **"come from their socks"**: *The West Wing*, Season 2, Episode 12, "The Drop In," April 4, 2014, accessed May 17, 2022, http://westwingtranscripts.com /search.php?flag=getTranscript&id=34&keyword=final%20draft.

259 **"second voice"**: Andrew Dlugan, "How to Use Quotes in Your Speech," Six Minutes, September 23, 2012, http://sixminutes.dlugan.com/speech -quotes/.

260 **"This election had many firsts"**: Sam Leith, *Words Like Loaded Pistols: Rhetoric from Aristotle to Obama* (New York: Basic Books, 2016), 243–44.

261 **"change is always possible"**: Freek Janssen, "Five Rules of Storytelling from Obama's Speechwriter," Team Lewis, March 19, 2014, accessed May 17, 2022, https://www.teamlewis.com/uk/magazine/five-rules-of-storytelling -from-obamas-speechwriter/.

263 **As the late American politician**: "They May Forget What You Said, But They Will Never Forget How You Made Them Feel," Quote Investigator, April 6, 2014, accessed May 17, 2022, https://quoteinvestigator.com/2014 /04/06/they-feel/.

264 **"exclamation point"**: Brian Tracy, "9 Tips to End a Speech with a Bang."

264 **ending is for summarizing**: "Conclusion," Lumens Learning, March 5, 2014, accessed August 29, 2022, https://lumen.instructure.com/courses /218897/pages/linkedtext54136?module_item_id=5006958.

264 **"back to attention"**: "Conclude Your Speech with the Seven Samurai," *SpeechCamp* blog, May 9, 2016, https://www.speechcamp.ie/blog/conclude -your-speech-with-the-seven-samurai.

264 **"Let us pray"**: Austin Phelps, *The Theory of Preaching: Lectures on Homiletics* (New York: Charles Scribner's Sons, 1881), 501.

264 **"Stay hungry. Stay foolish"**: Barnard, "Different Ways to End a Presentation or Speech."

265 **per one speech coach**: Dugdale, "3 Ways to Close a Speech Effectively."

265 **"one inescapable conclusion"**: Brett McKay and Kate McKay, "The Winston Churchill Guide to Public Speaking."

265 **"amid a thunder of assent"**: Winston Churchill, "The Scaffolding of Rhetoric" (unpublished essay, 1897). Retrieved on May 2, 2022, https:// winstonchurchill.org/images/pdfs/for_educators/THE_SCAFFOLDING _OF_RHETORIC.pdf."

ACKNOWLEDGMENTS

Simply put, neither my career nor this book would exist were it not for the many people on both sides of the Atlantic who taught me the art of debate and rhetoric, who granted me opportunities to use those skills, and who—*how should I put it?*—tolerated my lifelong obsession with arguing. In no particular order, I would like to thank:

My publisher and editor in the United States, Tim Duggan at Henry Holt, who had faith in me before any other major publisher did, and who cold-emailed me out of the blue in early 2021 to suggest we do a book together—before I had even had a chance to come up with a proposal! And my publisher and editor in the United Kingdom, Matthew Cole, at Pan Macmillan, who had such confidence in me that he outbid eight other publishers for the UK and Commonwealth rights.

The folks at United Talent Agency (UTA): my literary agent, the powerhouse Pilar Queen, who not only helped me come up with the idea, structure, and name for this book—but then sold it within a matter of *days*! Then she regularly sent me encouraging and funny one-line emails throughout the writing process to boost my morale and made sure I got this whole damn thing across the finish line in time. My brilliant TV agents, the dynamic duo Marc Paskin and Lia Aponte, who have been invaluable sounding boards/cheerleaders/friends, and who began planting the seeds for this book back in

2019. And, of course, UTA's Meredith Miller, who has helped take this book global.

The various bosses in the UK who hired me as a TV researcher and producer in my twenties and then allowed me to argue every issue under the sun, *behind* the camera, long before anyone was foolish enough to let me out in front of one: David Mapstone, Dave Sayer, and Rob Burley at ITV; John Ryley and Chris Birkett at Sky News; and Dorothy Byrne and Kevin Sutcliffe at Channel 4. Plus, Arianna Huffington, Carla Buzasi, and Stephen Hull at *HuffPost UK*, and Betsy Reed, Glenn Greenwald, and Michael Bloom at the Intercept/First Look Media. The editor of the *New Statesman*, Jason Cowley, who took a chance on me and offered a twenty-nine-year-old TV producer with zero experience in print journalism a prestigious magazine column in 2009. I persuaded him to do so over a lunch organized by my great friend and former colleague James Macintyre, who was convinced that I was meant for this line of work even before I was. James and I also coauthored a book on British politics back in 2011, at the request of publisher and radio presenter Iain Dale, another long-standing supporter of mine.

The folks at Al Jazeera English (AJE), where I developed my signature interview style, including: managing director Giles Trendle; head of talk shows and my good friend Salah Khadr; as well as my long-standing producer, protector, adviser, ally, and confidant Juan Pablo Raymond, who even moved countries with me; and, of course, the members of the *UpFront* and *Head to Head* editorial teams, who always made sure I was prepared for every interview. (A special shoutout to AJE guest booker Ryan Kohls, who had to awkwardly walk Vitali Klitschko, as well as a multiplicity of other peeved interview guests, out of the studio!)

Phil Griffin, the then president of MSNBC, who rang me out of the blue in the summer of 2020, while I was locked down at home during the pandemic, to offer me a dream gig: hosting a nightly show on NBC's streaming channel Peacock and a weekly show on the cable channel MSNBC. Rashida Jones, who took over from Phil, made good on his pledge of a weekly show on MSNBC, and has since supported and encouraged my own particular style of combative TV interviews and outspoken on-air commentaries. Jessica Kurdali, head of talent at MSNBC, who has been a vital ally throughout this project. And, crucially, my executive producers at Peacock and MSNBC—Laura Conaway, Ben Mayer, Patrick McMenamin, Kyle Griffin—plus all the hardworking segment producers and guest bookers. They continue to make me look good on a daily basis, and without them, I simply would *not* have been able to pull off many of my most viral and hard-hitting interviews. Thanks, especially, to Sujata Thomas and Kassandra Scheese for securing the Peacock interviewees mentioned in the book.

The legendary British television interviewers who I had the opportunity to work under, learn from, and befriend long before I had a show of my own: Jonathan Dimbleby, a mentor in the true sense of that word, as well as Jon Snow, Jeremy Vine, Kay Burley, and Eamonn Holmes, among many others.

Producer Kiran Alvi, who helped me develop some of the ideas behind this book long before I even had a publisher for it. Freelance editor Jon Cox, who helped transform my rambling thoughts into (what I hope is) the lucid prose you see in this finished book. Fact-checker Glenn Speer and his ever-so-keen eye. Former Oxford Union president Joey D'Urso, because there is no Oxford Union Islam debate without Joey persuading me to do it. The wonderful people at Intelligence Squared—especially Hannah Kaye and Farah Jassat—who invited me again and again to debate onstage in front of thousands of people. Author Johann Hari, who pushed me nonstop for six years to write this book, *a* book, *any* book!

The many authors, writers, and online speech coaches who developed or collated so many of the arguments and concepts outlined in this book—and, in particular, a special shout-out to authors Carmine Gallo (*Talk Like TED*), Sam Leith (*Words Like Loaded Pistols*) and Jay Heinrichs (*Thank You for Arguing*).

My closest cousin Saif and his wife, Reshma, who have tirelessly championed me over the years—as have my wife's parents, sisters, and brothers-in-law. So many other morale-boosting friends and family members across the United States, the UK, Canada, India, and beyond. You know who you are! My best friend Sameer, who has always had my back—and always believed in me. My sister, who was my argumentative foil growing up and has always supported me. My father and mother, who provided the intellectual and moral ballast for *everything* I have ever achieved in my life, both professionally and personally.

My kids, my two beautiful and eloquent daughters, my mini-Ciceros, who will debate and declaim for as long as it takes to cow their father into rhetorical submission! Perhaps above all else, however, my poor wife, who has had to put up with my love for debate and argument for almost two decades now. She can't get rid of me by switching off the television, or walking out of the auditorium. Then again, she happens to be a brilliant lawyer who, like me, wins arguments for a living and gives as good as she gets. (She also, I should add, helped come up with both the idea and the title for this book!)

The love, support, and affection that I get from my wife and kids day after day, ultimately, is what gives me the confidence, energy, and ability to do what I do.

And there is no arguing with that.

—*Mehdi Hasan, May 2022*

INDEX

ABOUT THE AUTHOR

Mehdi Hasan is an award-winning British American journalist, anchor, and author. He is the host of *The Mehdi Hasan Show* on MSNBC and NBC's streaming channel Peacock. Hasan is a former columnist and podcaster at the Intercept, as well as a former presenter at Al Jazeera English, and his op-eds have also appeared in the *New York Times* and the *Washington Post*.